Private Ratings, Public Regulations

This illustration is taken from the original etching in Thomas Hobbes' *Leviathan* of 1651. Palgrave Macmillan and the editors are grateful to Lucila Muñoz-Sanchez and Monika Sniegs for their help in redesigning the original to illustrate what 'transformations of the state' might mean. The inscription at the top of the original frontispiece reads *'Non est potestas Super Terram quae Comparetur ei'* (Job 41.33): 'there is no power on earth which can be compared to him'. In the Bible, this refers to the seamonster, Leviathan. (Original Leviathan image reprinted courtesy of the British Library.)

Transformations of the State

Series Editors: **Achim Hurrelmann**, Carleton University, Canada; **Stephan Leibfried**, University of Bremen, Germany; **Kerstin Martens**, University of Bremen, Germany; **Peter Mayer**, University of Bremen, Germany.

Titles include:

Outline of the themes of the series: Achim Hurrelmann, Stephan Leibfried, Kerstin Martens and Peter Mayer (*editors*)
TRANSFORMING THE GOLDEN-AGE NATION STATE

Moritz Weiss
TRANSACTIONS COSTS AND SECURITY INSTITUTIONS
Unravelling the ESDP

Michael Dobbins
HIGHER EDUCATION POLICIES IN CENTRAL AND EASTERN EUROPE
Convergence towards a Common Model?

Heinz Rothgang, Mirella Cacace, Simone Grimmeisen, Uwe Helmert, Claus Wendt
THE STATE AND HEALTHCARE
Comparing OECD Countries

Anna Holzscheiter
CHILDREN'S RIGHTS IN INTERNATIONAL POLITICS
The Transformative Power of Transnational Discourse

Kerstin Martens, Alexander-Kenneth Nagel, Michael Windzio and Ansgar Weymann (*editors*)
TRANSFORMATION OF EDUCATION POLICY

Steffen Schneider, Achim Hurrelmann, Zuzana Krell-Laluhová, Frank Nullmeier and Achim Wiesner
DEMOCRACY'S DEEP ROOTS
Why the Nation State Remains Legitimate

Anja P. Jakobi
INTERNATIONAL ORGANIZATIONS AND LIFELONG LEARNING
From Global Agendas to Policy Diffusion

Michael J. Warning
TRANSNATIONAL PUBLIC GOVERNANCE
Networks, Law and Legitimacy

Thomas Rixen
THE POLITICAL ECONOMY OF INTERNATIONAL TAX GOVERNANCE

Hartmut Wessler (*editor*)
PUBLIC DELIBERATION AND PUBLIC CULTURE
The Writings of Bernhard Peters, 1993–2005

Hartmut Wessler, Bernhard Peters, Michael Brüggemann, Katharina Kleinen-von Königslöw and Stefanie Sifft
TRANSNATIONALIZATION OF PUBLIC SPHERES

Jochen Zimmerman, Jörg R. Werner and Philipp B. Volmer
GLOBAL GOVERNANCE IN ACCOUNTING
Public Power and Private Commitment

Peter Starke
RADICAL WELFARE STATE RETRENCHMENT
A Comparative Analysis

Jens Steffek, Claudia Kissling and Patrizia Nanz (*editors*)
CIVIL SOCIETY PARTICIPATION IN EUROPEAN AND GLOBAL GOVERNANCE
A Cure for the Democratic Deficit?

Klaus Dingwerth
THE NEW TRANSNATIONALISM
Transnational Governance and Democratic Legitimacy

Kerstin Martens, Alessandra Rusconi and Kathrin Leuze (*editors*)
NEW ARENAS OF EDUCATION GOVERNANCE
The Impact of International Organizations and Markets on Educational Policy Making

Achim Hurrelmann, Steffen Schneider and Jens Steffek (*editors*)
LEGITIMACY IN AN AGE OF GLOBAL POLITICS

Joan DeBardeleben and Achim Hurrelmann (*editors*)
DEMOCRATIC DILEMMAS OF MULTILEVEL GOVERNANCE
Legitimacy, Representation and Accountability in the European Union

---

Transformations of the State

Series Standing Order ISBN 978–1–4039–8544–6 (hardback)
Series Standing Order ISBN 978–1–4039–8545–3 (paperback)

You can receive future titles in this series as they are published by placing a standing order. Please contact your bookseller or, in case of difficulty, write to us at the address below with your name and address, the title of the series and one of the ISBNs quoted above.

Customer Services Department, Macmillan Distribution Ltd, Houndmills, Basingstoke, Hampshire RG21 6XS, England

---

Private Ratings, Public Regulations

Credit Rating Agencies and Global Financial Governance

Andreas Kruck
Teaching and Research Associate, Geschwister-Scholl Institute for Political Science, Ludwig Maximilian University of Munich, Germany

Transformations of the State
CRC 597

palgrave macmillan

First published 2011 by
PALGRAVE MACMILLAN

Palgrave Macmillan in the UK is an imprint of Macmillan Publishers Limited, registered in England, company number 785998, of Houndmills, Basingstoke, Hampshire RG21 6XS.

Palgrave Macmillan in the US is a division of St Martin's Press LLC, 175 Fifth Avenue, New York, NY 10010.

Palgrave Macmillan is the global academic imprint of the above companies and has companies and representatives throughout the world.

Palgrave® and Macmillan® are registered trademarks in the United States, the United Kingdom, Europe and other countries.

ISBN: 978–0–230–28223–0 hardback

This book is printed on paper suitable for recycling and made from fully managed and sustained forest sources. Logging, pulping and manufacturing processes are expected to conform to the environmental regulations of the country of origin.

A catalogue record for this book is available from the British Library.

Library of Congress Cataloging-in-Publication Data

Kruck, Andreas, 1981–
Private ratings, public regulations : credit rating agencies and global financial governance / Andreas Kruck.
p. cm.
Includes bibliographical references and index.
ISBN 978–0–230–28223–0 (alk. paper)
1. Credit ratings. 2. Credit bureaus. 3. International finance. I. Title.

HG3751.5.K78 2011
332'.042—dc22 2011006612

10 9 8 7 6 5 4 3 2 1
20 19 18 17 16 15 14 13 12 11

Printed and bound in Great Britain by
CPI Antony Rowe, Chippenham and Eastbourne

Contents

Tables

Figures

Acronyms

ADR	American Depositary Receipt
APEC	Asia-Pacific Economic Cooperation
APRA	Australian Prudential Regulation Authority
BaFin	German Federal Financial Supervisory Authority/ 'Bundesanstalt für Finanzdienstleistungsaufsicht'
BCBS	Basel Committee on Banking Supervision
BIS	Bank for International Settlements
CAA	credit assessment agencies
CCR	central credit register
CDO	collateralized debt obligation
CDU	Christian Democratic Union of Germany/'Christlich-Demokratische Union'
CEBS	Committee of European Banking Supervisors
CEO	chief executive officer
CFSD	central financial statements databases
CME	coordinated market economy
CRA	credit rating agency
ECB	European Central Bank
EU	European Union
ERISA	US Employee Retirement Income Security Act
FD	Fair Disclosure
FDIC	US Federal Deposit Insurance Corporation
G-10	Group of Ten
G-30	Group of Thirty
HK	Hong Kong
HKMA	Hong Kong Market Authority
IASB	International Accounting Standards Board
IASC	International Accounting Standards Committee
ICBA	Independent Community Bankers of America
IMF	International Monetary Fund
IOSCO	International Organization of Securities Commissions
LME	liberal market economy
MBS	mortgage-backed security
NAISC	US National Association of Insurance Commissioners

NGO	nongovernmental organization
NRSRO	US Nationally Recognized Statistical Rating Organization
OCC	US Office of the Comptroller of the Currency
OECD	Organization for Economic Cooperation and Development
OTS	US Office of Thrift Supervision
S&Ls	savings and loans associations
S&P's	Standard & Poor's
SEC	US Securities and Exchange Commission
SolvV	German Solvency Regulation (on the Use of Credit Ratings in Regulation)/'Solvabilitätsverordnung'
SRP	Supervisory Review Process
UK	United Kingdom (of Great Britain and Northern Ireland)
US(A)	United States (of America)
USD	US dollar
VoC	varieties of capitalism

Series Editors' Preface

Over the past four centuries, the nation state has emerged as the world's most effective means of organizing society, but its current status and future are decidedly uncertain. Some scholars predict the total demise of the nation state as we know it, its powers eroded by a dynamic global economy on the one hand and, on the other, by the transfer of political decision-making to supranational bodies. Other analysts point out the remarkable resilience of the state's core institutions and assert that even in the age of global markets and politics, the state remains the ultimate guarantor of security, democracy, welfare and the rule of law. Do either of these interpretations describe the future of the OECD world's modern, liberal nation state? Will the state soon be as obsolete and irrelevant as an outdated computer? Should it be scrapped for some new invention, or can it be overhauled and rejuvenated? Or, is the state actually thriving and still fit to serve, just in need of a few minor reforms?

In an attempt to address these questions, the analyses in the *Transformations of the State* series separate the complex tangle of tasks and functions that comprise the state into four manageable dimensions:

- the monopolization of the means of force,
- the rule of law, as prescribed and safeguarded by the constitution,
- the guarantee of democratic self-governance, and
- the provision of welfare and the assurance of social cohesion.

In the OECD world of the 1960s and 1970s, these four dimensions formed a synergetic constellation that emerged as the central, defining characteristic of the modern state. Books in the series report the results of both empirical and theoretical studies of the transformations experienced in each of these dimensions over the past few decades.

Transformations of the State? (Stephan Leibfried and Michael Zürn (eds), Cambridge 2005) and *Transforming the Golden-Age National State* (Achim Hurrelmann, Stephan Leibfried, Kerstin Martens and Peter Mayer (eds), Basingstoke 2007) define the basic concepts of state transformation employed in all of these studies and provide an overview of the issues addressed. Written by political scientists, lawyers, economists and sociologists, the series tracks the development of the post-World War II OECD state. Here, at last, is an up-to-date series of reports on the state of the state and a crystal-ball glimpse into its future.

ACHIM HURRELMANN, STEPHAN LEIBFRIED,
KERSTIN MARTENS AND PETER MAYER

Preface and Acknowledgements

When I started work on this book, the US mortgage crisis was just beginning to unfold, and interest in credit rating agencies was still the preserve of a few, very knowledgeable, academic specialists. Some years and the greatest financial and economic crisis since World War II later, credit rating agencies have become known to even the casual newspaper reader. Innumerable articles have appeared blaming credit rating agencies for failing to properly evaluate the default risks of complex structured finance products, for entertaining unduly close relationships with their customers (the main critique being that it is the rated entities that pay rating agencies for their services) and for destabilizing whole countries through downgrades of sovereign ratings. The global financial crisis has demonstrated the critical role credit rating agencies play in global investment decisions and the powerful position they occupy in the global financial system. Politicians on both sides of the Atlantic have made a sport of scolding credit rating agencies for their lack of reliability and integrity. More or less ambitious regulatory steps towards stricter oversight and control of credit rating agencies have been taken. But US and European politicians have taken no or very little pain to explain why, before the great crisis, *state regulatory authorities* had further empowered credit rating agencies by making increasing use of private credit ratings in public financial regulation (e.g. through capital reserve requirements for banks that were contingent on credit ratings). I believe that this important and extremely interesting feature in the governance of financial markets has received too little attention in current debates about the power, reliability and accountability of credit rating agencies.

This is one reason why this book examines the driving forces for the regulatory use of credit ratings over time and across countries. But there was another, more general rationale for writing this book: the regulatory use of credit ratings is an interesting example of state-sanctioned and state-bolstered private governance. For the past three decades, the privatization of public policy functions in nearly all issue areas has stood out as one of the most significant transformations of governance and statehood in the western OECD world. At the same time, there have been considerable variations not only over time, but also across countries, types of governance tasks, and political issue areas in public actors' propensity to rely on private actors in the provision of governance. But what accounts for changing tides and cross-country variations in the privatization of governance? What makes states transfer political authority to private actors? In this book I propose a theoretical model of public authorities' use of credit ratings in their financial regulation, which I think can serve as a much more general model (or theory) of public authorities' delegation of public tasks to private actors. So I hope that this book will be insightful for both 'specialists' wanting to know more about the politics of credit rating agencies and 'generalists' interested in the contours, driving forces and implications of the transformation of governance and the state.

If this should be the case, much of the credit will go to colleagues and friends who have provided crucial assistance and critical input to this book project. I owe special thanks to Volker Rittberger and Bernhard Zangl for their invaluable intellectual and practical advice and support. I would also like to thank Ingvild Bode, Tine Hanrieder, Hans K. Hansen, Rainer Hülsse, Marina Karbowski, Dieter Kerwer, Alexander Kocks, Julia Maier-Rigaud, Thomas Nielebock, Andreas Nölke, Judith Renner, Alexander Spencer and Patrick Theiner, as well as the participants of the International Relations research colloquia at the universities of Tübingen and Munich for their very helpful comments at various stages of this project. Of course, all remaining omissions and errors of fact or interpretation are entirely my responsibility. I am grateful to the editors of the *Transformations of the State* series, Stephan Leibfried, Achim Hurrelmann, Kerstin Martens and Peter Mayer, for including my book in the series. I must also thank Liz Blackmore at Palgrave Macmillan for her support, assistance and patience in accompanying the publication of this book.

Very special thanks go to Anne Romund, not only for her detailed comments on the manuscript but also, and far more importantly, for her love and support, which have made writing this book much easier and a lot more enjoyable. Last, but certainly not least, I thank my parents, my sister and a few very close friends for their continuous encouragement and support over the years and decades.

1

Introduction: Private Ratings and Public Purposes

In the past three decades, public actors (i.e. states and intergovernmental organizations) have increasingly come to rely on private (business and civil society) actors' governance contributions in a wide range of political issue areas. A trend has emerged towards a partnering of state and nonstate actors in the provision of governance and a reallocation of political authority from public to private actors. This book examines processes of delegation of political authority from states to business actors in the vital public policy area of finance and seeks to uncover both structural, contextual and agency-related causes and conditions underlying these processes. More precisely, I develop and apply a synthetic theoretical model based on principal–agent theory, resource dependence theory and the varieties-of-capitalism approach in order to explain why public regulators in advanced OECD states have used credit ratings by private credit rating agencies (CRAs) for regulatory purposes. Credit rating agencies such as Moody's Investors Service, Standard & Poor's (S&P's) or Fitch Ratings are private firms that estimate and rate the creditworthiness of borrowers, for example firms, insurance companies, banks, municipalities, and sovereign states, as well as financial instruments, for example bonds, loans, and structured finance products such as collateralized debt obligations (Cutler et al. 1999b: 10–11; Fuchs 2005: 125; Kerwer 2002: 294). Credit rating agencies collect dispersed information on the financial situation of borrowers and the default risk of certain financial products, and condense it into a single measure of relative credit risk – a credit rating in the form of a letter grade (see Chapter 2). Credit rating agencies publish these condensed credit risk assessments, which have been widely used not only by private actors for investment decisions in the market place but also by public regulators in risk-sensitive financial regulation (Cantor and Packer 1994: 1; Kerwer 2002: 294; Nölke and Perry 2007: 129). This book is interested in exactly this latter regulatory use of private credit ratings. Through the regulatory use of private ratings for public purposes, public authorities have transferred (quasi-)regulatory authority to credit rating agencies. In explicating the causes and conditions for the use of credit ratings in financial regulation and the concomitant delegation of regulatory authority, this book addresses the more general overarching puzzle of why public actors from OECD countries have relied on private business actors for the provision of governance in key domains which affect crucial public policy goals.

The transformation of governance: decentralizing and privatizing political authority

This book draws upon and aims to complement a growing body of literature in international relations and comparative politics which is concerned with the emergence and consequences of transnational modes of governance and the transformation of statehood (Genschel and Zangl 2008; Hurrelmann et al. 2007; Koenig-Archibugi and Zürn 2006; Leibfried and Zürn 2005). In the face of globalization processes and the ensuing 'rise of transsovereign problems' (Cusimano 2000), which are propelling changes in the conditions for governance[1] in all policy domains of world politics, there is growing recognition that regulation is no longer the exclusive domain of states and intergovernmental organizations. Instead, scholars of global governance stress the regulatory capacities of nonstate actors[2] and point to the emergence of a variety of public–private and purely private modes of governance beyond the state. A broad range of public–private and private institutions create and implement rules for the collective management of trans-sovereign problems, which transcend state boundaries and cannot be solved by individual state actions alone, and take care of the provision of global public goods (Cusimano 2000: 3; Hutter 2006: 63; Koenig-Archibugi 2006: 1–3; Rittberger et al. 2008: 45; see also Bernstein and Cashore 2008; Graz and Nölke 2008a; Pattberg 2007).

However, while there can be no doubt that states are no longer the only or, at times, even the most important actors performing (global) governance activities, prophecies of the 'retreat of the state' (Strange 1996) from the provision of governance – most notably, though not exclusively, in the policy domain of welfare – have proved premature. Despite the proliferation of modes of governance involving nonstate actors, states seem to remain pivotal actors in world politics (Genschel and Zangl 2008: 430; Koenig-Archibugi 2006: 2). Pure forms of private transnational governance operating completely independently of states and/or intergovernmental organizations are relatively rare; the framework conditions which allow the emergence of meaningful private governance modes seem to be rather restrictive (Graz and Nölke 2008b: 23; Nölke and Graz 2008: 228). In many cases of so-called 'new', transnational modes of governance, an element of public involvement, support or oversight can be identified (Zürn and Koenig-Archibugi 2006: 242). In fact, nonstate governance institutions frequently operate in the 'shadow of hierarchy' (Héritier and Lehmkuhl 2008: 1). States may tacitly use, explicitly recognize and on occasion formally co-opt the governance capacities of nonstate actors contributing to several aspects of governance: information gathering (i.e. collection, processing and provision of information relevant for finding solutions to societal problems), rule setting (i.e. setting mostly 'soft' standards, aimed at guiding the behavior of social actors), behavior modification (i.e. ensuring the implementation of rules and changing individual or organizational behavior through monitoring and compliance mechanisms) and revision of rules (i.e. providing input concerning the adjustment of rules to changing circumstances) (Hutter 2006: 63–5).

The recognition and use of nonstate actors' governance capacities implies a 'decentralization' of governance from state to nonstate actors (Hutter 2006: 64), which seems to reflect a growing recognition of the limits of public law approaches and bureaucratic command and control strategies of regulation in the age of globalization. The growing recognition of alternative private methods and sources of regulation and the resulting broadening conception of regulation do not leave the state meaningless, though. In many cases, the effective functioning of transnational governance mechanisms is contingent upon states' recognition, support or even enforcement of private rules (Genschel and Zangl 2007, 2008). For example, transnational commercial dispute resolution ('lex mercatoria') is backed by the fact that private actors' decisions are recognized and, if need be, ultimately enforced by the state.

Thus, the state is not fading away; rather, the state itself and its relationship to nonstate actors are undergoing fundamental transformations, many of which are still difficult to grasp in conceptual and, even more so, in causal–analytical terms (Hurrelmann et al. 2007; Leibfried and Zürn 2005). As nonstate actors gain in importance, the state takes on new functions and new roles. The state is no longer the only political authority. Rather, it supports the political authority of nonstate actors and thus transforms itself from a 'monopolist' to a 'manager' of political authority (Genschel and Zangl 2008). The relationship of state and nonstate actors in the provision of governance can thus be described as a 'form of regulatory mix or partnering which involves the state overseeing or sharing regulatory responsibility' (Hutter 2006: 65) with private actors. Particularly in the realm of economic governance, the past two decades have seen the state increasingly harnessing corporate regulatory capacity with public recognition or even enforcement, and delegating regulatory duties (e.g. rule/standard setting or implementation) traditionally undertaken by public agencies to nonstate actors (ibid.: 63–5).

Deep involvement of private actors in governance processes, the recognition *by* the state of private modes and sources of regulation *beyond* the state and a 'decentralization' of governance from states to nonstate actors have been particularly evident in the global governance of financial, more precisely banking and securities, markets (Speyer 2006; Tsingou 2008). Financial market liberalization and deregulation, which can be traced back to initiatives of powerful states, first of all the US and the UK, in the early 1980s (Schirm 2004a: 75; see also Helleiner 1994), the cross-border integration of financial markets, and technological as well as financial product innovations, have substantially altered the operation of financial markets in the past decades and, consequently, fundamentally changed global financial governance (Tsingou 2008: 58). States have faced ever more significant constraints on the fulfillment of the public functions of financial market regulation and supervision, with 'financial market regulation' referring to the establishment of rules of behavior addressed towards financial market actors and 'financial market supervision' denoting the more general oversight of financial firms' behavior (ibid.).

States seem unable to oversee, let alone guide, the huge quantities of highly complex financial activities transcending national regulatory boundaries; in other words, when it comes to governing globalized financial markets, there is a particularly strong, widespread recognition of the limits of public law approaches and bureaucratic command and control strategies of regulation. At the same time, most states have been unwilling to substantially reverse patterns of liberalization, deregulation and integration of financial markets, for fear of harming their economic competitiveness. Proponents of financial market deregulation assert that an efficient allocation of resources achieved by liberalized financial markets will eventually entail middle and long-term market stability (Filc 2008: 4). However, contrary to overly optimistic assumptions, the deregulation and globalization of financial markets have not led to a level of market efficiency and stability which would relieve public authorities of their regulatory and supervisory responsibilities. Therefore, national and international regulatory and supervisory bodies have increasingly turned to private market actors and their know-how, using market-based methods of supervision and regulation for the provision of the (global) public good 'financial market stability' (Tsingou 2008: 58; see also Dieter 2004; Griffith-Jones 2003).

Thus, transnational private actors play a crucial and, in many cases, publicly sanctioned role in creating and implementing rules governing global financial markets (Speyer 2006: 101; Tsingou 2008: 59). This book sets out to describe and explain a particular feature of the governance of contemporary global financial markets: the use of credit ratings from private credit rating agencies in financial market regulation. This public use of credit ratings represents an institutional mode of state-sanctioned and state-bolstered involvement of private actors in governance processes, which is distinct from purely private provision of governance as well as from institutionalized participation of nonstate actors in 'open' intergovernmental or 'inclusive', public–private institutions for global governance (Rittberger et al. 2008; Staisch 2003). The use of credit ratings by national and international regulatory bodies constitutes a form of delegation of governance tasks and (quasi-)regulatory authority from public to private actors.

Why have states used credit ratings in regulation? The research question and its broader relevance

In the wake of the recent global financial crisis, which started out as a US mortgage crisis (2007) but went on to severely affect the banking industry, financial markets and real economies around the world, the recognition that credit rating agencies play a critical role in guiding the allocation of capital in global markets has moved beyond academic circles to enter public debates about the state of affairs and the future of the global financial system. In fact, credit rating agencies have become one of the main targets in the blame game for financial market losses caused by the financial crisis (Taylor 2008: 20).

A number of scholars have acknowledged – even before the 2007 US mortgage meltdown and the ensuing global financial crisis – that the credit rating agencies' powerful position in the global financial architecture raises crucial questions about their reliability, legitimacy and accountability (Gras 2003; Kerwer 2005; Partnoy 2006; Rousseau 2005). However, an important feature in the governance of (global) financial markets which has underpinned the power of credit rating agencies is still poorly understood. In the years and decades before the global financial crisis, national and international financial market regulators around the world – such as the US Securities and Exchange Commission (SEC) and other US regulatory bodies, the Basel Committee on Banking Supervision (BCBS) and EU legislators – came to use ratings by private credit rating agencies as risk measures for regulatory purposes on an increasing scale and scope (King and Sinclair 2003; Nicholls 2005; Rosenbaum 2004; Schwarcz 2001a, b; Strunz-Happe 2004).[3] While the use of credit ratings in financial market regulation has a long history in the US and some other countries (Kerwer 2002: 304–5; King and Sinclair 2001: 14–17; Rosenbaum 2004), it has gone global only in recent years (Nölke and Perry 2007: 131). From the 1980s onwards, as well as credit rating agencies' business activities, the regulatory use of credit ratings has spread geographically, and can now be found in most countries in the developed world (Estrella et al. 2000: 40–54; Kerwer 2005: 463). Credit ratings have been used by US and other national regulatory authorities, *inter alia*, to increase the risk sensitivity of investment restrictions for certain financial institutions (e.g. banks and pension funds), to define differential disclosure requirements for issuers of rated bonds with reference to the rating obtained from credit rating agencies, and to adjust capital reserve requirements for commercial or investment banks and institutional broker–dealers to their credit risk exposure (Kerwer 2002: 304; 2005: 463; Rosenbaum 2004: 11; Sinclair 2005: 42–5; see Chapter 2 for a more detailed overview of ratings-dependent regulation).

On the international level, the revised Basel Capital Accord of 2004 (Basel II) provided for the use of credit ratings from approved credit rating agencies, also referred to as 'external credit assessment institutions', in the calculation of banks' net capital reserve requirements (BCBS 2006: paras 50–1, 90–2). The Basel II Accord was developed in the late 1990s and early 2000s by the Basel Committee on Banking Supervision (BCBS), consisting of the central bank governors and representatives from the national credit market regulation agencies of 13 OECD states (Belgium, Canada, France, Germany, Italy, Japan, Luxembourg, the Netherlands, Spain, Sweden, Switzerland, the United Kingdom and the United States). The Basel II Accord of 2004 contains international standards for banking supervision – in particular, though not exclusively, relating to capital reserve requirements – which national regulatory and supervisory authorities should implement (see Chapter 2; Freund 2002; Macht 2007). The main function of all Basel Accords is to define internationally harmonized minimum capital reserve requirements which prescribe the minimum amount of capital banks are obliged to keep in reserve as a safety measure in the case of credit default. Notwithstanding spectacular failures, such as in the recent global financial crisis, the underlying idea of minimum capital requirements has remained uncontested: even in the case of some large-scale credit defaults, banks should still have enough capital 'put aside' to avoid a breakdown which might infect other financial institutions. Internationally harmonized capital reserve requirements should help to guarantee an 'international level playing field' for banks (Macht 2007). The crucial questions are how much capital should be put aside and how to calculate capital reserve requirements.

Unlike the original Basel Accord of 1988, the Basel II Accord proposed that regulation concerning banks' capital reserve requirements should be flexible and risk-sensitive. The amount of capital that banks needed to keep in reserve against the risk of credit default should no longer be calculated according to fixed formulae irrespective of the creditworthiness of their borrowers (BCBS 1999b: 9–10; Freund 2002: 63; Macht 2007: 60–3; Speyer 2006: 110–111). According to the Basel II Accord, whose main elements were put into force within the EU by the Capital Requirements Directive and Banking Directive in 2006, capital reserve requirements for banks should be dependent (among other factors) on the default risk of the credits banks issue. The Basel II Accord – and, consequently, the legally binding EU Capital Requirements Directive – provides for external measurement of credit risk by recognized credit rating agencies as one of two broad methodologies for banks' credit risk assessment (the standardized approach as opposed to the internal ratings-based approach). Banks that would like to deviate from the standardized approach and instead use their own internal rating procedures within the alternative framework of the internal ratings-based approach need to file an application with their national regulatory agency (see Chapter 2 for a more detailed discussion of Basel II; see also Asmussen 2005: 252–3; BCBS 2003, 2006: paras 50–1; Kerwer 2002: 305–6; 2005: 463, 470; King and Sinclair 2003: 349–51; Nölke 2004: 167–8; Nölke and Perry 2007: 130; Partnoy 2006: 83).

The use of private credit ratings by public national and international regulators constitutes a complex institutional mode of publicly sanctioned and publicly bolstered private governance of financial markets. As I will argue in more detail in Chapter 2, this arrangement is best conceived as a form of delegation of governance tasks and (quasi-)regulatory authority from public regulatory bodies to credit rating agencies. Once they are relied upon by public authorities, credit rating agencies fulfill governance functions for global financial markets in conjunction with public actors – more precisely, they perform state-sanctioned risk measurement, according to their own standard of creditworthiness, which allows risk-sensitive, flexible public regulation. Thus, a particular institutional mode of private participation in global governance can be observed that warrants not only careful conceptualization but also theoretical explanation. The use of credit ratings in financial market regulation raises crucial questions on how power and accountability are distributed within the interorganizational relationship between public regulators and credit rating agencies and how credit rating agencies' position on the markets, vis-à-vis other public and private market participants, is affected by the use of credit ratings in regulation (Cantor 2001: 178–80). However, the consequences of the use of credit ratings for regulatory purposes can only fully be grasped once the reasons for the reliance on private credit rating agencies in financial regulation are explained.

Therefore, this book seeks to provide a theory-based answer to the research question: *why public national and international financial market regulators, not only in the USA, but also on the international and particularly on the European level, came to use credit ratings by private rating agencies as risk measures in financial market regulation.* Providing a theory-based answer to this research question implies addressing the question of how the institutional mode of governance that is constituted by the public use of private credit ratings for regulatory purposes can be conceptualized and explained in more general theoretical terms.

Why should we care about finding an answer to this research question? In other words: what is the real-world and broader scientific relevance of this book? What kinds of political and scientific debates does it address? There are several rationales that make an investigation into the causes and conditions for the regulatory use of credit ratings appear worthwhile. First of all, studies dealing with credit rating agencies' influence on other financial market actors frequently discuss the use of credit ratings for regulatory purposes and its implications for credit rating agencies' power in transnational economic governance (Dittrich 2007; Gras 2003; Kerwer 2002, 2005; King and Sinclair 2001, 2003; Nicholls 2005; Nölke 2004; Nölke and Perry 2007; Rosenbaum 2004; Schwarcz 2001a, b). However, an in-depth, theory-guided analysis of public authorities' use of credit ratings in financial market regulation is still lacking. So far, there is no study that provides a theoretically grounded explanation for the regulatory use of private credit ratings by public authorities (the US SEC, the BCBS or EU legislators). This is all the more surprising as we are dealing with a phenomenon that is obviously 'important' in the real world *and* addresses broader conceptual and theoretical issues that are currently debated in a growing body of scholarly literature on (global) governance and the transformation of the state.

There can be no doubt about the real-world significance of credit rating agencies in general and the regulatory use of their ratings in particular. Credit rating agencies play a crucial role as collectors, processors and distributors of investment-related information that is relied upon by a large number of public and private financial market actors in the current global political economy. The influence of credit rating agencies has become manifest and widely recognized, at least since the US subprime and global financial crises (2007–10), the huge dimensions and global reach of which would not have been possible without credit rating agencies putting their 'stamp of approval' concerning adequate protection against default risks on mortgage-backed structured finance products (Lowenstein 2008; Taylor 2008: 20). Investors around the world relied on good or even very good credit ratings for collateralized debt obligations (CDOs)[4] backed by US mortgages, and bought those CDOs without being aware of the credit risks implied in those complex 'structured finance products'. Credit rating agencies have been blamed for downgrading mortgage-backed securities far too late and for failing to develop adequate risk models to identify risks and value those products properly (see Chapter 6; *The Economist* 2007a, b; Norris 2007; Osman 2007; Tomlinson and Evans 2007). The US subprime and global financial crises have demonstrated to a broader audience the critical role credit rating agencies play in global investment decisions and the powerful position they occupy in the current global financial system. Credit rating agencies, which for decades had merely caught the interest of financial market professionals and scholars of financial market governance, have become the object of rather extensive coverage in US and international media (see e.g. Hoffmann 2008; Kazim 2007; Lowenstein 2008; Osman 2007; Osman and Buchter 2007; Summers 2007; Zydra 2008). Notwithstanding this heightened public attention to credit rating agencies, their modes of operation, their sources of influence and, in particular, their relationship with state regulatory actors are still poorly understood by many people (e.g. politicians, small private investors, owners of small and medium-sized enterprises, and even employees) who might be affected by credit rating agencies (Friedmann 1995, Love 2008).

This is unfortunate, since the real-world importance of credit rating agencies is pronounced enough to raise considerable normative–prescriptive concerns that relate not only to questions of credit rating agencies' factual and interpretive reliability but also to more fundamental concerns with their 'unchecked power' in the current global financial governance architecture as well as their deficits of accountability and participatory legitimacy (Fuchs 2005: 125; Gras 2003; Kerwer 2005). The latter concerns become particularly salient, if not most relevant in terms of widespread 'structural' impact, when credit rating agencies rate sovereign states. Through so-called 'sovereign ratings' which constrain the financing opportunities of developing countries, credit rating agencies might even be in a position to influence economic and financial policies of states (Fuchs 2005: 125; Gras 2003: 23–4; Hillebrand 2001: 153–5; Murphy 2000). Credit rating agencies are assumed to have a substantial 'infrastructural' impact on corporate governance structures, not only in the US but also in Europe, by favoring short-term, shareholder-oriented business policies, which have been prevalent in Anglo-Saxon liberal market economies as opposed to Continental European coordinated market economies (Nölke and Perry 2007: 123). German small and medium-sized ('Mittelstand') companies feared that Basel II and the increasing role of credit rating agencies would make the financing model of German 'Mittelstand' companies, small and medium-sized enterprises, difficult to sustain, since highly indebted companies might face steep increases in credit costs due to their 'problematic' risk profile under Basel II (see Chapter 5). There have also been concerns that credit rating agencies may multiply pressures from shareholders to maximize dividends by concentrating on quarterly results and short-range return on investment variables (Nölke and Perry 2007: 131). At any rate, many people are actually, or might potentially be, affected by credit rating agencies and their relative position in the global financial architecture. Through the reallocation of governance tasks to transnational private expert bodies, the supervision of the financial economy has been further isolated from broad public scrutiny – at least as long as no major financial crises, such as the recent US subprime and global financial crises, occur (Nölke and Perry 2007: 136). It is crucial to note that the regulatory use of credit ratings bolsters credit rating agencies' influence. The use of credit ratings for regulatory purposes has further empowered credit rating agencies and contributed to 'enforcing' their standard of creditworthiness (Kerwer 2002: 303–4). Since the US subprime and global financial crises, public regulators in the US have expressed their worries that large-scale use of credit ratings in financial regulation may have contributed to investors' 'overreliance' on credit rating agencies (Ackerman 2008; SEC 2009b). Therefore the SEC has decided to stop referencing credit ratings in some of its securities markets rules (see Chapter 6 for the most recent regulatory developments since the financial crisis).

As far as the broader scientific relevance of this book is concerned, my study builds on and speaks to research on credit rating agencies and the transformation of governance and statehood. While, for the past 10 years in particular, a considerable amount of mostly empirical and prescriptive, but also some theory-guided, literature on credit rating agencies has accumulated,[5] a thorough theory-based explanation of the use of credit ratings by public regulatory bodies has not been offered yet. Faced with the failure of credit rating agencies to predict major financial crises and bankruptcies, the overall reliability of credit ratings has been questioned (Gras 2003: 30; see also Partnoy 1999; Reisen and von Maltzan 1999). A large number of proposals for stricter public oversight and control of credit rating agencies to increase the reliability of credit ratings have been voiced and discussed controversially (Covitz and Harrison 2003; Dittrich 2007; Fisch 2005; Partnoy 2001, 2006; Rousseau 2005; Smith and Walter 2001; Strunz-Happe 2005). Critics have argued that there are fundamental pathologies of the credit rating industry which contribute to *systematic* malperformance (Gras 2003).[6] However, at least until the recent global financial crisis, credit rating agencies were hardly held accountable for their performance. In fact, the lack of accountability of credit rating agencies has been the subject of scholarly work dealing with the 'accountability gap' (Kerwer 2005: 455) between the (quasi-)regulatory power of credit rating agencies and the lack of effective oversight and control of credit rating agencies (Fisch 2005; Kerwer 2005; Rousseau 2005; Smith and Walter 2001). In this book, I show that analyses of the politics of accountability in transnational governance can benefit from an in-depth, theory-guided investigation of the reliance of public regulators on credit rating agencies.

In analyzing the delegation of (quasi-)regulatory authority to credit rating agencies, this book aims to contribute to ongoing debates about the transformation of the state (Genschel and Zangl 2008; Hurrelmann et al. 2007; Leibfried and Zürn 2005) and the origins and dynamics of transnational private authority in global governance (Cutler et al. 1999a; Graz and Nölke 2008a; Hall and Biersteker 2002; Higgott et al. 2000; Nölke et al. 2007). Scholars of global governance argue that, by defining and monitoring a global standard of creditworthiness, credit rating agencies do not just disseminate 'informed opinions' about relative credit risk, but, rather, exercise private authority (Kerwer 2002; Nölke 2004; Schwarcz 2001a, b; Sinclair 2000, 2001). But things are more complicated than that. When private credit ratings are used by public national and international regulators, a particular institutional mode of publicly sanctioned and publicly bolstered private governance emerges which constitutes a public–private principal–agent relationship. The use of credit ratings by public regulators thus points to the variety of transnational governance arrangements that in one way or another include private nonstate actors (Koenig-Archibugi 2006; Rittberger et al. 2008). By conceptualizing and explaining the delegation of (quasi-)regulatory authority from public actors to transnational private agents, the book contributes to the literature on (the reasons for) the emergence of diverse public–private modes of global governance (Koenig-Archibugi 2006: 2–3).

The theoretical model proposed in this book draws upon and combines two main theoretical approaches that seem useful to advance our understanding of the decentralization and privatization of governance in the OECD world: principal–agent theory (see Hawkins et al. 2006a; Pollack 1997, 2003; Tallberg 2002) and resource dependence theory (see Brühl 2003; Edele 2006; Liese 2009; Nölke 2000; Pfeffer and Salancik 2003). There are a large number of studies that rely on principal–agent theory in order to analyze the delegation of competences from states to international organizations (Hawkins et al. 2006a; Mutschler 2008; Pollack 1997, 2006; Tallberg 2002).[7] This book seeks to show that principal–agent theory can fruitfully be applied to the relationship between public actors and private credit rating agencies conceived as transnational governance organizations which are explicitly recognized and harnessed in their regulatory authority by public actors. Research on the dependence of public actors on private actors' resources and its effect on the formation of public–private governance arrangements is a second major influence on the theoretical model. By increasingly taking actors' interests, incentives and resource endowments into account when trying to explain cooperative public–private relationships, scholars of 'new' modes of governance have explicitly or implicitly picked up resource exchange theory and resource dependence theory, which had first been used in (inter-)organizational research back in the late 1970s (Brühl 2003; Edele 2006; Liese 2009; Nölke 2000; see Aldrich 1975,

1979; Pfeffer 1981; Pfeffer and Salancik 2003). In particular, resource exchange theory has been used to explain the formation of (global) public–private partnerships, transnational policy networks and inclusive, multipartite institutions (Edele 2006; Nölke 2000; Rittberger 2008).[8] I apply a resource dependence perspective to the delegation of (quasi-)regulatory authority from states to private actors, showing that resource dependence theory and principal–agent theory can usefully be combined.

Finally, this book makes a contribution to research on 'new' modes of governance in that it seeks to complement agency-centered theoretical arguments derived from resource dependence theory and principal–agent theory with a structural framework that identifies particular macro-institutional socioeconomic contexts which condition public regulators' resource dependence. For that purpose, I draw on environmental approaches in organization theory (Blau 1987; Galbraith 1973, 1977; Hamilton and Woolsey Biggart 1994) and concepts of embedded and disembedded liberalism (Polanyi 1944; Ruggie 1982) as well as the varieties-of-capitalism approach (Coates 2005; Hall and Soskice 2001a; Schmidt 2002). These approaches capture how economic policies and the behavior of political and market actors are shaped by existing global and national/regional macro-institutional arrangements such as the structure of the global financial system and the prevalent modes of corporate financing.

Research design

The research design of this book essentially comprises three steps: a description of the object of investigation, that is, the regulatory use of credit ratings; the development of an explanatory theoretical model that purports to explain variations in the regulatory use of credit ratings over time and across countries; and, finally, a test of the proposed explanatory framework against empirical evidence, which also amounts to an account of both transformations in the governance of global financial markets and the persistent relevance of national (macro-)institutions in explaining states' positions on alternative modes of economic governance in an era of globalization.

First of all, due to the complexity of the subject matter, an in-depth description of credit rating agencies' activities and the regulatory use of credit ratings is a necessary prerequisite for developing an adequate explanation for this phenomenon (see Chapter 2). The basic idea is that we should first know *what* we are dealing with before we try to provide a satisfactory answer to the *why*-question that motivates the book. Thus, after a description of the regulatory use of credit ratings from the early 1930s to 2006 (before the US subprime crisis and the ensuing global financial crisis), the *explanandum* of this book, the regulatory use of credit ratings, will be conceptualized in more abstract terms in a *heuristic (what-)model* of ratings-dependent regulation.[9] This conceptual model is based on the principal–agent approach. Credit rating agencies are analyzed as transnational expert standard-setters whose standard of creditworthiness is authoritatively made binding by public regulators. Thus, the use of credit ratings in financial regulation constitutes a form of delegation of governance tasks and (quasi-)regulatory authority from public regulatory bodies to transnational standard-setters, in this case credit rating agencies. This conceptualization of the regulatory use of credit ratings in more abstract terms as a principal–agent relationship is useful because it avoids random ad hoc explanations of the observed phenomena and contributes to cumulative research on the transfer of political authority to nonstate actors. Thus, I argue that the theoretical model that builds on this public–private principal–agent relationship could be useful for the analysis of a broad range of situations where public actors delegate governance tasks and political authority to private actors.

Having described the empirical puzzle and conceptualized it in more abstract terms, the book explores what factors drive the delegation of political authority to credit rating agencies. For that purpose, a causal–theoretical (*why*-)model[10] is constructed. In order to arrive at an explanation which is both comprehensive and clearly framed, there is a need for some theory-generation or, more precisely, 'theory-re-engineering' rather than mere application of an existing theory. Therefore, theories and sets of concepts from different subfields of political science, namely principal–agent theory, resource dependence theory, environmental approaches in organization research and the concepts of embedded and disembedded liberalism as well as the varieties-of-capitalism approach, are modified and recombined for an explanation of a publicly sanctioned and publicly bolstered mode of private governance. This synthesis of different approaches serves to enhance the empirical explanatory power of this book and to make a theoretical contribution to the research on different institutional modes of transnational governance. The reasoning that connects the different theoretical and conceptual approaches into a single theoretical model in Chapter 3 is done in a mainly deductive manner and the proposed causal relationships are, to a large extent, phrased in general, rather than in case-specific, terms.[11] A positive corollary of this reasoning about causal relationships in abstract terms is that the validity of the *general* theoretical framework – which explains delegation of authority to transnational expert actors with recourse to a macro-institutionally embedded resource dependence argument – could well be tested in case studies that seek to explain delegation of authority to private (expert) actors other than credit rating agencies.

From the proposed theoretical model specific causal hypotheses are derived which are then applied to an intertemporal and interregional analysis of ratings-dependent regulation (see Chapter 4) and a case study that seeks to make sense of the Basel II provisions on external ratings in banking supervision (see Chapter 5). In doing so, I test whether the predictions made by the theoretical model are corroborated by empirical data. In this book, a test design is chosen that comprises an intertemporal and interregional congruence analysis as well as process tracing. The intertemporal analysis checks whether the values of the condition variable, the independent variable and the dependent variable of the theoretical model co-vary over (different points in) time. The interregional analysis checks whether the values of the condition variable, the independent variable and the dependent variable proposed by the theoretical model co-vary across (world) regions, namely the US and Continental Europe (see Collier 1993; Lijphart 1971; Van Evera 1997: 58–62). This intertemporal and interregional analysis is complemented by retracing a particular decision for the (limited) use of credit ratings in financial regulation: the inclusion of provisions for ratings-dependent banking regulation into the Basel II Accord. Empirical evidence is drawn from political science and economics research on the use of credit ratings in regulation and the broader development of global financial markets as well as from primary data including quantitative indicators of financial market development on a regional and global level, oral statements of public regulators on the role of credit rating agencies and consultative reports on the role and function of credit rating agencies in financial market governance by national and international regulatory bodies.

Core arguments and structure of the book

The aim of this book is to provide a theoretically and empirically grounded explanation for the regulatory use of credit ratings by national and international public regulatory bodies. For that purpose, a synthetic theoretical model of delegation to transnational private actors is developed and empirically applied. The macro-institutionally embedded resource dependence perspective on delegation to private actors that is advanced in this book should be useful not only for explaining trends and variations in the regulatory use of credit ratings but also for understanding a wide range of situations in which public actors have delegated political authority to private actors.

The book argues that, in the past few decades before the global financial crisis, public regulators not only in the US but in developed countries across the world increasingly perceived themselves as lacking essential analytical resources, that is, capabilities to cope with financial market uncertainty in a risk-sensitive way. Therefore, public regulators have delegated governance tasks and (quasi-)regulatory authority to specialized risk-measuring agents, namely credit rating agencies. Intertemporally and interregionally varying degrees of dependence on credit rating agencies' analytical resources cause diachronic and cross-country variations in the regulatory use of credit ratings: the higher the degree of public regulators' dependence on the analytical resources of credit rating agencies, the higher will be the degree of public regulators' use of credit ratings in regulation. Public regulators' dependence on the analytical resources of private credit rating agencies is a function of different global and national/regional macro-institutional settings; it is contingent on the (dis)embeddedness of the global financial system and the prevalence of different varieties of capitalism (Rhenish coordinated market economy vs. Anglo-Saxon liberal market economy). A move from embedded to disembedded liberalism in the global financial architecture leads to a higher overall degree of dependence on credit rating agencies, and an Anglo-Saxon variety of capitalism is linked to a considerably higher degree of dependence on the analytical resources of credit rating agencies than a Rhenish variety of capitalism.

The empirical tenability and analytical usefulness of the proposed theoretical model are underlined by an intertemporal and interregional analysis of ratings-dependent regulation (from 1931 to 2006) and by process-tracing the road to Basel II. The model is also useful for understanding regulatory change in the oversight of credit rating agencies and in the regulatory use of credit ratings after the US subprime and global financial crises, as the final chapter, Chapter 6, demonstrates.

These core arguments are developed in the following way. Chapter 2 is descriptive in nature and provides an empirical overview of the use of credit ratings by national and international regulatory bodies as well as a heuristic conceptualization of the regulatory use of credit ratings. In Chapter 3, a theoretical model combining principal–agent theory, resource dependence theory and concepts of embedded and disembedded liberalism as well as the varieties-of-capitalism approach is constructed. In Chapter 4, an intertemporal and interregional analysis of common trends and cross-country differences in the regulatory use of credit ratings is performed as an initial test of the empirical validity of the proposed theoretical framework. This congruence test, which checks whether the independent, dependent and condition variables of this study co-vary over time and across countries, is complemented in Chapter 5 by retracing the decision to include provisions for ratings-dependent banking regulation in the Basel II Accord. The aim of this process-tracing exercise is to examine whether the candidate hypotheses and the proposed causal mechanism are corroborated by an in-depth study of a particular decision for the use of credit ratings in regulation (see Bennett and George 2005; Eckstein 1975). Chapter 6 presents a summary of the main findings of the book and a brief discussion of its limits, open questions and directions for further research. Moreover, it offers a preliminary assessment and a tentative outlook on regulatory changes in the control of credit rating agencies and the use of credit ratings in financial regulation after the involvement of credit rating agencies in the US subprime and global financial crises (2007–10).

2
The Regulatory Use of Credit Ratings: Overview and Conceptualization

Credit ratings have been used for a number of public regulatory purposes in the US regulatory system and other national regulatory systems as well as in international financial market rules. In the three decades before the global financial crisis, national and international regulatory bodies made increasing use of ratings-dependent regulation. While the importance of ratings-based regulations has traditionally been particularly salient in the United States, all developed states came to use credit ratings for regulatory purposes to some extent. This chapter describes the regulatory use of credit ratings in national and international financial regulation. In a next step, the regulatory use of credit ratings is conceptualized in more abstract terms. Credit rating agencies set a private standard of creditworthiness which is made binding by a public third party when credit ratings are used in financial regulation. This public enforcement of credit rating agencies' standard of creditworthiness constitutes a delegation of regulatory authority from public regulators (principals) to a specific type of transnational expert standard-setters (agents).

However, before turning to a more detailed description of the use of private credit ratings by public regulators for regulatory purposes, a few words on the key features of credit ratings and the process of credit rating, the roles and functions of credit rating agencies in the global political economy, the structure of the credit rating industry, and the rise of credit rating agencies in the past three decades are in order. This should help to get a better grasp of what credit ratings mean, how and under what conditions ratings are produced, and why they are important for financial market actors (even if they were *not* used in financial regulation).

The credit rating industry: what ratings mean, how they are produced and why they are important

Key features of credit ratings and the rating process

As already indicated in Chapter 1, credit rating agencies are private companies that estimate and rate the creditworthiness of public and private borrowers (*issuer ratings*) and a wide range of financial products such as bonds, loans or CDOs (*issue ratings*). Credit ratings are measures of relative credit risk; they express, in the form of letter grades, credit rating agencies' assessment of the relative likelihood that there will be a credit default, that is, a missed or late disbursement of debt interests or principal sums (Moody's Investors Service 1991: 74). In other words, credit rating agencies assess the relative likelihood that payment requirements arising from the issuance of bonds will be serviced both in time and to full extent, that is, in accordance with the initially offered conditions (Peters 2001: 28). Inherent in the definition of ratings as indicators of *relative* credit risk is the notion that they are an ordinal measure of risk, but not necessarily a cardinal one (Gonzalez et al. 2004: 7). Credit rating agencies stress that their ratings are merely 'opinions' about comparative credit risk which do not amount to recommendations to buy, sell or hold a particular financial title, and do not address the suitability of a particular financial product/investment for a particular investor (Gonzalez et al. 2004: 7; Gras 2003: 7; Moody's Investors Service 1991: 73; Peters 2001: 67). By insisting that their ratings are nothing but opinions protected by the US Constitutional right to free speech, credit rating agencies seek to deny effective legal liability for their ratings, which is considered one of the reasons for their 'accountability gap' (Kerwer 2005: 455). The liability standard to which credit rating agencies are held in US courts is thus not mere 'negligence' but 'recklessness', which constitutes a very high hurdle for plaintiffs (Kerwer 2005: 469; for a detailed legal discussion see Husisian 1990 and Peters 2001). However, critics argue that, while credit rating agencies assert that rating determinations are opinions, they simultaneously seek to objectify and offer their views as 'facts', masking the inherent tentativeness of the rating process (Sinclair 2005: 47). In the wake of the global financial crisis, calls for legal liability of credit rating agencies in the case of gross negligence have been voiced (again). For example, it has been suggested that credit rating agencies should be liable for their credit risk assessments just as auditing firms are (Grass 2007). However, it remains highly doubtful whether legal practice will change so that credit rating agencies can effectively be held accountable before courts.

Different types of ratings can be distinguished, the most important distinctions being those between issuer and issue ratings, long-term and short-term ratings, confidential and published ratings, and solicited and unsolicited ratings. *Issue* ratings are assessments of specific financial products (e.g. bonds, loans and CDOs) while *issuer* ratings refer to the creditworthiness of borrowers (i.e. private as well as public financial market actors). *Long-term* ratings are ratings for bonds with a duration of more than one year, while *short-term* ratings refer to bonds with a duration of less than one year (Gras 2003: 7–8). While there are *confidential* ratings, the overwhelming amount of credit ratings are *published* by the credit rating agencies on their websites and in the relevant media and are available to financial market actors for free (Cantor and Packer 1994: 1; Kerwer 2002: 301–3; Nölke and Perry 2007: 129). The main revenue of credit rating agencies (around 80 to 95 percent of their overall income) comes from rating fees paid by issuers of bonds for solicited ratings. *Solicited* ratings are requested by and prepared in consultation with the issuer of the rated financial product. They are based on both public and confidential information which the issuer agrees to share with credit rating agencies, and borrowers, rather than investors, pay credit rating agencies for solicited ratings (Gonzalez et al. 2004: 6). In the less common case of (unpaid) *unsolicited* ratings, credit rating agencies produce a rating on their own initiative, using only publicly available data on the borrower or the financial product. Unsolicited ratings tend to be lower than solicited ones because they are exclusively based on public information, which implies that credit rating agencies consider it necessary to hedge against unknown risks (Gras 2003: 7–9).

The business model of credit rating agencies, which provides that borrowers pay fees for solicited ratings, has been the object of constant criticism. This has not always been the case. Until the 1970s, credit rating agencies earned their money by selling publications containing their credit risk assessments to investors. Investors interested in credit ratings needed to subscribe to newsletters published by credit rating agencies. In the 1970s, this business model came under pressure because ratings were increasingly available for free on the newly introduced electronic communication networks for finance. This is when rating agencies switched to charging borrowers (Kerwer 2005: 468). Critical observers argue that the current business model almost necessarily creates a conflict of interests and might provide incentives for 'rating-shopping', that is, choosing the credit rating agency that 'offers' the most favorable credit risk assessment (Dittrich 2007; Hartwall and Pettersson 2005; King and Sinclair 2003; Partnoy 2001). White (2001: 19) identifies a potential moral hazard due to the financing model of credit rating agencies: 'A rating firm might offer to improve an issuer's rating in return for a higher fee. Or it might threaten that an unsolicited rating would be substantially lower than a requested (fee-based) rating.' Credit rating agencies, and some scholars, reply that the main asset of credit rating agencies is their reputation and credibility as reliable measurers of risks. The business of credit rating agencies is contingent upon their reputation for high quality, excellent expertise, and an image of objectivity and independence (Covitz and Harrison 2003; O'Donovan 2004). According to this view, credit rating agencies cannot afford to endanger their reputation by giving their clients more lenient grades than would be appropriate. A reputation for high quality, accurate ratings is considered to be the overriding incentive of credit rating agencies, and it is this that disciplines their behavior (Gras 2003: 16). In response to criticism of credit rating agencies' business model, Raymond McDaniel, the CEO of Moody's, has argued that there would be conflicts related to the business model of credit rating agencies no matter who paid the fees, suggesting that a major investor paying a credit rating agency might put pressure on the agency to give high ratings to securities the investor already owned. However, critics reply that it is stretching the imagination to suggest that the conflict of interest would be comparable if credit rating agencies were being paid by the buyers of financial products (Norris 2008: 13).

The rating symbols through which credit rating agencies express the outcome of their credit risk assessments are letter grades or, more precisely, combinations of letters and so-called 'modifiers' (+/– or 1/2/3). These rating symbols more or less correspond to each other across rating agencies even if the exact combinations of letters and modifiers used by the single agencies differ (Gonzalez et al. 2004: 7; Gras 2003: 9). The scale for the evaluation of long-term bonds[1] ranges from Aaa (Moody's) or AAA (S&P's) – the best grade signifying very high safety against credit default – over numerous steps (22 with S&P's and 21 with Moody's) to C (Moody's) or D (S&P's), indicating high probability of credit loss[2] and 'extremely poor prospects for ever attaining any investment value' (Gras 2003: 9; Moody's Investors Service 1991: 74). Credit ratings are broadly categorized as either *investment grade* or *speculative grade* ratings: bonds rated Baa3 (BBB–) or higher obtain an investment grade while bonds rated Ba1 (BB+) or lower obtain a speculative grade and are sometimes referred to as 'junk bonds' (Everling 1991: 48–9; Schwarcz 2001a: 300). The investment vs. speculative grade threshold is significant for a number of reasons. First of all, it severely affects the costs of borrowing and the opportunities for getting access to capital. In addition to that, many institutional investors have their own business guidelines, which define minimal safety requirements and stipulate that financial titles whose rating drops below the investment grade threshold should be got rid of immediately. Dropping below the investment grade threshold thus triggers (quasi-)automatically the sale of the respective financial titles (Gras 2003: 18–19). Finally, the distinction between investment grade and speculative grade is significant because there are usually stricter regulatory requirements for issuers of speculative grade bonds (Gras 2003: 9). Table 2.1 shows the rating symbols used by the two major credit rating agencies, Moody's and S&P's, for long-term issue ratings and the meaning of the rating symbols.

Credit rating agencies' assessment of the creditworthiness of a borrower and/or the credit risk inherent in a certain financial product can be conceived as a fairly routinized multistep procedure (S&P's 2007b). Table 2.2 provides a typified overview of the credit rating process, which consists of five main elements.

The most complex step in the overall credit rating process is the credit analysis. In order to assess credit default risk, credit rating agencies use a broad set of economic criteria and employ both quantitative and qualitative methods for risk measurement, which differ

Table 2.1 Credit rating symbols (long-term issue credit ratings)

Moody's	S&P's	Meaning of the rating*	Categorization
Aaa	*AAA*	highest rating assigned; the obligor's capacity to meet its financial commitment on the obligation is extremely strong.	investment grade
Aa1 *Aa2* *Aa3*	*AA+* *AA* *AA–*	differs from the highest-rated obligations only to a small degree; the obligor's capacity to meet its financial commitment on the obligation is very strong.	
A1 *A2* *A3*	*A+* *A* *A–*	somewhat more susceptible to the adverse effects of changes in circumstances and economic conditions; the obligor's capacity to meet its financial commitment on the obligation is still strong.	
Baa1 *Baa2* *Baa3*	*BBB+* *BBB* *BBB–*	adequate protection parameters; adverse economic conditions or changing circumstances are more likely to lead to a weakened capacity of the obligor to meet its financial commitment on the obligation.	
Ba1 *Ba2* *Ba3*	*BB+* *BB* *BB–*	less vulnerable to nonpayment than other speculative issues; however, major ongoing uncertainties or exposure to adverse business, financial or economic conditions could lead to the obligor's inadequate capacity to meet its financial commitment on the obligation.	speculative grade
B1 *B2* *B3*	*B+* *B* *B–*	more vulnerable to nonpayment than obligations rated 'BB', but the obligor currently has the capacity to meet its financial commitment on the obligation; adverse business, financial or economic conditions will likely impair the obligor's capacity or willingness to meet its financial commitment on the obligation.	
Caa1 *Caa2* *Caa3*	*CCC+* *CCC* *CCC–*	currently vulnerable to nonpayment, dependent on favorable business, financial and economic conditions for the obligor to meet its financial commitment on the obligation; in the event of adverse business, financial or economic conditions, the obligor is not likely to have the capacity to meet its financial commitment.	

Continued

Table 2.1 Continued

Moody's	S&P's	Meaning of the rating*	Categorization
Ca	*CC*	currently highly vulnerable to nonpayment.	
C	*C*	obligations that are currently highly vulnerable to nonpayment, obligations that have payment arrearages allowed by the terms of the documents, or obligations of an issuer that is the subject of a bankruptcy petition or similar action which have not experienced a payment default.	
	D	in payment default; payments on an obligation are not made on the date due; used upon the filing of a bankruptcy petition or the taking of a similar action if payments on an obligation are jeopardized.	

Note: * The definitions are from S&P's (2008). Moody's definitions are similar. S&P's ratings from 'AA' to 'CCC' may be modified by the addition of a plus (+) or minus (–) sign to show relative standing within the major rating categories. Moody's uses the numbers 1, 2, 3 for that purpose. Only definitions for the major categories without modifiers are indicated in Table 2.1.

somewhat from agency to agency (Gras 2003: 8; S&P's 2007a, c; Sinclair 2005: 46–7). In general, credit rating agencies base their analyses of *corporate* credit risk on a company's financial statements, franchise value, management quality and competitive position in its industry, and seek to predict credit performance – the servicing of debt obligations in full and on time – under a range of macroeconomic and credit conditions, including stress situations (Gonzalez et al. 2004: 6). More precise criteria used by the credit rating agencies in determining credit default risks are available for registered users on the websites of the credit rating agencies; for example, the website of S&P's offers a collection of more than 200 documents specifying the criteria in credit risk assessment for diverse financial products (see www.standardandpoors.com). In the case of sovereign ratings, the criteria are less transparent and less straightforward to determine. Political criteria which are hard to quantify (e.g. political stability or the degree of political participation in a country) are often said to be taken into account, as well as macroeconomic and

Table 2.2 The credit rating process (solicited ratings)

Initiation of a credit rating: credit rating request from the issuer
Collection of information: from public and nonpublic sources (involving interaction with and provision of information from the issuer)*
Credit analysis: quantitative and qualitative analyses of the collected data according to the CRA's methodologies and criteria (e.g. country-specific risks, industry and/or economic data; historical and projected financial statements; history of defaults; management policies; features of the specific financial product, etc.)
Vote of the CRA's rating committee (comprised of senior analysts): on the credit rating → notification of the committee's decision and major considerations supporting the decision to the issuer → opportunity for the issuer to comment on the rating and to present further ('new and meaningful') information → review of the additional information and second vote by the rating committee → publication of the rating and dissemination to the media (in the case of confidential ratings, release of the rating to the issuer)*
Rating review: continued surveillance of the rating; if need be, reconsideration and revision of the rating (up-/downgrading)

Note: * In the case of unsolicited ratings, steps 2 and 4 are performed without the involvement of the issuer.

Source: Compiled by the author with data from Gras (2003: 8); Peters (2001: 29–35); S&P's (2007b).

fiscal indicators of a country (Gras 2003: 8; see also Hillebrand 2001), even though empirical studies have found no conclusive evidence that regime type significantly affects sovereign bond ratings (Archer et al. 2007).

Credit rating agencies collect vast amounts of information on borrowers and on relevant financial markets for a certain financial product. They use elaborate arithmetic models of risk assessment. Nonetheless, it is pretty clear that in the end subjective factors – such as the belief in a continued positive development of an industry or in the growth of the market for a certain type of financial product – also seem to count when the final credit rating is determined. It is in this sense that Hirsch, in an often-cited dictum, has characterized credit rating as being 'objectively subjective' (Hirsch 1996: 657, translation A.K.).

It is important to keep in mind that credit rating agencies do not just produce and publish condensed credit risk assessments which are then widely used by various public and private actors for investment decisions in the marketplace (Cantor and Packer 1994: 1; Kerwer 2002: 294; Nölke and Perry 2007: 129), but also continue to monitor the development of credit risk associated with the rated borrower or product. If need be, credit rating agencies adjust their initial rating (upgrading or downgrading). Quite obviously, these adjustments affect the market value of rated financial products and the opportunity for rated issuers to get access to new capital.

Roles and functions of credit rating agencies in the global political economy

The basic function credit rating agencies perform in the global political economy is to lower inefficient transaction costs and to reduce information asymmetries between borrowers and lenders in financial markets (Nölke and Perry 2007: 129). Credit rating agencies act as (inter-)mediators between capital supply and demand. They thus play a crucial coordinating role in the efficient allocation of capital. For investors, ratings are a means to reduce costs for the collection and processing of dispersed information. Credit rating agencies take on the task of collecting dispersed information on the financial situation of borrowers and/or the default risk of certain financial products and condense it into a single, widely available measure of relative credit risk. Credit rating agencies thus produce important benchmarks or standards providing orientation and facilitating the comparison of different issuers and financial products. Creditors and investors have found it efficient to use ratings opinions in initiating and monitoring their transactions because of the economies of scale achieved in gathering and analyzing information. This, in turn, has facilitated the access of borrowers to debt markets by widening the investor pool and reducing adverse selection problems resulting from information asymmetries between investors and issuers of debt (Gonzalez et al. 2004: 7).

It is important to keep in mind that credit rating agencies are private firms that are primarily interested in maximizing their own profits (Gras 2003: 16). However, as a reputation for high quality, excellent expertise and objectivity is crucial for the business of credit rating agencies, pursuing their own business interest *might* benefit all market participants. Even though credit rating agencies are private firms, they also fulfill supervisory quasi-public functions (Peters

2001: 39). It is important to note that it is not only credit rating agencies that ascribe these functions to themselves as part of a marketing strategy; on the contrary, other market actors, and a considerable number of public regulators, attribute these functions to credit rating agencies (Everling 1991: 203), so that credit rating agencies hold a 'quasi-public responsibility' (Hunt 2002). Credit ratings are important market surveillance mechanisms which, provided the ratings are performed diligently, have the *potential* not only to facilitate an efficient allocation of capital (Rosenbaum 2004: 8) but also, in a wider sense, to contribute to the production of the global public good 'financial market stability' (Dieter 2004; Griffith-Jones 2003). More precisely, the activities of credit rating agencies usually serve two important supervisory objectives (Gras 2003: 20). First, they are supposed to increase *market transparency and efficiency.* Credit rating agencies use their privileged access to internal information to disclose important information in the form of a credit rating to investors. They thus perform a 'fog piercing service' (White 2001: 5), which in turn improves market information and transparency, and thus helps to protect investors' interests. Due to their specialization and economies of scale and scope, credit rating agencies reduce transaction costs, avoid the duplication of information-generation efforts and thus achieve efficiency gains for the whole market. Second, credit rating agencies contribute to *financial market stability and market oversight/control.* By producing and publishing credit risk assessments, credit rating agencies contribute to reducing uncertainties and limiting systemic risks in the financial system. If they perform their market surveillance diligently, credit rating is a mechanism of crisis prevention which serves the overarching goals of financial market stability and smooth functioning of the entire financial sector. Ideally, credit rating agencies constitute an early warning system, a form of market control, and a protection institution (Gras 2003: 20–1; Hillebrand 2001: 163).

Credit ratings are crucial tools used by most investors for making investment decisions based on a calculation of returns on investment vs. risks of investment. The higher the default risk, that is, the lower-rated the financial title, the higher will be the interest rates and thus the returns on investment (Gras 2003: 7; Gündling and Everling 1994: 728). Through their ratings, credit rating agencies codetermine the cost of borrowing for a wide array of private and public financial market actors around the world. A good rating increases the acceptance for a certain bond, makes the bond attractive to a broader circle of investors, or may even be a prerequisite for access to capital markets by making the issue of a bond possible in the first place. Ratings document the creditworthiness of an issuer and thus create trust, which is a prerequisite for striking (good) credit deals (von Randow 1996: 548). On the other hand, bad ratings or (sudden) rating downgrades lead to steeply increasing interest rates and may even prevent actors (e.g. business enterprises, or even developing countries) from getting access to private capital (Gras 2003: 32; Hillebrand 2001). As ratings have considerable influence on the interest of a bond (the risk premium), bad ratings or rating downgrades make the mobilization of capital more difficult and more expensive. A bad rating may even have an impact on the overall financing opportunities of issuers beyond borrower–lender relationships, since ratings frequently affect stock market notation and client and/or supplier relationships. In short, the potential damage from bad ratings is considerable (Gras 2003: 17–18; Peters 2001: 30; Randow 1996: 567–8).

Scholars have argued that, through their influence on the investment decisions of financial market actors, credit rating agencies may even be in a position to constrain the choice of national economic and social policies. States that are dependent on the inflow of private capital face strong pressures to adjust their monetary, fiscal and socioeconomic policies to credit rating agencies' (actual or supposed) criteria of creditworthiness, which are not politically neutral, but rather favor 'investor-friendly' economic and social policies that put a premium on macroeconomic growth and fiscal austerity policies (Fuchs 2005: 124; Hillenbrand 2001: 165; Nölke and Perry 2007: 131; Schirm 2004a: 284).

The structure of the credit rating industry

In order to gauge the influence of single credit rating agencies on the global political economy and understand the economic conditions under which ratings are produced, we need to have a closer look at the structure of the credit rating industry. The credit rating industry is characterized by incomplete competition and an oligopolistic structure of the market for ratings. Thus, a small number of credit rating agencies (Moody's, S&P's and Fitch) exercise considerable influence on – some observers even say control over – the global flow of capital (Sinclair 2005). Though competition has intensified and the number of players in the credit rating sector around the world have increased since the 1990s (White 2001: 8), the major agencies Moody's and S&P's (and to a much lesser extent Fitch) continue to dominate the market, not only in the US but also in Europe and Asia (Nölke and Perry 2007: 130). There are some smaller and younger rating agencies, particularly in emerging Asian markets, that offer credit risk assessments in more specialized fields. However, they are not yet serious competitors to the market leaders (Gras 2003: 15). In the past few years, the creation of a European credit rating agency as a counterweight to the US agencies has been repeatedly recommended, by German Chancellor Angela Merkel among others (Barber et al. 2008; Kröger 2008). So far, no European credit rating agency has emerged as a serious competitor and counterweight to the market leaders from the US. Today, Moody's and S&P's still have a combined global market share of 80 percent (in terms of ratings issued). Together with Fitch Ratings, the number three in the credit rating sector, they have over 95 percent (*The Economist* 2007b; Gras 2003: 4; Hillenbrand 2001: 152). As Fitch's market share is considerably smaller than those of Moody's and S&P's, one might even be tempted to say that the rating industry is characterized by a duopolistic rather than an oligopolistic structure (*The Economist* 2001: 72; 2005).

Moody's and S&P's are US firms. Moody's has been independent since 2000; before that it was owned by the business information corporation The Dun & Bradstreet Corp. Moody's is highly specialized in rating activities. S&P's credit rating activities are only part of the broader financial information services that are provided by S&P's (White 2001: 6). S&P's belongs to the media corporation McGraw-Hill Inc., which is not involved in financial business services. So there seems to be no inherent conflict of interest resulting from ownership of the major credit rating agencies (Cantor and Packer 1994: 2; Gras 2003: 15). Fitch Ratings, which has grown out of a fusion of several European and US credit rating agencies, is an international rating agency dual-headquartered in New York City and London and is majority-owned by Fimalac, a French holding company. Fitch is the smallest of the Big Three in the rating business, but may sometimes position itself as a 'tiebreaker' when the other two agencies have similar, but not equal, ratings.

Credit rating is a business with very high profit margins (White 2001: 14, 17–18). The rating fees for issue ratings, the main source of revenues, are calculated as a share of the overall volume of the financial product issue. At the turn of the century (more recent data are unfortunately not available), Moody's and S&P's had the following 'list prices' for requested ratings: 3.25 basis points on issues up to 500 million US dollars, with a minimum fee of 25,000 US dollars and a maximum of 125,000 US dollars (S&P's) or 130,000 US dollars (Moody's); both Moody's and S&P's charged an additional two basis points on amounts above 500 million US dollars. S&P's capped the amount at 200,000 US dollars; it also had a onetime fee of 25,000 US dollars for first-time issuers. Both Moody's and S&P's offered negotiated rates for frequent issuers. The fees charged by Fitch were slightly lower (White 2001: 14).

The rise of credit rating agencies in the 1980s and 1990s

We can observe a significant increase in credit rating agencies' scope of activities and relevance in the past three decades. The first credit rating agencies were established in the United States as early as the beginning of the twentieth century. Moody's was established in 1909; Fitch Ratings was founded as the Fitch Publishing Company in 1913. S&P's traces its history back to 1860, when its founder Henry Varnum Poor published a comprehensive account of the financial and operational state of US railroad companies. The company as it is known today was formed in 1941 with the merger of Poor's Publishing and Standard Statistics. After an early phase of business expansion and growing significance of credit ratings in the US capital market, investor demand for ratings dwindled in the late 1930s. After that, it took the rating industry until the 1970s to regain momentum and reassert its influential role in the US capital market. In the past three decades in particular (starting from the early 1980s), credit rating agencies have considerably expanded their business activities in several regards (Adams et al. 1999: 188; Cantor and Packer 1994: 3; Peters 2001: 37). Moody's growth serves as a good example: Moody's *staff* has grown from a 'handful of analysts' at the beginning of the 1970s (Sylla 2001: 24) to 1,000 analysts (plus additional advisory staff) employed by Moody's today. The *number* and *scope* of rated issuers and financial products have also increased tremendously. Today, Moody's ratings cover more than 100 sovereign states,

12,000 corporate issuers, 29,000 public finance issuers and 96,000 structured finance obligations (Moody's Investor Service 2008). In 1980, Moody's produced around 10 sovereign ratings; by the turn of the century this number had risen above 110 (Kerwer 2002: 305). In the wake of the deregulation and integration of global financial markets (see Adams et al. 1999; Cerny 1994; European Commission 2002), credit rating agencies, which had originally focused on the US market, have also expanded *geographically* to cover virtually the whole globe (Fuchs 2005: 124; Schirm 2004a: 282; Sylla 2001).

According to Gras (2003: 11–14), the increasing relevance of credit rating agencies for investors and their business expansion since the 1980s can be traced back to several changes in the context conditions in financial markets. The breakdown of the Bretton Woods System (1973), the ensuing liberalization and deregulation of capital transfers in the US and the UK, and, more broadly speaking, the globalization of financial markets have stimulated the demand for ratings and favored the rise of credit rating agencies (Gras 2003: 10–11). The end of the Bretton Woods System and the transition to a system of floating exchange rates paved the way for an increasingly unrestricted transfer of capital around the world, led to a dramatic increase in the volume of transnational flows of capital, and thus spurred the demand for ratings.

Further interrelated reasons also contributed to the rise of credit rating agencies in the 1980s and 1990s. First, qualitative structural changes of actor constellations and the types of products in financial markets – an increasing number of diverse public and private market actors offering and seeking capital, a trend towards internationalization of portfolios, and the emergence of new financial instruments – created higher market complexity and a growing need for reliable information and orientation in financial markets. Second, tendencies towards disintermediation and securitization, in the form of a shift from banks to markets (Everling 1991: 67–9; Peters 2001: 23–5), in corporate financing have created great incentives for investors *and* borrowers to use the services of credit rating agencies. While traditionally banks served as intermediators between borrowers and lenders and were also the bearers of credit default risk, the credit risk and the task of collecting information on the creditworthiness of a borrower have shifted to the investors themselves in a system where corporations frequently rely on the issuance of securities, a mode of securing financing directly from investors in capital markets. Not only have investors intensified their use of the credit rating agencies' expert risk assessments in their investment decisions. Due to the business model of credit rating agencies, it is even more important that ratings facilitate, or rather open up, access to the capital market, including the advantages of capital market-based financing, which in turn has driven up borrowers' demand for ratings. Third, there has been a similar shift towards capital market-based financing of states. Securing access to transnational capital flows has become a main objective of governments not only in developed countries but also in emerging economies and developing countries. The latter have attributed increasing importance to meeting their capital needs in transnational financial markets rather than relying on Official Development Assistance and World Bank/IMF loans. Therefore, many states have requested a credit rating, causing the demand for sovereign ratings to skyrocket in the 1990s (Adams et al. 1999: 202–3; Hillebrand 2001: 164). Fourth, Gras (2003: 12–13) argues that the integration of financial markets has been accompanied by a partial assimilation of market conditions and a transfer of market practices predominant in the leading US capital market to the global capital market (Everling 1991: 64). This diffusion process has also entailed an expansion of the use of ratings and an increasingly important position of credit rating agencies in the coordination and governance of financial markets beyond the US (Gras 2003: 11–14). Thus, credit rating agencies have tremendously profited from the globalization and deregulation of financial markets. But, at the same time, credit rating agencies have greatly facilitated financial market integration through their information-providing activities (Everling 1991: 65).

The use of credit ratings in national and international regulatory systems

State actors essentially deal with credit rating agencies in three ways. First, states are themselves the object of credit risk assessments conducted by credit rating agencies (sovereign ratings). Second, state legislators and other regulatory authorities (such as securities market authorities) set the legal framework for the business activities of credit rating agencies. Third, states use the credit risk assessments conducted by credit rating agencies in financial market regulation.

It is this third type of relationship between public actors and credit rating agencies that is addressed by this book – even though the use of credit ratings in regulation may have ramifications for how the legal framework for the business activities of credit rating agencies is designed. In the past three decades, the interest in and the demand for credit rating services have significantly grown, not only among banks, bondholders, pension fund managers and insurance companies, but also among public financial regulators. National and international regulatory bodies have made increasing use of 'ratings-dependent regulation' (Bruner and Rawi 2005: 191; Cantor and Packer 1994: 1; Gonzalez et al. 2004: 8). Generally speaking, credit ratings are used in financial 'safety and soundness regulation' (or 'prudential regulation' as it is termed in Europe), which is aimed at securing the stability of the financial system. The bottom line is that the use of credit ratings allows the design and implementation of 'risk-sensitive' regulation of financial markets (Kerwer 2002: 294). Ratings-dependent regulation is based on flexible rules which allow a (quasi-)automatic adjustment of regulatory requirements to different degrees of risk (Adams et al. 1999; Gras 2003: 19; Gündling and Everling 1994: 730; Peters 2001: 45–6; White 2001: 20). The importance of ratings-based regulations has traditionally been particularly salient in the United States. However, while ratings-based regulation is less common overall in Europe and other world regions, all developed states use credit ratings for regulatory purposes to some extent. The EU states have mainly done so in the area of banking regulation within the framework of the 2006 EU Banking Directive and Capital Adequacy Directive. The first Capital Adequacy Directive was passed in 1993 and contained an opt-out clause (which Germany used) concerning the use of ratings in banking regulation. The 2006 Capital Adequacy Directive and Banking Directive put into force the main provisions of the Basel II Accord within the European Union. The Basel II Accord (2004), in its 'standardized approach to credit risk', relies explicitly on 'external credit assessments institutions' in the calculation of credit risk weights (Gonzalez et al. 2004: 9).

The use of ratings in the US regulatory system

The United States has a long history of using private credit ratings in financial regulation (Estrella et al. 2000: 44). The origins of the use of credit ratings for the purposes of risk regulation in the US date back to the New Deal regulations of the 1930s. While in the emerging, hardly regulated US capital market of the late nineteenth century credit rating agencies were not used as an instrument of capital market regulation, this changed in 1931, when banks were obliged by US regulators to rely on credit ratings in fulfilling regulatory balance sheet requirements (Rosenbaum 2004: 10). The Great Depression produced a sharp decline in credit quality, and the consequent problems of domestic financial institutions led the US Office of the Comptroller of the Currency (OCC) to rule in 1931 that bank holdings of publicly rated bonds had to be rated BBB[3] or better to be carried on bank balance sheets at their face or book value. Otherwise, the bonds were to be written down to market value ('marked to market'), imposing losses on the banks. A lot of US state banking departments subsequently adopted this rule. New OCC rules in 1936 prohibited banks from holding 'speculative securities', bonds rated below BBB by the (then) two credit rating agencies Moody's and S&P's (Estrella et al. 2000: 44; King and Sinclair 2003: 348). This condition had far-reaching consequences, because almost half of the approximately 2,000 listed bonds were rated below BBB at the time. This high-yield or junk bond market was effectively closed for the next 40 years, until the end of the 1970s (Sinclair 2005: 42). Initially, the use of credit ratings for regulatory purposes was restricted to the supervision of banks. However, in particular since the mid-1970s and early 1980s, the use of ratings in regulations has expanded into other areas of financial regulation and supervision. Credit ratings have been used by various US public authorities (e.g. the OCC, the SEC, the Federal Reserve, the Federal Deposit Insurance Corporation (FDIC), the Office of Thrift Supervision (OTS) and the Department of Labor) for a broad range of specific regulatory purposes. Thus, the public regulatory and supervisory bodies of nearly all US financial market actors use – in one way or another – credit risk assessments from credit rating agencies for regulatory purposes (Gras 2003: 14). This implies that ratings-based regulations affect not only banks, but also insurers, pension funds, mutual funds, broker–dealers and other financial market actors (Gonzalez et al. 2004: 9).

For a systematic overview of the use of ratings in the US regulatory system, four main types of ratings-dependent regulatory requirements can be distinguished. First, ratings have allowed public regulators to impose risk-sensitive *investment restrictions* on certain financial institutions. In this case, a certain minimum credit rating (usually 'investment grade') serves as regulatory threshold for the investment in and/or the trading of securities; for example, pension funds have been restricted to investing exclusively in bonds of low credit risk, that is, bonds which were rated at least 'investment grade'. Second, US regulators have defined *differential disclosure requirements* for issuers of rated bonds with reference to the rating obtained from credit rating agencies. Credit ratings thus serve as criteria for disclosure requirements: the lower the rating, the stricter the requirements. This means that a financial institution with risky investments will have to disclose more information about its operation in its quarterly reports to the SEC than a firm with a lower-risk profile. Third, credit ratings have been used in defining the *conditions for the issuance of certain financial titles* (e.g. mortgage-backed securities). Credit ratings serve as criteria for the regulatory administrative requirements that have to be fulfilled before these titles can be issued; for example, the Secondary Mortgage Market Enhancement Act of 1984 eased the regulatory administrative requirements for the issuance of highly-rated mortgage-backed securities (MBS). Finally, US regulators have used credit ratings to adjust *capital reserve requirements* for banks and institutional broker–dealers to their credit risk exposure. Financial institutions get a discount on their capital reserve requirement if their transaction partners or securities they hold have a high credit rating. In 1994, the capital requirements on banks' holdings of different tranches of asset-backed securities were made a function of their rating. In 1999, the ability of national banks to establish financial subsidiaries was restricted based on their rating (Adams et al. 1999; Estrella 2000: 44; Gonzalez et al. 2004: 9; Gras 2003: 19; Gündling and Everling 1994: 730; Kerwer 2002: 304; 2005: 463; Rosenbaum 2004: 11; Sinclair 2005: 42–5; White 2001: 20).

In the past 80 years, the use of ratings for regulatory purposes has manifested itself in a large number of US laws and rules issued by several regulatory authorities (Cantor and Packer 1994: 6; Estrella et al. 2000: 54; Gonzalez et al. 2004: 9). In the year 2004, at least eight federal statutes and around 50 federal regulations, along with over 100 US state laws and regulations, referenced credit ratings as a benchmark in financial regulation (Rosenbaum 2004: 10). Table 2.3 provides a fairly comprehensive overview of the major US federal regulations that have made use of credit ratings from 1931 to 2006

Table 2.3 Use of credit ratings in the US regulatory system (1931–2006)

Year	Ratings-dependent regulation	Minimum rating	Regulator/Regulation
1931	requires banks to mark-to-market lower-rated bonds (where mark-to-market means recording the price or value of a security on a daily basis); obliges banks to write down bonds rated lower than BBB.	BBB	Office of the Comptroller of the Currency (OCC) and Federal Reserve examination rules
1936	prohibits banks from purchasing speculative securities.	BBB	OCC, FDIC and Federal Reserve joint statement
1951	imposes higher capital reserve requirements on insurers' lower-rated bonds; applies to insurers' bonds not rated investment grade.	Various	National Association of Insurance Commissioners (NAIC) mandatory reserve requirements
1975	imposes higher capital reserve requirements on broker–dealers' below-investment-grade bonds; the rating must be performed by a nationally recognized statistical rating organization (NRSRO).	BBB	SEC amendment to Rule 15c3-1: Uniform net capital rule (on the basis of the Securities and Exchange Act)
1982	eases disclosure requirements for (issuance of) investment grade bonds.	BBB	SEC adoption of Integrated Disclosure System (Release #6383)
1984	eases issuance of high-rated mortgage-backed securities (MBSs).	AA	Secondary Mortgage Market Enhancement Act of 1984
1987	permits margin lending against MBSs and (later) foreign bonds, recognition of MBSs as collateral.	AA	Federal Reserve Regulation T
1989	allows pension funds to invest only in high-rated asset-backed securities.	A	Department of Labor relaxation of Employee Retirement Income Security Act (ERISA) Restriction (PTE 89–88)
1989	prohibits savings & loans associations (S&Ls) from investing in below-investment-grade bonds.	BBB	Financial Institutions Recovery and Reform Act of 1989

Continued

Table 2.3 Continued

Year	Ratings-dependent regulation	Minimum rating	Regulator/Regulation
1991	requires money market mutual funds to limit holdings of low-rated (speculative) paper/bonds.	B1	SEC amendment to Rule 2a-7 under the Investment Company Act of 1940
1992	exempts issuers of certain asset-backed securities from registration as a mutual fund.	BBB	SEC adoption of Rule 3a-7 under the Investment Company Act of 1940
1994	imposes varying capital charges on banks' and S&Ls' holdings of different tranches of asset-backed securities.	AAA & BBB	Federal Reserve, OCC, FDIC, Office of Thrift Supervision (OTS) Proposed Rule on Recourse and Direct Credit Substitutes
1998	Department of Transportation can only extend credit assistance to projects with an investment grade rating.	BBB	Transport Infrastructure Finance and Innovation Act 1998
1999	restricts the ability of national banks to establish financial subsidiaries; when creating financial subsidiaries banks must rely on ratings by CRAs.	A	Gramm-Leach-Biley Act of 1999 (Title I, p. 91)
2000	exemption from Regulation 'Fair Disclosure' (FD) requirement to disclose investment-related information to public, as long as information is for purposes of making a rating.	Entity's rating must be public.	SEC Rule 100(b) (2)
2002	Call for comprehensive review of the role and function of CRAs, *inter alia*, in financial market regulation.	n.a.	Section 702(b) of the Sarbanes-Oxley Act of 2002
2006 (before financial crisis)	General confirmation of the use of CRAs' ratings in regulation, but: stricter criteria for the recognition of CRAs as nationally recognized statistical rating organization (NRSRO); formal registration system.	n.a.	Credit Rating Agency Reform Act of 2006

Source: Compiled by the author with data from Cantor and Packer (1994: 6); Estrella et al. (2000: 54); Rosenbaum (2004: 11) and Sinclair (2005: 43–4).

(for a discussion of the future regulatory use of credit ratings after the US subprime and global financial crises see Chapter 6).

The requirements imposed by public regulators on credit rating agencies to qualify as external credit assessment institutions whose ratings may be used in financial regulation have increased slowly but progressively over the decades. Three major steps can be distinguished. At the beginning of the regulatory use of credit ratings, credit rating agencies had to fulfill no particular requirements; quite simply, as a matter of fact, Moody's and S&P's ratings were considered the only serious, trustworthy options for ratings-based regulation. Since 1975, only 'nationally recognized statistical rating organizations' (NRSROs), not just any credit rating agency, have been eligible for US regulators to rely on (Sinclair 2005: 42). This constituted the introduction of a highly informal 'certification' system for raters (Sinclair 2005: 45). In 2006, the Credit Rating Agencies Reform Act introduced a formalized registration procedure instead of the previous rather informal 'no-enforcement action letter' approach for the designation of NRSRO status (see Chapter 6 for more recent developments after the global financial crisis).

The 1975 SEC rule on ratings-dependent capital reserve requirements stipulated that only ratings by NRSROs were recognized for SEC regulatory purposes (Peters 2001: 144–6, 180; Schwarcz 2001a: 297–8). This had a significant impact on further developments in the rating industry, the oversight and control of credit rating agencies, and the use of credit ratings in regulation (Rosenbaum 2004: 10). Critics argue that this kind of government regulation of credit rating agencies reinforced an oligopolistic ratings market and made it harder for new entrants to launch ratings businesses, since only credit rating agencies with large market shares were recognized as NRSROs and, in turn, only 'government-certified' NRSROs could amass large market shares because they were considered more reliable and more 'useful' in terms of fulfilling regulatory requirements by other market actors (Sinclair 2005: 42). The NRSRO system thus creates a 'regulatory catch 22' (Kerwer 2002: 309) and 'clearly favors incumbents' (Cantor and Packer 1994: 8), because new entrants to the rating business cannot hope to become 'nationally recognized' without NRSRO status (Sinclair 2005: 45; White 2001: 27).

Initially, the SEC did not define the substance of an NRSRO in any detail. Nonetheless, the NRSRO concept has since 1975 been incorporated into many regulatory initiatives by the SEC and other US regulatory bodies. The NRSRO concept remained relatively vague and unspecified in law but significant in practice for a long time (Sinclair 2005: 42, 44). The most important criterion is widespread acceptance as a credible and reliable source of information by the most important capital market actors in the US (Gras 2003: 17). Explicit statements on NRSRO criteria were contained in SEC 'no action' letters to the credit rating agencies Fitch Investors Service, Thompson Bankwatch and IBCA, which later merged into Fitch Ratings. The SEC 'no-enforcement action letters' indicated that the SEC would take no enforcement action if ratings from these agencies were used to satisfy the SEC capital reserve requirements of 1975. The criteria the SEC mentioned in these letters were: conflict of interest scrutiny; appropriate intra-organizational separation to avoid mixing investment advice and rating; adequate financial resources; adequate staff; and sufficient training. The precise meanings of 'adequate' and 'sufficient' were not defined. Moody's and S&P's were also deemed to be NRSROs. In the 1990s, the SEC undertook several unsuccessful initiatives (SEC 1994, 1997) to introduce formal procedures for designating and monitoring NRSROs and to set up a formal 'list of attributes' to consider in designating NRSROs and in the NRSRO application process (Gras 2003: 17; Sinclair 2005: 44–5). The performance of credit rating agencies in the Enron bankruptcy (2001) revived the NRSRO issue. In 2002 the Sarbanes-Oxley Act was passed, which called for an investigation into the role and function of credit rating agencies in US capital markets to be conducted by the SEC (Rosenbaum 2004: 10; Sinclair 2005: 46; see also SEC 2003a). After the SEC's investigation into the role and function of credit rating agencies and proposals for new rules on the recognition of NRSROs (SEC 2003b, 2005), the Credit Rating Agencies Reform Act was passed in 2006. The Credit Rating Agencies Reform Act provided for the introduction of a codified process for the designation and monitoring of NRSRO status under the auspices of the SEC (SEC 2007a, b, c). Credit rating agencies now have to apply for NRSRO status with the SEC through a formal procedure. The SEC decides whether to grant NRSRO status on the basis of a given set of criteria aiming at ensuring the factual and interpretive reliability of rating methods, the adequacy of personnel capacities and the integrity of the rating process (including avoidance of conflicts of interest). So far, 10 credit rating agencies (including the Big Three: Moody's,

S&P's and Fitch) have been granted NRSRO status under the formalized procedure (SEC 2008).

The use of ratings in other national regulatory systems

While the use of ratings in financial regulation is most developed in the US, over the past 20 years ratings have increasingly become a key regulatory tool beyond the US (Nicholls 2005: 15–6, 28–31; Sinclair 2005: 46). Particularly since the 1990s, the use of credit ratings for regulatory purposes has expanded to other developed economies (i.e. most EU member states, Switzerland, Australia, Canada and New Zealand) and emerging markets, particularly in the Latin American and Asian areas (Gonzalez et al. 2004: 9; Gras 2002: 13–4).

Unfortunately, comparative empirical research on the use of credit ratings in national regulatory systems outside the US is scarce. However, the study by Estrella et al. (2000) is still a good and often-referenced guide to the use of credit ratings in national regulatory systems. Estrella et al. (2000) conducted a cross-country survey of the use of credit ratings in financial regulation, particularly, though not exclusively, in banking supervision, across 18 countries. The countries selected were the members of the BCBS and the nonmembers Australia, Argentina, Chile, Hong Kong, Mexico and New Zealand. The latter fulfilled one or more of the following criteria: an innovative approach to financial regulation, a relatively recent experience of financial instability, a known significant use of credit ratings in their regulations and/or general importance to the world financial system. On the basis of the study by Estrella et al. (2000) and supplementary data from Sinclair (2005: 47–50), Gonzalez et al. (2004: 9), Nicholls (2005: 15–6) and the Asian Development Bank (ADB 2001: 154–5), as well as additional studies that *en passant* mention the use of ratings in regulation, a fairly comprehensive overview of ratings-dependent regulation in major national regulatory systems can be provided. While some of the following information is rather technical, it should nevertheless give an impression of the considerable scope of the regulatory use of credit ratings in national financial regulatory systems, while also demonstrating that the amount of ratings-dependent regulation in the US is unmatched.

At the turn of the century, credit ratings were incorporated into regulation in all but one of the (then) 12 BCBS member states, with

Germany being the only exception (Estrella 2000: 41; King and Sinclair 2003: 348; Sinclair 2005: 47–50). This exceptional position of Germany ended when the new EU Capital Adequacy Directive and the Banking Directive of 2006 were passed, putting the main Basel II provisions into force within the EU. Germany immediately transposed the EU Directives into German law, and the German Central Bank and the Federal Financial Supervisory Authority (BaFin) now jointly use credit ratings in banking regulation within the standardized approach to credit risk assessment of banks.

However, it should be noted that the 2006 Capital Adequacy Directive and Banking Directive were not the first EU directives providing for the use of credit ratings in European banking regulation. Within the European Union, the regulatory use of credit ratings started with the (first) Capital Adequacy Directive of 1993 (Adams et al. 1999: Annex 6; Gras 2003: 14; Randow 1996: 546). From 1993 to 2006, all the European BCBS members except for Germany used credit ratings in their prudential supervision of banks in order to determine what was a qualifying debt security or other interest-rate-related instrument for the calculation of the capital requirement for specific interest rate risk. This was also referred to as the 'market risk amendment' since it addressed banks' capital reserve requirements for *market* risks as opposed to *credit* (default) risks. Market risk refers to the risk that the value of investments may decline over a given time period simply because of economic changes or other events that impact large portions of the market. Credit (default) risk refers to the risk that borrowers are not able to pay back their debts in time and to the full extent, for example because of bankruptcy (Becker 2007: 82). The 1993 Capital Adequacy Directive applied to both credit institutions and investment firms (Estrella 2000: 41; Gonzalez et al. 2004: 9). EU member states were allowed to waive the ratings-based regulation part of the 1993 Capital Adequacy Directive, if they 'judge[d] it inappropriate in the light of, for example, the characteristics of the market, the issuer, the issue, or some combination of those characteristics' (Estrella et al. 2000: 41). It was this waiver which Germany opted to exercise until the 2004 Basel II Accord and subsequently the 2006 Capital Adequacy Directive and Banking Directive were passed. The ratings-based provisions on market risk of the 1993 Capital Adequacy Directive have meanwhile been incorporated into the new, considerably enlarged 2006 Capital Adequacy Directive.

Some BCBS members have used private credit ratings in their prudential regulation of banks for purposes other than market risk even before the 2006 Capital Adequacy Directive was passed. In *Belgium*, banks have been required to provide information on the composition of parts of their securities portfolio, split by rating. In *Switzerland*, ratings have been used in the definition of the risk weights for credit risk, where the appropriate risk weight depends on the counterparty's location. The (important) definition of what constitutes an OECD country in this context has an additional pretty complex criterion, which, phrased in somewhat simplified terms, excludes countries with a lower-than-investment-grade rating by a recognized credit rating agency on their long-term foreign currency liabilities. In the *UK*, banks are allowed to rely on private credit ratings when fulfilling specific liquidity monitoring requirements (Estrella 2000: 41).

A closer look at non-BCBS member states (ADB 2001: 154–5; Estrella et al. 2000: 44; Sinclair 2005: 47–50) reveals that Australia and Hong Kong use ratings to judge a qualifying debt security for market risk. In *Argentina*, the central bank constructs a list of banks permitted to receive time deposits from institutional investors (e.g. pension funds) and a bank's rating is one of the factors on which the central bank bases its decision on membership. In addition to this, all banks and financial institutions in Argentina must obtain a rating from a recognized agency. Each bank is required to provide a copy of the associated report to any customer requesting one, free of charge. In *Australia*, ratings play important roles in determining banks' capital requirement. First, the Australian Prudential Regulation Authority (APRA) recognizes mortgage insurance by insurers that have a rating of A or higher by a recognized credit rating agency. Second, ratings have a role in determining the adequacy of credit enhancements provided to securitization schemes. In *Hong Kong*, ratings are used to determine what is a liquefiable asset in the liquidity requirements regime. In *New Zealand*, the authorities make use of agencies' ratings of banks in their regulation. Ratings are used to provide information to the banks' creditors and thereby facilitate market discipline. A registered bank is required to include in its quarterly disclosure statements information on whether it has a rating (and, if it has, specific details) on its senior long-term debt. Ratings are regarded by New Zealand's financial authorities as being a particularly useful indicator of relative bank credit quality for 'prudent but not expert investors' because they are relatively easy to understand. Each bank is required to display a statement on its own credit rating (a so-called Key Information Statement) and make it available immediately in all its branches. It must also be displayed on the bank's internet site (Estrella et al. 2000: 44; Sinclair 2005: 47–50). Legislative and regulatory use of credit ratings is also well developed in *Canada*. References to ratings obtained from credit rating agencies appear in at least 10 so-called National Instruments or National Policies in the area of Canadian securities regulation as well as in various provincial securities rules and regulatory instruments. In addition to securities laws, at least eight other federal statutes or regulations promulgated under federal legislation, and at least 37 Canadian provincial statutes or regulations, refer to credit ratings. These regulations affect, among others, banks, insurance companies, and savings & loans associations (Nicholls 2005: 15–16).

Table 2.4 provides an overview of the use of credit ratings by national regulatory authorities in selected OECD and Asian Pacific Economic Cooperation (APEC) countries mainly for the purposes of securities and banking regulation.

The criteria and the procedures used by financial supervisory authorities in the various countries to recognize credit rating agencies as eligible for ratings-based regulation vary considerably. An in-depth study of the diverse approaches is clearly beyond the scope of this book. Table 2.5 displays the main results of a survey on national regulatory bodies' criteria for recognition of credit ratings. The findings by Estrella et al. (2000: 49–51) have been complemented with additional, more recent information, in so far as this was publicly available. It is particularly noteworthy that, at least within the EU, criteria for the recognition of credit rating agencies whose ratings may be used for regulatory purposes have become somewhat harmonized now that the Committee of European Banking Supervisors (CEBS) has developed European-level guidelines (CEBS 2006) for the recognition of external credit assessment institutions in the wake of Basel II and the 2006 Capital Adequacy Directive and Banking Directive.

Overall, ongoing monitoring of the performance of credit rating agencies has been limited in most regulatory systems (Estrella et al. 2000: 50). France, Italy and Japan claimed that their public supervisors undertook regular ongoing monitoring of the credit rating

Table 2.4 Regulatory use of credit ratings in selected countries

Country	Contents of regulation
Argentina	Banks and financial companies must seek a rating from an authorized CRA. The rating reflects the ability of the financial institution to repay its medium and long-term liabilities. Financial institutions must provide copies of the reports free of charge to customers who request them. However, they cannot be used in advertising campaigns or printed documents. The central bank prepares a list of banks that can receive time deposits from institutional investors (e.g. pension funds). Banks with weak ratings are excluded from this list. The Argentine stock market supervisory authority does not extend authorization for the public offer of a security unless its issuer has sought two ratings. In addition, pension funds are not allowed to invest in assets that do not exceed a certain rating threshold, which is set at BBB for domestic credit ratings and B for ratings issued by international agencies on securities of resident issuers. The same provisions are extended to the insurance industry. In this case, the insurance industry is asked to invest in rated securities with a minimum rating, and also to seek a rating as policies issued by them are increasingly being sold to pension funds.
Australia	Credit ratings are used in regulations on mortgage insurance. Reference to credit ratings is also made in a number of securities regulations. Credit ratings are used to determine capital requirements for banks.
Belgium	Capital Adequacy Directive / Market risk amendment. In prudential reporting, the description of the composition of a bank's securities portfolio requires information on securities' ratings and the credit rating agencies which issued the ratings.
Canada	Market risk amendment. Various securities laws and regulations. Regulation of banks, insurance companies, S&Ls etc.
Chile	Companies that issue equities in American Depositary Receipts (ADRs) must have a minimum rating. Chilean institutions are only permitted to invest in overseas securities that have a minimum rating.
France	Capital Adequacy Directive / Market risk amendment.
Germany	Capital Adequacy Directive. Implementing National Regulation: Solvency Regulation (SolvV).
Hong Kong	Liquidity regime: Authorized Institutions' (AIs') holdings of marketable debt securities may be regarded as liquefiable assets for the calculation of the liquidity ratio if the debt securities satisfy the qualifying credit rating. Capital adequacy regime: Under the market risk capital adequacy framework, debt securities that satisfy minimum ratings carry lower-risk weightings compared with 'unrated' securities.

Continued

Table 2.4 Continued

Country	Contents of regulation
Indonesia	Regulations from the Bank of Indonesia require ratings for bonds and commercial papers.
Italy	Capital Adequacy Directive / Market risk amendment.
Japan	Market risk amendment.
Luxembourg	Capital Adequacy Directive / Market risk amendment.
Malaysia	In 1992, Malaysia introduced a restriction that no private debt securities could be issued unless they were rated BBB or higher for long-term debt. From July 2000, while the rating requirement is retained, the minimum credit rating requirement for issuance of private debt securities has been removed, so that below-investment-grade private debt securities can be issued.
New Zealand	Banks are required to disclose credit ratings on their senior unsecured long-term New Zealand dollar debts in their quarterly disclosure statements. Information to be disclosed must include the name of the credit rating agency, the date of the rating, the nature of the rating nomenclatura used and changes to ratings over the previous two years. In the event that a bank does not have a rating of specified debt obligations, it is required to state this fact in its quarterly disclosure statements.
Philippines	The Securities and Exchange Commission of the Philippines requires issuers of long-term commercial papers to obtain a rating from the local credit rating agency.
South Korea	The Korean Securities and Exchange Commission (SEC) requires issuers of unguaranteed bonds to obtain ratings from at least two agencies, while any bonds issued overseas are required to have a rating. Only companies rated A or higher are allowed to issue unguaranteed bonds.
Sweden	Capital Adequacy Directive / Market risk amendment.
Switzerland	Market risk amendment. Credit risk: calculation of risk weights for some banks depends in part on counterparty's ratings. Investment funds: Funds managers are restricted as to with whom they may conclude certain derivative transactions, depending on the counterparty's credit rating.
Thailand	Unsecured debt issues must be rated.
The Netherlands	Capital Adequacy Directive / Market risk amendment.
UK	Capital Adequacy Directive / Market risk amendment. Liquidity reporting guidelines for non-clearing banks.
USA	See Table 2.3.

Source: Compiled by the author with data from ADB (2001: 154–5); Estrella et al. (2000: 42–3) and Sinclair (2005: 47–50).

Table 2.5 Recognition criteria for the use of credit ratings

Country	Criteria for eligible credit rating agencies
BCBS members	
Belgium	Credit rating agencies are recognized on the basis of a general assessment of their credibility (*inter alia*, their effective use by Belgian credit institutions) and an examination of their organization and methodology, with particular attention to their integrity and independence. EU-level CEBS Guidelines (2006): objectivity, independence, international access, transparency, disclosure, resources and credibility.
Canada	No explicit criteria for eligible credit rating agencies are set out in Canadian regulatory guidelines. According to Canadian regulators, the list of credit rating agencies that are used in regulation represents those firms that are internationally recognized for having accurate and fair ratings while maintaining a long history.
France	Information about national recognition criteria not available in the public domain. EU-level CEBS Guidelines (2006): objectivity, independence, international access, transparency, disclosure, resources and credibility.
Germany	EU-level CEBS Guidelines (2006): objectivity, independence, international access, transparency, disclosure, resources and credibility. National implementing regulation: Solvency Regulation (SolvV).
Italy	Eligible credit rating agencies are selected on the basis of their credibility, objectivity, transparency and role played in the Italian market. EU-level CEBS Guidelines (2006): objectivity, independence, international access, transparency, disclosure, resources and credibility.
Japan	Rating performance, management structure, organization, rating methodology and independence from capital structure.
Luxembourg	According to regulators, the main criteria are the CRAs' international recognition and their market presence. EU-level CEBS Guidelines (2006): objectivity, independence, international access, transparency, disclosure, resources and credibility.
Sweden	No specific national criteria have been developed regarding which credit rating agencies are eligible. However, Swedish regulators would only allow any of the major agencies that have a long standing track record and whose performance could be checked if needed. The three credit rating agencies that are considered to be eligible are those used by Swedish banks when rating their debt instruments.

Continued

Table 2.5 Continued

Country	Criteria for eligible credit rating agencies
	EU-level CEBS Guidelines (2006): objectivity, independence, international access, transparency, disclosure, resources and credibility.
Switzerland	Objectivity, experience, reputation, independence, and coverage of counterparties located in Europe, North America and Japan.
UK	Market recognition.
	EU-level CEBS Guidelines (2006): objectivity, independence, international access, transparency, disclosure, resources and credibility.
USA	Credit rating agencies must apply for registration as NRSRO (under a formalized registration procedure since the CRA Reform Act of 2006) and meet the following criteria:
	Recognition as being credible and reliable from the predominant users of securities ratings in the US;
	Ability to operate independently of economic pressures or control of the companies being rated (e.g. having sufficient financial resources);
	Employing an adequate number of staff members with the education and experience necessary to competently evaluate an issuer's credit;
	Utilizing systematic rating procedures designed to produce credible and accurate ratings;
	Practicing internal compliance procedures to prevent the misuse of nonpublic information.
Nonmembers of the BCBS	
Argentina	As far as the central bank registry is concerned, there are two conditions for participation: The credit rating agency must provide ratings in at least 10 countries and five of them must be in Latin America. Their report must follow guidelines set by the central bank.
	As far as Argentine stock market supervision is concerned, the requirements are: Credit rating agencies must be organized as a limited company. Their sole object must be credit rating activities. They must have a minimum capital of 250,000 US dollars. Shareholders' names must be disclosed. Rating procedures and manuals must be approved by the public securities market supervisor. The directors of the credit rating agencies cannot be shareholders, directors or employees of those companies they rate.

Continued

Table 2.5 Continued

Country	Criteria for eligible credit rating agencies
Australia	There are no formal criteria for determining acceptance of credit rating agencies. The status and acceptance of credit rating agencies in the market and by other regulators, as well as the performance of the credit rating agency, are used as benchmarks for regulators' decision on eligible rating agencies.
Chile	Coverage, reputation, history and position in the market.
Hong Kong	Ownership, history and background of the credit rating agency; methodology and coverage of the ratings; market acceptance; regulatory acceptance.

Source: Compiled by the author with data from Estrella et al. (2000: 51); CEBS (2005) and CEBS (2006).

agencies they recognized. In Japan, rating performance is one of the legally based criteria for recognition. In Belgium, files containing significant information on different credit rating agencies are kept up to date by regulatory authorities. In the US, responsibility lies with credit rating agencies themselves to report any changes in their organizational structures or rating practices. If any changes affect an agency's credibility, NRSRO designation may be withdrawn. In Canada and Switzerland, public authorities would investigate if there was evidence that a credit rating agency was making an increasing number of rating errors or its performance was 'truly questionable', which could cost the credit rating agency its recognition. The Hong Kong Market Authority (HKMA) does not undertake ongoing monitoring, but reviews the recognized status of a credit rating agency if it becomes aware of a marked deterioration in the performance and/or market acceptance of the agency. Some public supervisors seem to rely on market acceptance as a criterion that acts as a substitute for ongoing public monitoring (Estrella et al. 2000: 50).

The use of ratings in regulation on the international level: Basel II and its implementation in the EU

On the international level, the revised Basel Capital Accord (Basel II), developed by the BCBS, provides for the use of credit ratings from approved credit rating agencies (eligible 'external credit assessment institutions') in the calculation of banks' net capital reserve requirements (BCBS 2006: paras. 50–1, 90–2). Basel II is an example of ratings used as a regulatory tool internationally, allowing ratings to be employed as a means of specifying banks' credit risk exposure (Sinclair 2005: 46; see also King and Sinclair 2003). The Basel II Accord highlights the increased role that nonstate actors – credit rating agencies for external-ratings-based regulation but also banks themselves for internal-ratings-based regulation – play in creating and implementing rules governing global financial markets (Speyer 2006: 101). However, to fully understand the relevance of the ratings-based provisions in Basel II, some brief remarks on the BCBS, the rationale for international banking supervision standards, and, in particular, the differences between the first Basel Capital Adequacy Accord (1988) and the Basel II Accord (2004) are in order.

The Basel Committee consists of the central bank governors and representatives from the national credit market regulation agencies of Belgium, Canada, France, Germany, Italy, Japan, Luxembourg, the Netherlands, Spain, Sweden, Switzerland, the United Kingdom and the United States (see Table 2.6). Governments of countries represented in the BCBS have the right to instruct the representatives to grant or withhold their consent to any agreement reached within the BCBS – a right that is, at least occasionally, being exercised, as was shown in the context of disputes on capital requirements for credits to small and medium-sized enterprises under Basel II (Speyer 2006: 115). The BCBS was established in 1974 by the central bank governors and regulatory authorities of the Group of Ten (i.e. the above-mentioned states except Switzerland, Luxembourg and Spain) in order to foster international coordination and harmonization of banking supervision. The BCBS meets regularly four times a year. It has four main working groups (the Accord Implementation Group, the Policy Development Group, the Accounting Task Force and the International Liaison Group), which also meet regularly. The BCBS is situated within the institutional framework of the Bank for International Settlements (BIS), which is an intergovernmental organization for the promotion of international cooperation in financial policies (Becker 2007: 81–2; Macht 2007: 28–9, 54–8). The Bank for International Settlements was established in 1930 and is thus the oldest international financial institution. It has a secretariat in Basel, which also supports the BCBS, and two subsidiaries in Hong Kong and Mexico City (Becker 2007: 81).

The main function of the BCBS is the development of international standards for banking supervision that national supervisory

Table 2.6 Membership in the BCBS

	Members	
Country	**Central Banks**	**Supervisory/Regulatory authorities**
Belgium	National Bank of Belgium	Banking, Finance and Insurance Commission
Canada	Bank of Canada	Office of the Superintendent of Financial Institutions
France	Bank of France	General Secretariat of the Banking Commission
Germany	German Central Bank	BaFin (German Federal Financial Supervisory Authority)
Italy	Bank of Italy	–
Japan	Bank of Japan	Financial Services Agency
Luxembourg		Surveillance Commission for the Financial Sector
Spain	Bank of Spain	–
Sweden	Sveriges Riksbank	Swedish Financial Supervisory Authority
Switzerland	Swiss National Bank	Swiss Federal Banking Commission
The Netherlands	Netherlands Bank	–
UK	Bank of England	Financial Services Authority
USA	Board of Governors of the Federal Reserve System	Office of the Comptroller of the Currency
	Federal Reserve Bank of New York	Federal Deposit Insurance Corporation

authorities should implement. The cornerstone of the BCBS's work in this area is the development of international capital adequacy standards (summed up in Basel I and Basel II), which provide formulae for the calculation of the minimum amount of capital that banks have to keep in reserve (Kerwer 2006: 94). Even though agreements of the BCBS are not legally binding, they have been shown to contribute to internationally harmonized norm creation and modification in the issue area of banking supervision (Kapstein 1991; Simmons 2001; Wood 2005). In fact, the BCBS capital adequacy standards for internationally active banks were one of the most successful sets of global financial standards, at least in terms of widespread acceptance and implementation (Kerwer 2006: 93–4; see also Kapstein 1994; Porter 1993). While some adversely affected member states have questioned the basic approach of the Basel Committee from time to time, the Basel Committee has overall been highly successful in securing the acceptance of its rules (Freund 2002: 57–9). The implementation rate of BCBS agreements is very high, in general – not only as regards the member states of the BCBS but also among banking supervisors around the world (Karacadag and Taylor 2000: 11; Speyer 2006: 110–11). Around 100 states have implemented the 1988 Basel Capital Adequacy Accord. Before the global financial crisis (2007–10) a similar number of states had announced their readiness to implement the 2004 Basel II Accord (BCBS 1999a: 1; Becker 2007: 81–2; Freund 2002: 57–9; Macht 2007: 20–2; Pattison 2006: 443). Notwithstanding this broad acceptance, the collapse of several major banks in the US and in Europe during the latest global financial crisis has obviously raised fundamental questions as to whether the Basel II capital adequacy requirements and their implementation have been adequate. Major revisions of the Basel standards have been undertaken, amounting to the announcement of a new Basel III framework which supplements and in some points tightens the Basel II capital adequacy provisions (see Chapter 6 for a more detailed discussion of regulatory responses to the global financial crisis).

In general terms, there are several rationales for the development of international standards for banking supervision, the necessity of which has been impressively highlighted by the global financial crisis. First, the stability of international financial markets can be conceived of as a global public good whose production requires international and transnational cooperation (Becker 2007: 82; Speyer 2006: 101). Banks sometimes face strong incentives to take greater risks than might be considered optimal, not only from the perspective of a single bank but also in systemic terms. Given the interlinkage of domestic financial markets, the effects of banking insolvencies have frequently not been limited to a bank's country of origin, but, rather, have spilled over to impact financial systems in other countries (El-Shagi 2008: 16). This potential negative externality warrants international cooperation aimed at the prevention of large bank bankruptcies and the spilling over of their effects into other markets. Second, international standards aim at preventing a regulatory race to the bottom which would increase the vulnerability of the overall financial system. Third, the development of international banking supervision standards is expected to serve the purpose of creating a 'level playing field' (Macht 2007) for internationally active banks (Speyer 2006: 101).

In order to mitigate systemic credit risk, to prevent a regulatory race to the bottom and to ensure the existence of an 'international level playing field' with regard to regulatory requirements imposed on banks, a first Basel Capital Adequacy Accord was passed in 1988 (Bieling 2007: 152; Nölke and Perry 2007: 130). The basic idea behind its core element (standards of minimum capital requirements that should be imposed on banks) is that, when it is stipulated that a bank's equity base must meet a minimum percentage of that bank's assets, the equity base becomes a constraining factor, limiting the bank's potential leverage. Equity capital can be considered the 'ultimate bearer of unexpected losses. The more capital a bank holds relative to its asset base, the less likely it is that assets will not be sufficient to satisfy the demands of depositors and other creditors' (Speyer 2006: 109). On the other hand, equity capital is costly. Shareholders demand a sufficient return for the risk that they take, and meeting these demands becomes more difficult if the capital base is large relative to return-generating assets. Ideally, therefore, the equity base should be proportionate to the risk content of the assets. Minimum capital requirements oblige banks to keep a certain amount of capital in reserve (in the Basel Accord usually 8 percent of issued credit volumes) as a safety measure in case of credit default. The idea was that, even in the case of some large-scale credit defaults, banks should still have enough capital 'put aside' to avoid a breakdown which might infect other financial institutions.

The internationally harmonized minimum capital reserve requirements proposed by the 1988 Basel Accord acquired nearly global applicability, in part *because* Basel I was a relatively simple framework. It addressed some major issues endangering global financial stability. Indeed, Basel I achieved the objective of raising capital ratios of internationally active banks (BCBS 1999a: 6–8; Speyer 2006: 111). However, the Basel I Accord proved to have some serious limits and shortcomings that reduced its effectiveness (Bieling 2007: 152). The 1988 Basel Accord concentrates on credit risk only, with other types of risk – market risk, interest rate risk, liquidity risk and operational risk – being ignored.[4] Moreover, there were no internationally standardized methods for the disclosure of risk-relevant information and for the banking supervisory process. Finally, Basel I was a fairly crude rule system that set capital requirements ('the 8 percent rule') according to a very simple differentiation of credit risk categories (Speyer 2006: 110). Capital reserve requirements for banks were determined not on the basis of the creditworthiness of individual clients/borrowers, but on the basis of the broad economic segment (e.g. corporate firms vs. individual private customers) to which the borrower belonged. This created incentives for banks to give credits to high-risk borrowers because in that way higher interest rates could be demanded and greater returns relative to banks' equity capital could be generated. In other words, when banks have to put aside the same amount of capital for credits to a certain class of borrowers irrespective of their creditworthiness, there are incentives to give credits to borrowers with low creditworthiness, because they can be charged higher interest rates. This in turn means that the returns on the capital that had to be put aside for the credit are higher than in the case of a very safe, low-interest-rate credit (BCBS 1999a: 3; Becker 2007: 82; Macht 2007: 61).

Towards the end of the 1990s, there was broad consensus – among public regulators, scholars and most actors from the financial industry – that there was a need to reform the Basel I Accord in order 'to eliminate the distortions caused by Basel I, to better align market practice and the regulatory framework and to catch up with changes in financial markets' (Speyer 2006: 111). Therefore, negotiations on a revised Capital Accord, which was to include lessons learnt from the application of the original Basel Accord and broaden the scope of international banking supervision standards, started in the late 1990s (Karacadag and Taylor 2000: 11–14).

In 2004, they led to the adoption of a revised Basel Capital Accord (Basel II), a comprehensive version of which was published by the BCBS in 2006 under the official title 'International Convergence of Capital Measurement and Capital Standards – A Revised Framework' (BCBS 2006; Becker 2007: 82). At the EU level, the implementation of Basel II as binding law occurred with the publication of the Banking Directive (2006/48/EC) and the Capital Adequacy Directive (2006/49/EC) in June 2006 (Deutsche Bundesbank 2008a; see also European Parliament and Council of the European Union

2006a, b). In Germany, Basel II was transposed into national law by means of changes to the Banking Act and by means of additional regulations, in particular the 2006 Solvency Regulation ('Solvabilitätsverordnung') on the implementation of the first pillar of Basel II (Deutsche Bundesbank 2008a, b). Implementation of the Basel II Accord in the US was originally scheduled to begin in 2008, but even before the global financial crisis it was further delayed (Bieling 2007: 152). During the final stages of the drafting of the accord, US regulators also announced a reduced applicability of the accord in the US, with only the largest internationally operating institutions expected to adopt the relevant requirements and practices. Tsingou (2008: 62–3) argues that 'this came about as a result of sharp divisions among the US regulatory community where at a technical level, the emphasis [was] on safety and soundness, whereas at the political level, the focus shift[ed] to competition.' Nonetheless, before the global financial crisis (2007–10), most observers predicted that Basel II would achieve near-universal applicability even faster than Basel I had done. While Basel II was mainly directed at large, internationally active banks, the basic concept was considered to be suitable for application to banks of varying levels of complexity and business activities. More than 100 countries had indicated that they would apply Basel II (Pattison 2006: 443; Speyer 2006: 113). At the time of writing this book (September 2010) it remains to be seen how many countries will implement the successor agreement Basel III, which reflects lessons learnt from the global financial crisis and tightens the Basel II quantitative requirements for banks' core capital reserves.

The 2004 Basel II Accord was developed on the basis of a three-pillar framework, the second and third pillars of which were completely new compared with Basel I (see Figure 2.1). The three pillars (minimum capital requirements, supervisory review process, and enhanced disclosure/market discipline) should complement each other (Deutsche Bundesbank 2008a).

Pillar Two outlines qualitative standards for an adequate supervisory review process (SRP). It sets up a framework for active supervision of banks' internal practices that requires a regular review of the business procedures of banks. The SRP aims mainly to identify the overall risk of an institution and the main influential factors on its risk situation and to evaluate them from a supervisory perspective.

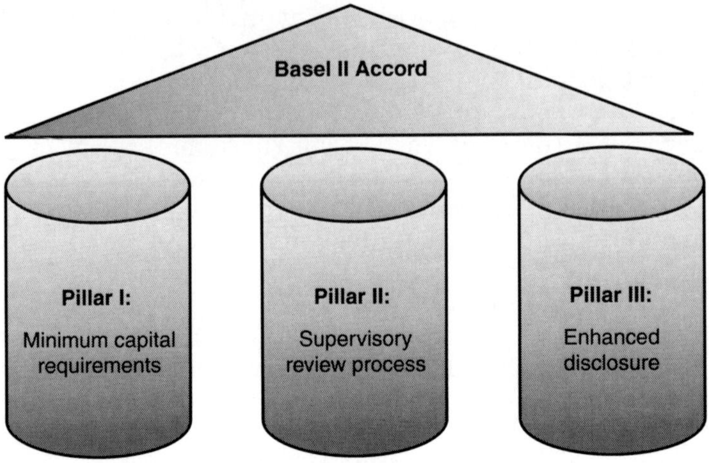

Figure 2.1 Basic concept of Basel II: The three pillars

Pillar Three is aimed at enhancing market discipline by providing guidelines for improved disclosure and transparency of banks' businesses.

However, it is Pillar One of Basel II that is most relevant for this study. It contains a capital requirements framework that provides for quantitative minimum capital reserve requirements to be calculated in accordance with the banks' exposure to credit risk, operational risk and market risk (Becker 2007: 83; Deutsche Bundesbank 2008a; Macht 2007: 68–96; Paul 2006: 298–300; Tsingou 2008: 60). Reliance on ratings from recognized credit rating agencies is one option for the calculation of banks' minimum capital requirements underlying credit risk.

While under the original Basel I rules all commercial loans had been subject to the same capital reserve requirement – irrespective of their relative default risk (Jackson 2001: 8) – the Basel II Accord stipulates that capital reserve requirements for banks should be dependent (among other factors) on the default risk of the credits banks give. In other words, if a bank is heavily invested in highly liquid and very safe securities, it should need to keep less capital in reserve than a bank that holds bonds from creditors with low creditworthiness.

For the sake of accuracy, and in order to present the changes under Basel II in technically correct regulatory terms, it is worth noting that the 8 percent capital coefficient rule of Basel I for the calculation of underlying minimum capital reserves for banks' credits has remained unchanged. What did change, though, was credit risk measurement, that is, the computation of the denominator of the capital reserve formula. More precisely, the asset base, on the basis of which the amount of minimum capital reserves is calculated, is now risk-weighted, and the risk weight is determined with reference to an internal or external rating. In other words, depending on the (external or internal) rating of a certain credit, a specified percentage share (e.g. 20 percent, 50 percent, 100 percent or 150 percent) of the overall credit volume (plus capital charges for market risk and operational risk) constitutes the basis on which the 8 percent share of minimum capital reserves is calculated. Beyond these technical regulatory details, the main thrust of Basel II is clear: capital reserve requirements should be contingent upon the quality of credits banks give; the quality of these credits must be measured either by internal rating procedures or by external rating procedures recognized by public banking supervisors. This was a major reform effort, aiming to make banking regulation and supervision more responsive to the risks of financial markets, thus keeping regulation in tune with markets (Gras 2003: 33–4; Kerwer 2006: 93). The use of ratings for the calculation of credit (default) risks was supposed to serve this purpose of flexible regulation.

Overall, it should be noted that the role of credit rating agencies in the final Basel II Accord is less pronounced than originally proposed by some of the BCBS members, first of all the US regulatory authorities (see BCBS 2001: para. 69 in contrast to BCBS 2006: para. 50). It does not equal the position of credit rating agencies in the US national financial regulatory system; Germany in particular has been reluctant to accept proposals by US authorities to use credit ratings even more extensively and as an almost exclusive source of risk measurement. Germany has also succeeded in curbing the influence of credit rating agencies on German public sector banks, a vital source of finance for small and medium-size enterprises (Becker 2007: 86–7; Buiter 2007; Kerwer 2002: 306; 2005: 470). The possibility of internal ratings conducted by the banks themselves was included as an alternative to external credit risk assessment from credit rating agencies. That being said, the Basel II Accord – and, consequently, the legally binding EU Capital Adequacy Directive and Banking Directive – provides for external measurement of credit risk by recognized credit rating agencies as *one* of two broad methodologies for banks' credit risk assessment (Macht 2007: 71–5). Banks can use the credit assessments of external rating agencies when determining the credit risk weights that are used for the calculation of capital requirements in the standardized approach as long as the credit rating agencies are recognized by the national banking supervisors. The national supervisory authorities assign the ratings of the recognized credit rating agencies in a routinized procedure to the risk weight categories fixed in the Basel II provisions on the standardized approach ('mapping process') (BCBS 2006: paras. 91–108; Deutsche Bundesbank 2008c). Table 2.7 shows how credit ratings

Table 2.7 Determination of risk weights in Basel I and Basel II

Credit rating	**AAA to AA–**	**A+ to A–**	**BBB+ to BBB–**	**BB+ to B–**	**Below B–**	**Unrated**
Claims on sovereigns						
Risk weight Basel II (%)	0	20	50	100	150	100
Risk weight Basel I	0% for OECD and 100% for non-OECD countries					
Claims on banks						
Risk weight Basel II (%)	20	50	50	100	150	50
Risk weight Basel I	20% for OECD or remaining repayment period of less than one year, otherwise 100%					
Credit rating	**AAA to AA–**	**A+ to A–**	**BBB+ to BB–**	**Below BB–**	**Unrated**	
Claims on corporate firms						
Risk weight Basel II (%)	20	50	100	150	100	
Risk weight Basel I (%)	100					

Source: Compiled by the author with data from Macht (2007: 74) and BCBS (2006: 19–23).

are used to determine the risk weights for the calculation of capital requirements for different credit categories – claims of banks on sovereigns, claims on other banks and claims on corporate firms. The main point of the use of credit ratings is nicely illustrated by the table: in the standardized approach, the risk weights (and consequently the minimum capital reserves to be put aside) for credits that banks give to states, to other banks or to firms depend on the credit rating of the relevant credits or borrowers.

Banks that would like to deviate from the standardized approach need to file an application with their national regulatory agency (Deutsche Bundesbank 2008d). The general expectation was that many smaller, less sophisticated banks that lacked extensive analytical capacities would calculate their capital reserve requirements on the basis of external credit ratings, while larger banks would more often use internal rating procedures within the alternative framework of the internal ratings-based approach (King and Sinclair 2003; Nölke 2004: 167–8; Nölke and Perry 2007: 130; Sinclair 2005: 46). While there are no robust, broad-based empirical findings detailing how many banks (in EU countries) use the alternative internal ratings-based approach, there is at least superficial evidence that many of the larger banks in Germany do indeed favor the internal-ratings-based approach (Osman 2007).

According to the Basel II Accord, external credit assessment institutions have to fulfill certain minimum requirements in terms of 'objectivity', 'independence', 'international access/transparency', 'disclosure', 'resources' and 'credibility' (BCBS 2006: paras. 91–3). Credit rating agencies are granted recognition as external credit assessment institutions by the competent national supervisory authorities (in Germany, for example, this is the BaFin jointly with the German Central Bank). However, there are European-level guidelines to ensure harmonized recognition criteria and procedures (BCBS 2006: para. 91; CEBS 2005, 2006). The Basel recommendations for recognizing external rating agencies have been implemented in the EU Banking Directive. In addition, CEBS published the Guidelines on the Recognition of External Credit Assessment Institutions (CEBS 2006) in order to achieve a maximum of consistency in the interpretation of the Banking Directive in this regard. These guidelines also lay down which standards are to be used to assess whether the recognition criteria have been fulfilled (Deutsche Bundesbank 2008c).

In the case of credit rating agencies seeking recognition in several EU member states, a joint assessment process is carried out among the EU member states concerned. A central contact and coordinator ('process facilitator') is appointed within this informal process. The joint evaluation and coordination in the joint assessment of the application by all of the supervisory authorities involved is intended to ensure that a shared view is reached across member states, while at the same time reducing the bureaucracy involved for the applicant. However, the ultimate decision on recognition of credit rating agencies still lies with the relevant national supervisory authority. In Germany, the Solvency Regulation (Art. 41), which transposes the EU Banking Directive into German law, states that a credit rating agency must be recognized by the supervisory authority before credit institutions can use credit ratings prepared by the agency when determining the risk weights of counterparty risk positions for the standardized approach. The credit rating agency itself must file the application for recognition. The application must be accompanied by evidence that at least one institution intends to use credit assessments from the credit rating agency for determining risk weights. The German Central Bank and the BaFin jointly examine whether the requirements for recognition have been met on the basis of the CEBS Guidelines. Recognized external credit assessment institutions pursuant to the German Solvency Regulation are Moody's, S&P's, Fitch Ratings, Dominion Bond Rating Service (DBRS) and Japan Credit Rating Agency (JCRA) (Deutsche Bundesbank 2008c).

Rating agencies' standard of creditworthiness and its public enforcement

After this detailed description of the use of credit ratings in financial regulation on both national and international levels, it can be shown on a more abstract conceptual level that credit rating agencies set a private standard of creditworthiness which is made binding by a public third party when credit ratings are used in financial regulation. This public enforcement of credit rating agencies' standard of creditworthiness constitutes a delegation of authority from public regulators to a specific type of transnational expert standard-setters, and is thus best captured by a principal–agent conceptual framework.

Credit rating agencies do not just disseminate 'informed opinions' about the creditworthiness of borrowers, even though it is crucial for the success of credit rating agencies, which is clearly based on a reputation for expertise and an image of objectivity, to present themselves as nothing more than neutral providers of information (Gras 2003: 16). Viewing credit rating agencies as neutral financial information providers overlooks the fact that credit rating involves a process of transnational standardization and certification (Gras 2003: 17; Kerwer 2002: 294; 2006: 91), which in turn constitutes an important instance of private governance (Nölke 2004; Nölke and Perry 2007). As such, the process of standardization is a highly political matter with considerable regulatory and (re-)distributive consequences for followers of the standard and third parties. This merely reflects the general insight that it is always problematic to regard expert knowledge as politically neutral (Jacobsson 2002: 47).

Generally speaking, standards are rules 'based on expertise that can be adopted voluntarily' (Kerwer 2002: 297; 2006: 81, 94). Regulation by standards can be contrasted with regulation by directives. Directives are coercive. They are accepted because they are issued by those who have the legal authority to do so, because they are adopted according to legally defined procedures and because they can ultimately be enforced through sanctions. By contrast, standards become binding by virtue of their expertise, not by virtue of the formal legal authority of the issuer and the adoption process, as in the case of directives. On an abstract level, standards constitute voluntary rules about what those who adopt them should do (Brunsson and Jacobsson 2002a: 4). Standards are rules issued without reference to formal authority. Rather, they are frequently based on expertise and adopted because of a belief in the expert knowledge of the standardizer (Jacobsson 2002: 40; Kerwer 2006: 81; see also Brunsson and Jacobsson 2002b: 135–6).

Those who issue standards are unable (or unwilling) to make others follow them by exploiting any formal authority they may possess (Brunsson and Jacobsson 2002a: 13). However, even though standardizers cannot authoritatively oblige people to follow their standards, other parties may do this for them, as the case of credit rating agencies demonstrates (Brunsson and Jacobsson 2002a: 14). We will consider this kind of third-party enforcement of (formerly) voluntary standards in detail on the next few pages. But, before doing so, it is important to note that, even without authoritative enforcement, standards (including credit rating agencies' standard of creditworthiness) may reach very high levels of compliance. This is because the fact that standardizers as such cannot claim hierarchical authority does not mean standards are ineffective. On the contrary, standards generate a strong element of global order in the modern world. They contribute to creating similarity and homogeneity even among people and organizations far apart from one another (Brunsson and Jacobsson 2002a: 1; see also Brunsson 2002b). Standards are considered useful and are frequently followed voluntarily because they render a highly complex and opaque world more ordered, making it easier to orientate ourselves (Brunsson and Jacobsson 2002c: 170). Standards reduce the amount of information we need to make decisions: 'If we know that a ship has been classified as conforming to certain safety standards, we are perfectly happy to sail on it, often without knowing anything about the exact content of the standards concerned' (ibid.: 169). It should also be noted that the degree of *actual* voluntariness of a standard may vary in practice. While standardization does not rely on formal positions of authority, actors will sometimes have no choice but to follow certain standards; the success of a business enterprise may de facto depend on following certain established standards, since some market players might demand that certain standards be observed before they agree to enter into a transaction (Brunsson and Jacobsson 2002b: 134; Kerwer 2006: 82; see also Brunsson 2002a: 33).

By defining and monitoring criteria of credit risk for private and public actors around the world, credit rating agencies have managed to establish an important, widely recognized and nearly global private standard for creditworthiness which is based *per se* (without public regulators' interference) on their reputation as experts and their ensuing legitimacy in the eyes of other financial market actors (Nölke 2004: 163–4). To be sure, the reputation and legitimacy of credit rating agencies have suffered from their failure to adequately rate the 'toxic' structured finance products which were a main contributor to the US subprime crisis and the global financial crisis. However, it remains doubtful whether this blow to credit rating agencies' expert reputation will have a more durable impact than previous rating miscalls. At least, the expert reputation of credit rating agencies still seemed strong enough to trigger massive capital flight after sovereign rating downgrades of European states in the 2010 Euro crisis. At any rate, the recent damage to credit rating agencies' reputation does not invalidate the argument that (without public enforcement) the acceptance of credit rating agencies' standard of creditworthiness essentially depends on their expert reputation and the ensuing legitimacy of 'those who know best' in the eyes of financial market actors. Because of the presumed expert status of credit rating agencies, investors relied and, to a large extent, continue to rely extensively on credit rating agencies for screening non-transparent capital markets (Kerwer 2006: 91). In times of financial crises it becomes most evident that many investors have indeed happily sailed on a ship which had been classified as conforming to a certain standard of creditworthiness without knowing anything about the exact content of the standards concerned.

Credit rating agencies publish, for instance on their websites, the criteria that guide their assessment of credit risk in the rating process. 'The standard [of credit-worthiness, A.K.] provides a set of criteria which defines, for a general audience, what credit quality is about and how it can be enhanced' (Kerwer 2002: 300). Financial market actors are aware of credit rating agencies' criteria for credit risk assessment and tend to adjust their behavior to conform to them, since – by assigning and constantly reviewing credit ratings – credit rating agencies do not only *define* a standard of creditworthiness, but also *verify* compliance with the standard and promote its adoption (Gras 2003: 25–6). Credit rating agencies' standard of creditworthiness thus becomes a benchmark for other market actors (King and Sinclair 2001: 4–5). Even if some actors may depart from these marks, they must be aware that the marks are still the standards for the work of other actors. The letter grade assigned by credit rating agencies marks a seal of approval or a certification for the creditworthiness of a borrower and, consequently, for adopting and living up to the credit rating agencies' standard of creditworthiness (Gras 2003: 17; see also Brunsson and Jacobsson 2002a: 5). This seal of approval is vital for borrowers' financing conditions and their access to capital. The criteria credit rating agencies set for the assessment of creditworthiness are in effect 'access rules for financial markets' (Kerwer 2006: 91). This gives credit rating agencies considerable leverage over other financial market actors.

From this perspective, credit rating agencies should be conceived as representatives of the broader category of 'coordination service firms' and as incumbents of private authority (Cutler et al. 1999b; Nölke 2004; Nölke and Perry 2007; Sinclair 1999, 2001). Coordination service firms set and promote compliance with standards of behavior, primarily for other firms, but occasionally also for public market participants. The relevance of those standards is not limited to the business sectors of the coordination service firms (in the case of credit rating agencies, the financial industry), but affects the wider private economy. This (potential) impact of credit rating agencies on the wider private economy became obvious in the negotiations for the Basel II Accord. German small and medium-sized enterprises and politicians (up to the German Chancellor at the time, Gerhard Schröder) warned that the Basel II provisions in general, and credit risk assessments from credit rating agencies in particular, would tend to disadvantage small and medium-sized enterprises, which in turn might undermine their competitiveness and eventually cost jobs (Becker 2007: 86–7). As well as credit rating agencies, accounting firms are another good example of coordination service firms that exercise private authority (Cutler et al. 1999b: 10; Nölke and Perry 2007: 121).

Authority can be defined in general terms as the ability of an actor or an institution to induce relevant addressees to take note of, and comply with, its rules (Rittberger et al. 2008: 2). More specifically, Cutler et al. (1999b: 19) name three criteria through which transnational private authority can be empirically identified: 'First, those subject to the rules and decisions being made by private sector actors must accept them as legitimate, as the representations of experts and those "in authority". Second, there should be a high degree of compliance with the rules and decisions. Third, the private sector must be empowered either explicitly or *implicitly* by governments with the right to make decisions for others.' Credit rating agencies meet all of these three criteria (Nölke and Perry 2007). First, acceptance of their standard of creditworthiness clearly is based on the expert reputation of credit rating agencies. Credit rating agencies' expert capacities to condense the overwhelming amount of information available to financial market actors into one (seemingly straightforward and comparable) measure of credit risk and the legitimacy that is derived from this expert status in the perception of market participants are an important source of the private authority credit rating agencies hold. This is in line with more general findings of organizational research that standardization is usually closely linked to expertise and is frequently motivated by the view that there are 'some persons who know best' (Jacobsson 2002: 40; see also Brunsson and Jacobsson 2002b: 135–6). Reference to expert knowledge is thus used to give legitimacy to the standardization activities of credit rating agencies. Second, there is indeed a high degree of compliance with credit rating agencies' standards. A wide range of public and private market actors do not only rely on their credit risk assessments when making investment decisions but also tend to adjust their behavior to meet the criteria of creditworthiness set by credit rating agencies, since credit rating agencies' risk assessment is crucial for their financing conditions. Finally, as this book argues, credit rating agencies have explicitly been empowered in their authority by governments or other public actors (Nölke and Perry 2007; Schwarcz 2001a: 296–7).

Credit rating agencies *exercise* their authority in two ways. First, credit rating agencies shape the behavior of financial market actors by limiting their thinking to a range of possibilities which correspond to credit rating agencies' criteria of creditworthiness and are therefore considered 'legitimate' in the eyes of market participants. On the other, more obvious but overall less frequent side, credit rating agencies may even be in a position to exercise an explicit veto over certain options (in the corporate governance of firms or the economic policies of a state) by using a ratings downgrade (King and Sinclair 2001: 4; Nölke and Perry 2007: 130). Most companies, and even states, cannot afford a low rating: 'For firms, a downgrade by a credit rating agency can lead to restructuring and mass lay-offs. For public borrowers such as municipalities and regional governments, and so-called "sovereign borrowers", that is, nation states, the consequences of a downgrade can be fiscal stress and, as a result, a lower supply of social security and other public goods' (Kerwer 2006: 91–2; see also Sinclair 1994). Even states might thus consider changing their behavior to suit the preferences of credit rating agencies, that is, to meet the criteria of credit rating agencies' standard of creditworthiness. However, while credit rating agencies' evaluation of public institutions (sovereign states, municipalities, etc.) has received a lot of attention because this kind of credit assessment constitutes the most obvious display of their political relevance (Hillebrand 2001; Sinclair 2003: 151–155), it should not be forgotten that the core task of credit rating agencies is to rate the quality of other companies' debts. It is here that credit rating agencies exercise the largest 'infrastructural impact' (Nölke and Perry 2007: 131). Credit rating agencies exercise authority over other companies, since most companies depend on reasonably cheap access to capital (i.e. a good rating) and will therefore consider adjusting their activities (or even corporate governance structures) to credit rating agencies' standard of creditworthiness. As ratings upgrades and downgrades are not confidential but, rather, made available to all investors, the impact of credit rating agencies is deeper than the confidential assessment of banks in a system of intermediated finance (Nölke and Perry 2007: 131).

The role of credit rating agencies as standardizers is highlighted and publicly bolstered by ratings-dependent regulation. The increasing use public regulators have made of ratings-based constraints in their rules is one of the main reasons why ratings increasingly act as creditworthiness standards, far beyond their initial purpose (Gonzalez et al. 2004: 8). When ratings are used in financial regulation, credit rating agencies emerge as publicly sanctioned 'judges of prudent economic and financial behavior' (Sinclair 2005: 46). It is not only that the regulatory use of credit ratings merely reinforces the expert authority of those issuing the standard, which in turn should increase the perceived legitimacy of credit rating agencies and thus the further dissemination of, and compliance with, credit rating agencies' standard of creditworthiness (see Brunsson and Jacobsson 2002b: 136). Instead, the nature of the standard of creditworthiness changes. In the use of credit ratings in financial regulation we can observe a 'decoupling of rule-setting and rule-enforcement' (Zürn and Koenig-Archibugi 2006: 249). Once public regulators use private credit ratings for regulatory purposes, the standard is not only adopted by public regulatory authorities but also *enforced* by a public third party. In abstract terms, the standard becomes coercive in practice because parties other than the potential adopter believe it to be reasonable to follow and have the means to authoritatively enforce it (Brunsson and Jacobsson 2002b: 134). It becomes mandatory for financial market actors to observe the credit rating agencies' standard for creditworthiness (Kerwer 2002: 303–4; 2005: 463–4); it is no longer voluntary. Public third-party enforcement of the private standard thus reinforces the alignment of investors' and borrowers' behavior along the lines of credit rating agencies' standard of creditworthiness (Gras 2003: 14). Arguably, it also increases the demand for ratings (Gras 2003: 34; White 2001: 30), causing an 'artificial lift in their business' (White 2001: 22).

Therefore, while the expert reputation of credit rating agencies and their ensuing legitimacy in the eyes of market participants should indeed be considered *one* source of (genuinely) private authority, this is far from providing the complete picture of credit rating agencies' sources of authority. Instead, the widespread use of credit ratings as instruments of financial market regulation is a key source of credit rating agencies' authority to influence the allocation of capital. The role of credit rating agencies as gatekeepers determining access to capital and costs of borrowing is, to a significant extent, supported by the fact that the private standard of creditworthiness defined by the agencies is enforced by public regulation (Kerwer 2006: 90; Partnoy 2006). In other words, public regulation, that is, public authority, is crucial in constituting the authority of a particular type of transnational standard-setters and turning them into 'de facto regulators' (Schwarcz 2001a: 297), in fact even 'coercive regulators' (Kerwer 2006: 92). When public regulators use and thus recognize credit rating agencies' standard of creditworthiness, regulatory authority is conferred upon credit rating agencies. 'The regulatory use of CRAs turns them into quasipublic regulators' (Kerwer 2005: 464). This does not just happen incidentally; rather, public actors are well aware of the transfer of authority being implied in the use of credit ratings in regulation, as the dictum of US Senator Joe Lieberman that credit rating agencies' power is 'government-conferred power' (Lieberman 2002) betrays. The wider implication is that financial regulation and oversight are, 'in effect, being privatized' (Gras 2003: 1), since the competence and capacity to set rules and to promote compliance with them for the sake of the provision of the (global) public good 'financial market stability' is transferred from state actors to private actors (ibid.: 25–8, 32–3; Sinclair 2005: 46).

This mode of public recognition and enforcement of private standards is not a unique phenomenon that occurs only with credit rating agencies (see e.g. Brunsson and Jacobsson 2002a: 3; Bundgard-Pedersen 1997; Kerwer 2006: 82–3). Rather, it can be found in a growing body of literature dealing with the public recognition of private sources of economic regulation (Hutter 2006: 64–6) and with publicly supported 'transnational expert-driven standardization' (Botzem 2008: 44; see Brunsson and Jacobsson 2002a: 8; Jacobsson 2002: 45;

Kerwer 2006: 82–3). While transnational expert-driven standardization is on the rise in a globalizing economy and the importance of private actors in regulation has increased, transnational standardization ultimately still relies on public authority to a large extent. Besides credit rating agencies' standard for creditworthiness, another well-researched example is accounting standards. In fact, transnational accountancy governance has been seen as a process characterized by an interaction of private and public actors, with public actors providing recognition and legitimacy, granting authority, and thus complementing private actors' expertise-based sources of (genuinely) private authority with publicly conferred authority (Botzem 2008: 44–5, 56). Thus, the EU actively supported the creation of private international accounting standards by the International Accounting Standards Committee (IASC) and its successor organization, the International Accounting Standards Board (IASB). The IASB is an independent, privately funded accounting standard-setter based in the UK (Hutter 2006: 70–1). The EU took regulatory steps to secure the adoption of the IASB standards by making the use of international accounting standards obligatory for all group accounts of listed companies in Europe (Botzem 2008: 52).

In a similar vein, Jacobsson has shown that within the EU there have been several cases, for example in the areas of health, safety and the environment, where regulatory matters have been largely delegated to standardizing organizations and private standards have become virtually mandatory by being linked to directives (Jacobsson 2002: 45–6; see also Joerges et al. 1999; Kerwer 2006: 82–3).

The regulatory use of credit ratings and the delegation of political authority

The dependent variable of this study 'use of private credit ratings by public regulators for regulatory purposes' can be conceptualized in more abstract terms. In fact, it can be conceived as a principal–agent relationship between public regulators and credit rating agencies that implies the delegation of governance tasks, namely risk measurement according to credit rating agencies' standard of creditworthiness for the purpose of flexible, risk-sensitive regulation, and the transfer of (quasi-)regulatory authority. Note that the principal–agent approach is used, in this context, as a conceptual framework for a heuristic pre-theoretic model of ratings-dependent regulation (or 'regulation by ratings') on the basis of which a theoretical explanation can be developed. In Chapter 3 principal–agent theory will be introduced as a causal theory providing hypotheses on when and why delegation occurs.

The principal–agent approach defines delegation as 'a conditional grant of authority from a principal to an agent that empowers the latter to act on behalf of the former' (Hawkins et al. 2006b: 7). This grant of authority is limited in time and/or scope and must be revocable by the principal. Typically, a principal decides upon a certain policy and delegates its implementation to an agent (Richter and Furubotn 2003: 173–4). Principal and agent are mutually constitutive: an actor cannot be a principal without an agent, and vice versa; the actors are thus defined by their relationship to each other. A principal must, by definition, be able to both grant authority and rescind it. The relationship between a principal and an agent is governed by a contract. This is not necessarily a formal written document but can also be an implicit (never formally acknowledged) and informal (unwritten) agreement (Hawkins et al. 2006b: 7; Mutschler 2007: 12–13). In terms of institutional economics, a principal delegating regulatory authority to an agent in a vertically integrated setting is an extreme form of a relational contract (Milgrom and Roberts 1992). The principal and the agent enter into a contractual arrangement, in which the principal chooses to delegate certain functions to the agent in the expectation that the agent will act in ways that produce outcomes desired by the principal (Tallberg 2002: 25).

It is important to note that a principal need not be a single actor: Lyne et al. (2006) distinguish between a single principal, multiple principals (i.e. several principals acting independently from one another delegate competences to an agent), and collective principals (i.e. a collective of several actors enters into a common contract with an agent). Finally, while the principal–agent approach, in international relations, has mainly been used with reference to the relationship between states and international (and in particular supranational) organizations, states might 'also delegate authority to private firms, NGOs, or a third state rather than a formal international organization' (Hawkins et al. 2006b: 11; see Cooley and Ron 2002; Martens et al. 2002).

The main conceptual features of principal–agent relationships can be identified in the use of credit ratings by public regulators in financial market regulation. Public authority plays a crucial role in constituting the regulatory authority of credit rating agencies (Kerwer 2001: 295). When credit ratings are used by public regulators in financial market regulation, the (genuinely) private authority of credit rating agencies, which is based on the expert character and the resulting supposed legitimacy of credit ratings in the eyes of market participants, becomes enmeshed with and substantially reinforced by public regulatory bodies' recognition and enforcement of credit rating agencies' standards of creditworthiness (Nölke 2004: 167–8; see also Gras 2003: 25; Jackson 2001: 1–3; Kerwer 2002: 303–6; 2005: 463–4). By rendering the credit rating agencies' standards of creditworthiness binding in financial market regulation, public third parties, such as the SEC, BCBS or other supranational and national legislators, confer (additional) regulatory authority on credit rating agencies. Credit rating agencies have explicitly been empowered in their authority by governments and international regulatory bodies such as the BCBS in various laws, rules and regulations that constrain the behavior of financial market actors (Nölke and Perry 2007: 124).

At first glance, the credit risk assessments conducted by credit rating agencies may look like nothing more than providing an information collection and processing service which public regulators make use of. However, this conception fails to recognize that credit rating agencies perform crucial governance tasks on behalf of the regulators – they measure credit risk according to their own standard of creditworthiness. In doing so, credit rating agencies promote the adoption of, and compliance with, their standard of creditworthiness. This kind of 'standardising as governance' (Kerwer 2002) becomes all the more significant and consequential when it is made binding by regulators and when credit rating agencies are given a publicly sanctioned regulatory function.

From this perspective, credit rating agencies' risk measurement and certification of creditworthiness is not merely some information provision service but a governance activity which in turn is an integral part of publicly designed risk-sensitive financial regulation. Making use of private credit ratings (i.e. the expression of credit rating agencies' standardization and certification activities) makes it possible for public regulators to design and effectively implement flexible, risk-sensitive financial market regulation (Kerwer 2005: 463–4; 2006: 95). Financial market regulators on their own would not be able to collect and process the necessary information to assess the credit risks of all borrowers they seek to regulate. Rather than conduct the risk assessments needed for risk-sensitive regulation *themselves*, public regulators have implicitly transferred this task to credit rating agencies when providing for the use of credit ratings in regulation.

Thus, to summarize, credit rating agencies have been empowered and granted political authority by public regulators. Moreover, they are expected to conduct a governance activity on behalf of public authorities. Thus, the constitutive elements of a principal–agent relationship can be observed in the case at hand. Neither the absence of an explicit instruction to credit rating agencies to conduct credit risk assessment on behalf of public regulators nor the fact that public regulators do not create a new actor to perform this task, but rather rely on preexisting actors and rating processes, would in any way contradict the conception of the relationship between public regulators and credit rating agencies as a principal–agent relationship, since a principal–agent relationship can also be constituted by an implicit arrangement (Hawkins et al. 2006b: 7). In fact, delegation in this case is based on an implicit contract that gives credit rating agencies (agents) considerable discretion in how to achieve the expected outcome. In economics, the principal–agent approach has frequently been applied to situations where no formal contract between principal and agent exists (Richter and Furubotn 2003: 174–8). Nothing in the core assumptions of the principal–agent conceptual framework would preclude applying it to the relationship between public actors and a preexisting private actor whose activities are given a new regulatory quality by being granted a degree of authority he had not enjoyed before public recognition and use. Once their ratings are used by a regulator in financial regulation, credit rating agencies turn into agents of the principal 'public regulator' and, through their credit risk assessment activities, perform a governance task on behalf of public regulators. We thus witness an allocation of regulatory tasks from public actors to transnational private actors (Nölke and Perry 2007: 136). Public regulators grant credit rating agencies (quasi-)regulatory authority through the use of ratings in regulation and expect them to act on their behalf *as if* they had explicitly ordered them to do so.

In accordance with the principal–agent approach, financial market regulators are in the formal position to withdraw the (quasi-) regulatory authority they have bestowed upon credit rating agencies in the relevant regulatory document (e.g. national laws and regulations, supranational directives or the Basel II Accord) and thus to terminate the contractual relationship. This possibility has been raised and in part also realized after the dismal performance of credit rating agencies in the US mortgage crisis (see Chapter 6 on regulatory change after the global financial crisis; see also Ackerman 2008; Reuters 2007). In this vein, the finance policy spokesman for the parliamentary group of the German Christian Democrats (CDU), Otto Bernhardt, said as early as summer 2007 that either Germany's financial supervisory authorities would have to stop using credit rating agencies' risk assessments 'or we'll fold the rating agencies' voluntary code of conduct into a reform by law' (Bernhardt, quoted in Reuters 2007). The SEC issued a regulation in 2009 stipulating that the use of credit ratings in some securities regulations be terminated (SEC 2009b; see Chapter 6).

While the topic of this book is the *causes* for public regulators' use of credit ratings in financial regulation, it is nonetheless noteworthy that many assumptions of the principal–agent approach on control mechanisms in principal–agent relationships are also applicable to the relationship between public regulators and credit rating agencies. In the following, I will briefly outline how far the need to control agents through different mechanisms manifests itself in the principal–agent relationship between public regulators and credit rating agencies (Hawkins et al. 2006b: 8–11, 26–8). This does not only support my argument that the use of credit ratings by public regulators indeed constitutes a principal–agent relationship. It also contributes to adequately grasping the relationship between public and private actors in the particular mode of public–private governance we are dealing with here. The possibility of 'recontracting' (Alter 2008: 34), that is, 1) strengthening oversight and control of agents by stricter recognition criteria and/or more extensive oversight, 2) changing the rules so as to reduce the reliance on private credit ratings or 3) even rescinding the delegation of authority by completely renouncing the use of ratings in regulation, is an inherent feature of this mode of public–private governance which underlines its essentially *hierarchical* nature. Arguably, the possibility of recontracting might even contribute to the attractiveness of using credit ratings in regulation. The transfer of quasi-regulatory authority to credit rating agencies is ultimately revocable – this might have reduced public actors' resistance to sharing regulatory prerogatives with private actors.

According to the principal–agent approach, control of agents is necessary because delegation entails the risk of *agency slack* (Mutschler 2007: 26–7). Agents are to be conceived as actors that have preferences of their own which may diverge from the preferences of their principals. Usually, they also have resources 'to strike out on [their] own should the opportunities arise' (Moe 1990: 121; see also Kiewiet and McCubbins 1991: 5, 24). As a result, agency slack may occur; that is, agents may behave opportunistically, in ways undesired by the principal. Agency slack occurs in two primary forms: *shirking,* when an agent minimizes the effort it exerts in the implementation of tasks on its principal's behalf, and *slippage,* when an agent shifts policy away from its principal's preferred outcome and toward its own preferences. In the case of slipping, agents pursue goals that are not congruent, or not even compatible, with the goals of their principals (Hawkins et al. 2006b: 8). Costs that arise for principals from the undesired behavior of agents are termed *agency losses* (Hawkins et al. 2006b: 8–11; Kiewiet and McCubbins 1991: 5; Mutschler 2007: 26–7; Pollack 1997: 108; 2003: 26). The crucial point is that, in any principal–agent relationship, information about the agent and its activities is asymmetrically distributed in favor of the agent, making control or even evaluation by the principals difficult. In fact, in the economics account of the principal–agent approach, the existence of asymmetrically distributed information is *the* defining feature of a principal–agent relationship (Richter and Furubotn 2003: 174–5). The principal cannot permanently and thoroughly monitor the *activities* of the agent (e.g. the intensity of its efforts in fulfilling a task). The agent may be in a position to make observations that the principal has not made, thus gaining an *informational advantage* which it might exploit to the detriment of the principal. In the former case *hidden action* occurs; in the latter case the principal faces the problem of *hidden information* (Arrow 1985: 38; Richter and Furubotn 2003: 174). Without means of acquiring the necessary information to evaluate the agent's performance the principal seems to be at a permanent disadvantage, and the likelihood of agency losses seems large (Pollack 2003: 26–7; see also Arrow 1985: 38–9; Richter and Furubotn 2003: 174–5).

To avoid agency losses principals employ *screening and selection procedures*. They seek to choose an agent whose (presumed) preferences are as close to those of the principal(s) as possible. For that purpose, principals may choose among different existing agents or 'create' a new agent (e.g. institution). The latter option, of course, entails (usually considerable) start-up costs (Hawkins et al. 2006b: 28–9). Furthermore, principals may adopt ex ante *administrative procedures*, which define more or less narrowly the competences and the scope of agency activity and the procedures to be followed by the agent. They may also rely on ex post *oversight procedures* in order to rectify, or at least mitigate, informational asymmetries through various institutional mechanisms of monitoring, and constrain or shape the incentives of the agents through the use of positive or negative sanctions. Two kinds of oversight procedures can be distinguished. In the case of *police patrol*, the principal monitors the agent himself. In the case of *fire alarm*, the principal leaves this task to other actors external to the principal–agent relationship. These external actors alert the principal in the case of agents' misbehavior (McCubbins and Schwartz 1984). Of course, this oversight mode only works properly if and when other actors are affected by the agents' misbehavior (Hawkins et al. 2006b: 29–30; Mutschler 2007: 27).

A principal may sanction a 'rogue agent' by (the threat of) changing the contract, for example by rewriting the contractual terms to undercut the agent's realm of authority, curbing the agent's competences, and overruling policies designed by the agent, thus damaging the agent's reputation (Alter 2008: 34; Pollack 1997: 109). Yet control and sanctioning mechanisms are themselves costly and are unlikely to be perfectly effective in preventing agents from behaving opportunistically and from pursuing their own preferences (Hawkins et al. 2006b: 26–9; Mutschler 2007: 27–8; Pollack 2003: 7, 27). Too much control undermines the very sense of delegation (Kiewiet and McCubbins 1991: 27). Strict administrative controls, narrowly defining the scope and flexibility an agent possesses in the execution of its functions, tend to produce rigid or inefficient policies. Oversight procedures may consume considerable resources, and sanctions may impose costs upon principals as well as agents (Pollack 2003: 27). The mode and intensity of control must fit the specific tasks and functions the agent is supposed to perform (Mutschler 2007: 28). In some situations of delegation, tight oversight and control of agents' behavior might be counterproductive for the fulfillment of functions such as enhancing the (long-term) credibility of policy commitments. This has led scholars to argue that there are 'principal–trustee' relationships, which should be conceived as a mode of delegation distinct from principal–agent relationships (Alter 2008; Majone 2001). In principal–trustee relationships a lack of effective control of trustees by principals follows necessarily from the very rationale for delegation (and properties of the trustees).

At this point some remarks on the need for control of credit rating agencies as agents in financial regulation and the (lack of) adequate control mechanisms are in order (Bottini 1993; Champsaur 2005; Dittrich 2007; Fisch 2005; Hartwall and Pettersson 2005; Kerwer 2005, 2006; King and Sinclair 2003; Rousseau 2005; Smith and Walter 2001). Indeed, there seems to be an agency problem in the relationship between public regulators and credit rating agencies. This is caused by informational asymmetries of both the *hidden action* and the *hidden information* type. It is very hard for public regulators to keep track of the activities of credit rating agencies and to 'measur[e] the measurers' in terms of the adequacy and integrity of their rating methodologies (*The Economist* 2007b). In other words, it is very difficult and costly for public regulators to monitor whether credit rating agencies are doing a good job or not – unless some major crisis uncovers misbehavior on the part of the credit rating agencies. This makes for a high potential for *hidden action*. Similarly, credit rating agencies will almost necessarily acquire information unavailable to their principals, the public regulators, which implies a high potential for *hidden information*. Actually, one of the main rationales for relying on credit rating agencies in regulation is the expectation that 'they know better' than a bureaucrat designing inflexible, rather crude financial rules. The substantial degree of autonomy enjoyed by credit rating agencies derives not only from the authority delegated to them by principals, but also from the authority that comes from a belief in their superior expertise (for a general elaboration on this point see Koenig-Archibugi 2006: 8). However, the question of whether these quite obvious informational asymmetries translate into actual agency slack in the form of shirking or slipping is less straightforward to answer. It is not evident *a priori* that credit rating agencies should have any incentives for shirking – such as spending less-than-adequate efforts on credit risk assessment – and/or slipping – such as giving better rating grades to a (large) corporate borrower than justified in both single-business and systemic terms in order to keep it as a fee-paying client. On the contrary, the optimistic assumption on which public regulators' use of credit ratings in regulation has been based is that the dependence of credit rating agencies on a reputation as reliable and credible experts, which is vital for their business success, would discipline their behavior (Gras 2003: 27–8). Thus, market competition between credit rating agencies would ensure that there would be some kind of 'de facto accountability of rating agencies through reputation' (Schwarcz 2001a: 303). Monitoring by reputation and competition would therefore preclude agency slack, because shirking and slippage would undermine the viability of the business of credit rating agencies. From this perspective, regulators could rely on the belief that the profit-maximizing motives that are driving the behavior of a private enterprise such as credit rating agencies, and the disciplining forces of the market, would make credit rating agencies act in ways desired by the regulators. Essentially, reputational concerns would prevent agency slack and the market would do the monitoring for public regulators. However, this reasoning has some serious flaws.

The main problem is the oligopolistic (or even duopolistic) market structure of the rating industry. The impact of the disciplining forces of market competition is therefore limited (Gras 2003: 29). Concerns for reputation only partly constrain credit rating agencies' (potential mis-)behavior, because reputation is assessed *mainly* in relative terms, that is, in relation to (a small number of) competitors (*The Economist* 2002a: 76). Empirical evidence shows that – at least before the major industry-wide failure in the most recent US mortgage crisis – performance of credit rating agencies in relation to other credit rating agencies accounted for their reputation (Gras 2003: 29; *The Economist* 1997: 87). This has created incentives for credit rating agencies to adjust their ratings to the ratings of the other big agencies and thus to undermine the control function of market competition. Therefore, mere reliance on reputational concerns and market discipline seem to be insufficient for adequate control of the activities of credit rating agencies. Given the significant impact and the regulatory function of credit rating agencies, some kind of public administrative and oversight procedures would appear necessary. However, many observers argue that the 'light regulation' model, which the US, the most important public regulator for credit rating agencies, has pursued with the (until 2006 rather informal) NRSRO registration procedure, has done more harm than good in terms of holding credit rating agencies accountable. It has created market access barriers, reinforced the oligopolistic market structure and thus reduced economic pressure to avoid misbehavior (Adams et al. 1999: 191; Cantor and Packer 1994: 2; Gras 2003: 29; Jackson 2001: 322; Kerwer 2002: 309; Randow 1996: 551; Sinclair 2005: 42; White 2001: 5, 25). As the reputational concern and market discipline mechanisms, as well as 'light regulation' through an informal, procedurally loose NRSRO certification mechanism (or similar approaches which were common in other countries until the global financial crisis), failed to guide the behavior of credit rating agencies in ways desired by public regulators, the consequence seems to be either to 'take agencies out of the framework of financial regulation' (*The Economist* 2002b: 76) or to design and implement more rigorous public control procedures (Gras 2003: 29–30, 34–5; Randow 1996: 563–4). But it took the great US subprime and global financial crises to induce regulators to pursue stricter oversight and control policies towards credit rating agencies and to at least reduce their reliance on credit ratings in financial regulation (see Chapter 6).

In general terms, to date, no adequate public accountability structure for the activities of credit rating agencies in general, and for their contributions to financial regulation in particular, has been institutionalized. The continual demands for more accountable credit rating agencies have led to only limited changes (Kerwer 2005, 2006). At the same time, it seems there has been a trend toward (somewhat) stricter control mechanisms for credit rating agencies whose ratings are to be used in financial regulation.

It can be observed that *screening and selection procedures* and ex ante *administrative procedures* have become more formal and rigorous. This applies to the US Credit Rating Agencies Reform Act 2006, which ordered the SEC to develop a formal registration procedure and called for more frequent (though not procedurally institutionalized) oversight of credit rating agencies; to the Basel II Accord, which provides for certain minimum requirements in terms of 'objectivity', 'independence', 'international access/transparency', 'disclosure', 'resources' and 'credibility'; to the European level (see CEBS 2006) and to national recognition criteria and procedures (German SolvV). At the same time, oversight has so far been ad hoc: in the US, for example, through inquiries conducted by the SEC or by the appropriate Committees of Congress. By the time of the global financial crisis (2007–10), the relevant regulatory agencies had failed to establish an institutionalized supervisory regime (Kerwer 2006: 96; see Chapter 6 for a detailed discussion of recent regulatory developments).

There is one established institutional mechanism which evokes *fire alarm* conceptions of oversight. The International Organization of Securities Commissions (IOSCO) drafted and eventually passed a Code of Conduct Fundamentals for Credit Rating Agencies in 2004 that was to ensure the integrity and reliability of the rating process. The IOSCO comprises the national securities market watchdogs from over 100 countries (including the US, Japan and the EU). Its main tasks are to promote the establishment and consistent implementation of internationally harmonized standards of securities markets regulation and surveillance and to assist in the exchange of information among national supervisory bodies to ensure effective oversight of transnational securities transactions. IOSCO members agree to apply and enforce guidelines they jointly adopted in order to promote the integrity of financial markets (IOSCO 2008a; Reuters 2008: 12). The IOSCO Code of Conduct Fundamentals for Credit Rating Agencies (IOSCO 2004, 2008b) as well as the broader IOSCO Principles Regarding the Activities of Credit Rating Agencies (2003a, b) were developed out of consultations of IOSCO members and other major financial market stakeholders. In this context, it should be emphasized that representatives of the BCBS were not only supportive of, but also closely and actively involved in, the drafting of the IOSCO Code of Conduct (IOSCO 2008b). In this vein, the IOSCO Code of Conduct could be conceived as some kind of external accountability mechanism that was supposed to serve the BCBS's interest in ensuring the accountability of those agents the BCBS empowered in the same year in the 2004 Basel II Accord. However, the IOSCO Code of Conduct Fundamentals provides merely broad guidelines that credit rating agencies should integrate into their own codes of conduct. If credit rating agencies fail to do so, they should at least explain why there is a deviation of their codes of conduct from the IOSCO provisions, and how any deviations nonetheless achieve the objectives contained in the IOSCO provisions ('comply or explain'). There is no third-party monitoring or enforcement mechanism. This has not changed for the revised Code of Conduct for Credit Rating Agencies, which was published by IOSCO in 2008 and contained lessons learnt from credit rating agencies' miscalculations of structured finance products in the context of the US subprime crisis (IOSCO 2008b; Reuters 2008). The impact of the IOSCO Code of Conduct has been modest at best. This has led European-level and German politicians to demand public oversight of credit rating agencies rather than self-regulation through a voluntary code of conduct. Financial supervisory authorities would thus 'fold the rating agencies' voluntary code of conduct into a reform by law' (Bernhardt, quoted in Reuters 2007).

The involvement of credit rating agencies in the global financial crisis (2007–10) has indeed led to regulatory moves towards increased oversight of credit rating agencies in both the US and the EU. The SEC has devised additional disclosure, transparency and reporting requirements for NRSROs (SEC 2009a), going beyond the previous requirements of the Credit Agencies Reform Act 2006 and concretizing 2007 SEC rules. On the EU level, even more stringent regulations have been devised. A European Commission regulatory initiative that was approved by the European Parliament in April 2009 puts in place a European registration and external oversight regime for credit rating agencies whereby European regulators will supervise the policies and procedures followed by credit rating agencies active in Europe. Besides procedural provisions on the new mandatory registration process coordinated by the Committee of European Securities Regulators (CESR), the Regulation also imposes further regulatory requirements on credit rating agencies, including measures to prevent conflicts of interests through in-house rotation, disclosure requirements concerning the risks models of credit rating agencies, their rating methods and basic assumptions, a ban on rating consultancy services for companies that are to be rated, and the issuance of transparency reports that list large customers and outline the measures taken by the agency to ensure the quality of its ratings (see also Chapter 6).

3

The Theoretical Model: An Embedded Resource Dependence View on Delegation

In the preceding chapter the regulatory use of credit ratings has been described and conceptualized as a principal–agent relationship. In this chapter, a synthetic theoretical framework for analysis is developed which yields hypotheses that purport to *explain* the use of private credit ratings by national and international public regulators in financial market regulation. In essence, I suggest a macro-institutionally embedded resource dependence view on the delegation of regulatory authority from public actors to private credit rating agencies. The proposed model is designed to explain the regulatory use of credit ratings; however, its gist should be useful for analyzing a broad range of situations where political authority has been delegated to private actors.

In order to (re-)construct this model, I proceed as follows. First, I examine the different reasons for delegation that proponents of principal–agent theory have identified so far. Delegation to a 'specialized agent' that is supposed to perform a certain governance task more efficiently than an (overmatched and under-informed) principal appears as a fruitful candidate explanatory approach from principal–agent theory that could help to make sense of the regulatory use of credit ratings. In particular, it echoes the resource dependence argument of resource dependence theory. Therefore, in a second step, I seek to combine principal–agent theory and resource dependence theory. The value-added of a joint principal–agent and resource dependence framework – in terms of both the empirical explanatory power of this study and its theoretical contribution to the existing literature on different institutional modes of public–private governance – promises to be worth the effort of combining these theories. According to both resource dependence and resource exchange theory, organizations, conceived as rational, selfish and goal-oriented actors, will seek to establish relationships with other organizations if, for the attainment of their goals, they are dependent on resources which those organizations control and which are hard to obtain elsewhere.[1] If one applies a joint principal–agent and resource dependence perspective to the relationship between public regulators and credit rating agencies in financial market governance, the following argument can be advanced. Public regulators lack essential analytical resources for measuring credit risk and, thus, for implementing risk-sensitive regulation. Therefore, they delegate governance tasks and regulatory authority to specialized risk-measuring agents, that is, transnational expert standard-setters. Both principal–agent theory and resource dependence theory are rationalist theories. The supposed causal mechanism is, therefore, 'cost–benefit analysis': public regulators delegate governance tasks and regulatory authority if the (perceived) benefits of making use of credit rating agencies' resources through delegation are greater than the (perceived) agency losses.

Finally, I argue that resource dependence in general, and public regulators' dependence on credit rating agencies' analytical resources in particular, should be analyzed not as something that is exogenously given but rather as a phenomenon that is activated and magnified by the relevant socioeconomic macro-institutional context, which can be conceived as a condition variable. Drawing on environmental approaches in (intra- and inter-)organizational research and the studies by Nölke (2004) and Nölke and Perry (2007), I seek to embed the principal–agent/resource dependence theory argument on the establishment of public–private governance arrangements into a macro-institutional socioeconomic context. Applied to the case of credit rating agencies, this means that the essentiality and substitutability of their analytical resources are a function of, or in other words are conditioned by, prevailing national or regional socioeconomic macro-institutional settings, in the form of different varieties of capitalism (Hall and Soskice 2001a).

Principal–agent theory revisited: causes of delegation

Why do principals delegate? Generally speaking, delegation of authority by a principal (such as a group of domestic regulators or a group of member states) to an agent (such as a regulatory agency or a supranational institution) is a special case of the more general problem of institutional choice. The basic approach of principal–agent theory to the question of institutional choice is functionalist: that is, it explains institutional choices in terms of the functions a given institution is expected to perform and the effects on policy outcomes it is expected to produce (Pollack 1997: 102; see also Keohane 1984: 80). Principals expect to benefit from the delegation of competences, which is the reason why they delegate. Several functions performed by agents, and different rationales for delegation, can be distinguished. In the following, the six most important rationales for delegation, frequently mentioned in the principal–agent literature, are summarized (Abbott and Snidal 1998; Hawkins et al. 2006b: 13–23; Mutschler 2007: 14–15; Pollack 1997: 103–4; 2003: 20–4; Tallberg 2002: 26; Thatcher and Stone Sweet 2002: 4).[2]

First, collective principals may delegate *agenda-setting competences* to an *agenda-setting agent* to 'avoid endless cycling among alternative policy proposals' (Pollack 2003: 24) that might occur in a system where all principals would retain agenda-setting rights for themselves. The argument is that any majoritarian system in which each and every legislator had the right to initiate policy proposals would encourage an endless series of proposals from disgruntled legislators who had been in the minority in a previous vote. No decision would be an equilibrium; instead we would witness 'endless cycling among alternative policy proposals'. Thus, there should be an incentive for any legislature to develop rules governing which actors can initiate proposals, and when (Kiewiet and McCubbins 1991: 23–4; Pollack 2003: 24–5; Shepsle 1991).

Second, agents can help to solve problems of *incomplete contracting* among principals. In this case, 'filling in' and interpreting incomplete international agreements dealing with very complex and/or disputed issues is delegated to agents. Many contracts are incomplete in that they do not spell out in explicit detail the precise obligations of all parties in all conceivable circumstances. Rather than writing a complete contract anticipating all possible contingencies, the contracting parties agree on a framework agreement which contains general performance expectations, procedures to govern decision-making in situations where the contract is not explicit, and provisions on how to adjudicate disputes where they arise (Milgrom and Roberts 1990: 62; Pollack 2003: 22–3). Particularly when uncertainty about future developments relevant for the contract is great and/or agreement among the principals on the precise obligations of the contract is hard to achieve, contract parties may delegate the elaboration and amendment of rules and the arbitration of disputes dealing with the interpretation of the contract to an agent. This *arbitrating agent* is supposed to impartially interpret the agreement, fill in the details of the incomplete contract, and adjudicate disputes of interpretation that might arise (Hawkins et al. 2006b: 17–18; Pollack 2003: 23).

Third, principals may delegate competences to certain *policy-biased agents* in order to *lock in their preferences*. Principals that are in the power position to do so might choose to allocate agenda control, (limited) decision-making rights, and/or policy implementation competences deliberately to agents whose interests coincide with theirs, so as to bias future policymaking and implementation outcomes in particular directions favorable to their interests (Hawkins et al. 2006b: 19–20; Pollack 2003: 25).

Fourth, principals can delegate *monitoring of compliance* with policy agreements and contractual obligations, and in some cases even sanctioning of noncompliance, to agents. The underlying idea is that *monitoring* (or even *enforcing*) *agents* reduce transaction costs under conditions of imperfect information and help to overcome collective action problems. Agents do so by providing information on principals' compliance with agreements, which in turn facilitates decentralized sanctioning by the principals themselves. Monitoring principals' compliance with agreements thus mitigates concerns about noncompliance by would-be partners and encourages mutually beneficial cooperation among principals. In some cases, agents may even undertake sanctioning breaches of obligations (Hawkins et al. 2006b: 15–16; Pollack 2003: 21–2).

A *fifth*, closely related, reason for delegation is that agents may *resolve credible commitment problems*, as agents allow politicians (principals) to jointly tie their hands. In fact, the demand for credible commitments has been singled out as one of the most important motivations for delegation (Pollack 2003: 28). *Independent, insulated agents*, such as regulatory bureaucracies (Gilardi 2008), central banks (Rogoff 1985) and international courts (Alter 2008), are granted competences to adopt regulation or to adjudicate disputes in areas where the principals would obviously be biased. By delegating (regulatory or judiciary) authority to independent agents, principals tie their hands and thus establish the credibility of their policy commitments among constituents and market actors. This is rational in areas where the principals themselves have difficulties in credibly promising to apply policies consistently to powerful constituents because there are strong incentives for principals to renege on agreements or policy commitments. A classic example of delegation for credible commitment reasons is delegation of monetary authority to independent central banks which would be insulated from political pressures to stimulate the economy (thereby creating inflationary pressures) prior to elections (Pollack 2003: 24).

The 'credible commitment' rationale for delegation has been picked up by Majone (2001) and Alter (2008), who have coined the term 'fiduciary principal–trustee relationship', meant to designate a conceptually distinct type of delegation.[3] Fiduciary delegation serves to increase the legitimacy and credibility of the principal and of political decision-making (Alter 2008: 38–9; Majone 2001: 110–11). In fiduciary delegation to 'trustees', the main goal is to convince some third party that their interests are being protected.

Principals deliberately grant substantial discretion to trustees, because they seek to ensure the credibility of their own policy commitments where problems of strong political incentives for noncompliance, time inconsistency (i.e. a divergence between short-term and long-term preferences) or concentrated costs and diffuse benefits of keeping to commitments would otherwise undermine that credibility (Majone 2001: 105–7; Pollack 2003: 31). In other words, the demand for credible commitments leads principals to deliberately insulate their agents or 'trustees', in Alter's and Majone's term. For the purpose of credibility-enhancing delegation, the best strategy is 'to choose a delegate whose policy preferences differ systematically from the preferences of the delegating principal' (Majone 2001: 104), to make these agents highly independent and to refrain from meddling because 'an agent bound to follow the directions of the delegating politicians could not possibly enhance the credibility of their commitment' (Alter 2008: 38–9; Majone 2001: 110). Independence does not mean only that the principal's and the delegate's preferences *may* diverge, but rather that in general it is not in the principal's *interest* to minimize such difference, since 'a perfect alignment of preferences would destroy the usefulness of delegation' (Majone 2001: 110). For example, the 'optimal' central banker should be more conservative (i.e. value ex post inflation less) than the government or the median voter. This implies that the banker must be independent; otherwise he or she could be overruled, and his or her policy preferences would be irrelevant (Majone 2001: 104; Rogoff 1985). Credibility-enhancing 'fiduciary' delegation thus follows a logic of delegation, distinct from delegation to agents, that is aimed at reducing policymaking costs, capturing effectiveness and efficiency gains, and improving the quality of policymaking in terms of problem-solving (Majone 2001: 103, 110–11, 115).

The logic of delegation for the purpose of reaping efficiency and effectiveness gains manifests itself most clearly in the *sixth and final* reason for delegation that principal–agent theorists have identified: principals may not always have all the *policy-relevant information and expertise* at their disposal that are necessary to perform a certain governance task. Apart from expertise and adequate information, they may simply lack time to promulgate detailed (expert) regulation. In particular, when the task keeps recurring, principals may delegate this task to an agent that is specialized in this field (delegation to a *specialized agent*). In this case, the rationale for delegation is informational, that is, a demand for policy-relevant information (Hawkins et al. 2006b: 13–15; Mutschler 2007: 15; Pollack 2003: 23, 28–9, 31): Agents adopt expert regulation of specific economic activities in areas where principals are ill-informed; thus, the agents reduce the informational demands and workloads of their principals. In complex and technical issue areas in particular (e.g. environmental protection, trade, competition and antitrust policy), regulation is simply too detailed and too complex to be undertaken effectively by legislative principals in national parliaments or in multilateral negotiations. It is, therefore, delegated to regulatory agencies, which are assumed to provide policy-relevant expertise and thus to enhance the quality, effectiveness and efficiency of regulation (Pollack 2003: 23; see also Epstein and O'Halloran 1999a, b; Gilardi 2008). Epstein and O'Halloran (1999a) argue that specialized agents' discretion will largely be determined by the complexity and inherent uncertainty of an issue area. In areas of scientific or technical uncertainty, agents will, in general, be allocated greater discretion.

When we now examine these rationales for delegation in the light of the in-depth description of the *explanandum* (see Chapter 2) in order to judge which of them merit(s) closer consideration or even testing, *delegation to a specialized agent* emerges as the most promising approach for an explanation of the regulatory use of credit ratings.

The preselection made here is not too difficult to justify. Rationales one and four (*delegating agenda-setting, monitoring compliance of principals to overcome collective action problems*) quite obviously cannot contribute to the explanation of the research question, since credit rating agencies do not obtain competences for agenda-setting or monitoring compliance of their principals. Similarly, approach two (*solving problems of incomplete contracting*) is not applicable. 'Filling in incomplete contracts' may at first glance appear similar to what credit rating agencies do. However, it is *not* the task of credit rating agencies to close gaps in multilateral agreements which allow for different interpretations. Solving problems of incomplete contracting clearly refers to resolving potential disputes arising from unclear or controversial (international) contracts among collective principals. This would certainly not apply in cases of delegation to credit rating agencies in national regulatory systems. One might make a case for examining more closely rationale three (*delegation to policy-biased agents*), at least with respect to the Basel II negotiations, arguing that the US was interested, but eventually only partly successful, in fixing banking supervision standards which, through heavy reliance on credit rating agencies, should favor both US banks and US corporate enterprises. On the other hand, this approach does not promise to offer any help in explaining delegation of regulatory authority to credit rating agencies in national regulatory systems in and beyond the US.

This leaves us with approaches five (*resolving credible commitment problems / fiduciary delegation*) and six (*delegation to specialized agents due to information rationales*). While the apparent functional closeness of credit rating agencies to central banks might invite at least probing the applicability of a credible commitments (principal–trustee theory) explanation, the 'information rationale' argument evidently trumps the 'credible commitments' argument sufficiently to reject the latter without a more rigorous empirical test. First of all, there is broad agreement that the objective of relying on credit ratings in regulation is enhancing regulatory *effectiveness* rather than credibility (*The Economist* 1996: 20; Gras 2003: 34; Hunt 2002; Kerwer 2002: 306; 2006: 94–6). In addition, the broad discretion credit rating agencies have enjoyed has been a consequence of public regulators' long-held (if dubious) belief that credit rating agencies are adequately policed by the market (Kerwer 2006: 92–3). It does not result from a conscious decision to delegate competences to a trustee that *must* enjoy considerable leeway to digress from the principals' preferences in order to fulfill the very rationale of delegation (making a credible commitment), as principal–trustee theory would have us believe.

Thus, this preselection has shown that 'delegation to specialized agents due to information rationales' appears to be the most promising approach to explain the regulatory use of credit ratings. There is a plausible case to make that public regulators have delegated regulatory authority to credit rating agencies conceived as specialized agents that, due to their professional expertise and informational advantages over their overmatched and ill-informed principals, were expected to enhance the effectiveness and efficiency and thus the overall quality of regulation. Principal–agent theory's assumption that delegation for policy-relevant information rationales is particularly salient in very complex and technical policy areas would also correspond to the case at hand.

A resource dependence view on delegation to specialized agents

The case for combining principal–agent theory with resource dependence theory

What is even more striking is that the notion of 'delegation to a specialized agent' due to informational resource constraints strongly echoes arguments of resource dependence theory, which postulates that organizations dependent on the (material or immaterial) resources of another organization will seek to establish interorganizational relationships with it (Pfeffer and Salancik 2003). In fact, it seems surprising that the resource dependence argument underlying the 'information rationale for delegation' (Pollack 2003: 7) has so far gone unnoticed. Principal–agent theory and resource dependence theory can usefully be combined for an explanation of the delegation of regulatory authority from public regulators to transnational standard-setters, namely credit rating agencies. However, before undertaking the labors of combining two theories, we should be clear about what the value-added of developing a joint principal–agent and resource dependence framework for analysis would be, compared with merely relying on the principal–agent explanation of delegation to specialized agents. There are several points to make in favor of a combined principal–agent / resource dependence framework.

First of all, principal–agent 'theory' is a framework of related concepts and different explanatory approaches rather than a coherent theory: 'As causal theory – that is, as an integrated body of concepts, operationalisable variables, and testable propositions – it [principal–agent theory] remains incomplete' (Thatcher and Stone Sweet 2002: 3). In a similar vein, Hawkins et al. (2006b: 9–10) note that 'the propositions about why principals delegate and how they control agents build on existing theories' and 'the theoretical variation among those who study principal–agent relationships is large', implying that 'it would be a mistake to discuss "the" theory of delegation.' Thus, the bundle of reasons for delegation identified by proponents of principal–agent theory betrays the (mostly implicit) reliance of principal–agent theory on a number of causal assumptions taken from other theories. Making use of resource dependence theory rather than solely relying on a principal–agent explanation would mean explicating implicit theoretical assumptions underlying the argument of principal–agent theory on delegation to specialized agents. This would in turn contribute to the formulation of more clearly framed causal hypotheses and help to advance the principal–agent research program by enhancing its (causal–)theoretical saturation.

Furthermore, there are serious methodological concerns associated with explaining institutional choice exclusively with functional arguments, as principal–agent theory does. Functional arguments are particularly prone to the post hoc ergo propter hoc fallacy, since functional arguments are almost always post hoc arguments (Mutschler 2007: 12). In contrast, applying resource dependence theory would accommodate criticism on the inherent functionalism of principal–agent theory and allow the formulation of testable and falsifiable ex ante predictions on delegation to specialized agents – provided that the independent variable, the dependent variable and the causal hypothesis are conceptualized and operationalized carefully.

Furthermore, combining principal–agent theory and resource dependence theory builds a bridge from principal–agent theory via resource dependence theory to environmental approaches in organizational research that postulate that the macro-institutional environment of organizations structures their interactions to a considerable extent (see below and Blau 1987). This would allow us to capture the structural conditions conducive to the delegation of governance tasks to a particular type of specialized agents (credit rating agencies conceived as transnational expert standard-setters). These structural conditions are neglected by individualistic, agency-centered theories such as principal–agent theory (Hawkins et al. 2006b: 7) and resource dependence theory (Edele 2006: 84).

In sum, principal–agent theory and resource dependence theory complement each other. Resource dependence theory, which remains very unspecific about *which institutional type* of interorganizational relationship an organization depending on the resources of another one will seek to establish (Theiner 2008), provides a robust causal hypothesis explaining *why* public regulators will seek to establish interorganizational relationships with credit rating agencies for the attainment of their goals. The principal–agent approach allows us to conceptually grasp *the institutional form of delegation* taken by the interorganizational relationship between public regulators and credit rating agencies. Principal–agent theory's causal reasoning on delegation to specialized agents is placed on a much stronger theoretical footing when framed in terms of resource dependence theory. If the developed causal framework were to be corroborated, this would demonstrate that hypotheses from resource dependence theory can be applied fruitfully not only to the establishment of public–private partnerships (Edele 2006), inclusive, multipartite institutions (Rittberger 2008) or the granting of 'extended, but varying participation rights' for nonstate actors in open multilateral institutions (Brühl 2003: 186–230; Liese 2009), but also to the delegation of regulatory authority from public actors to transnational standard-setters.

Core assumptions of resource dependence and resource exchange theory

Both resource dependence theory and resource exchange theory are organization theories. Organization theory is based on the view of organizations as rational,[4] self-interested actors that are oriented toward the effective and efficient[5] attainment of specific organizational goals (Aldrich 1975: 50; Edele 2006: 42; Pfeffer and Salancik 2003: 23; Scott 1981: 57).[6] It should be noted, though, that the underlying concept of rationality used in this study is one of 'bounded and intentional' rather than perfect 'classical' rationality (Milgrom and Roberts 1992: 129–30). The notion of bounded and intentional rationality has gained widespread acceptance in more recent research in the fields of institutional economics (Milgrom and Roberts 1992: 129–30; Richter and Furubotn 2003: 192–3, 203; Simon 1982: 415), international relations (Keohane 1984: 114; Zürn 1992: 78–136) and global governance in particular (Brühl 2003: 197–9; Edele 2006: 52–3). The notion of bounded and intentional rationality is based on the assumption that 'real' actors are not omniscient or perfectly far-sighted (Milgrom and Roberts 1992: 129). In a world with frictions, an actor trying to make a decision cannot acquire and process all necessary information without the expenditure of costs and time. Due to limited cognitive capacities and considerable costs of information collection and processing, actors choose *subjectively* from a limited set of behavioral options rather than taking all possible behavioral options, including all their consequences, into account (Brühl 2003: 197–8; Richter and Furubotn 2003: 192–3). This means that '[a]ctors are *boundedly rational,* and they know it.... They then act in an *intentionally rational* manner, trying to do the best they can given the limitations under which they work' (Milgrom and Roberts 1992: 129–30; see also Zürn 1992: 78–136). With uncertainty increasing in their task environment, actors will rely more heavily on 'rules of thumb' in their decision-making (Richter and Furubotn 2003: 193). Applied to resource dependence and resource exchange theory, this means that, while organizations are assumed to act rationally in the sense that they calculate and weigh the costs and benefits of alternative courses of action to accomplish their organizational goals, they do not consider all imaginable options, but rather select them from a limited set of alternatives. This applies particularly in areas which are very complex and/or inherently uncertain and thus place very high demands on organizations' information processing capacities. Rather than maximizing their utility in the classical sense, organizations 'satisfice', that is, they evaluate alternative courses of action only until they find one that satisfies their utility (Edele 2006: 53; Simon 1982: 415; see also Keohane 1984: 114).

While organization theorists initially focused on the emergence, structure, behavior and effectiveness of individual organizations on the basis of a *closed* system model, researchers later adopted an organization–environment perspective (Aldrich 1975; 1979; Aldrich and Pfeffer 1976), which took the relationships of organizations, conceived as *open* systems, with their structural and actor environment as units of analysis (Edele 2006: 42). The open systems model in organization theory holds that organizations should be conceived as open entities, whose behavior is constrained by both structural characteristics of their task environment, such as environmental complexity and uncertainty (Thompson 1967), *and* other external organizations relevant to the attainment of the organizations' goals (Aldrich 1975: 51; Pfeffer and Salancik 2003: 1; Scott 1981). From an open system's perspective, interchange with the environment is an essential factor underlying the organizational system's viability (Cook 1994: 363). In other words, organizations, as open social systems, require certain environmental inputs in order to survive and achieve their goals (Pfeffer 1981: 124; Scott 1981: 116).

From the conception of organizations as boundedly and intentionally rational as well as open actors, one can deduce that organizations will make conscious, intentional decisions to establish and maintain relationships with other organizations in their task environment if this serves the accomplishment of their organizational goals (Oliver 1990: 241–2). Researchers have developed several more specific theoretical approaches dealing with the formation, nature and maintenance of interorganizational relationships. In this context interorganizational relationships are defined as transactions, flows and linkages that occur between an organization and one or more organizations in its environment (Edele 2006: 42; Oliver 1990: 241). Many studies have examined the *evolution* of interorganizational relationships and addressed the question of why and under what conditions organizations (e.g. business enterprises, social service organizations or public agencies) establish interorganizational relationships (Börzel 1998: 259; Edele 2006: 42–3; Jansen 1993: 95–6; Oliver 1990: 241–4; Scharpf 1978; Van de Ven 1976; Van de Ven et al. 1975).

A broad consensus among scholars has emerged that the underlying rationale for establishing relationships with other organizations is an organization's need for access to specific resources which are crucial to achieve its particular objectives (Jansen 1993: 97). Resources have commonly been defined in interorganizational analysis as 'generalized means, or facilities, that are potentially controllable by social organizations, and that are potentially usable – however indirectly – in relationships between the organization and its environment' (Yuchtman and Seashore 1967: 900; see also Emerson 1981: 41). This includes material resources such as funds, technical material and personnel, as well as immaterial resources such as information, expertise and legitimacy (Aldrich 1975: 52; Edele 2006: 44; Pfeffer 1981: 101; Scharpf 1978: 354). In general terms, the more liquid, transportable, stable over time and universally applicable resources are, the more precious they are (Jansen 1993: 99). The key to organizational success is the ability to acquire and maintain valued resources. This problem would be simplified if organizations were in complete control of all the components necessary for their operation and the accomplishment of their organizational objectives. However, organizations are usually not (completely) self-contained or self-sufficient (Pfeffer and Salancik 2003: 2, 43–4). Organizations often do not themselves possess all the resources required for organizational goal attainment (Jansen 1993: 97), but rather depend to some varying degree on getting access to resources controlled by organizations in their task environment in order to successfully fulfill their organizational functions (Oliver 1990: 241–2). Limitations on the availability of resources and organizations' inability to generate all needed resources themselves create resource dependencies. Organizations in the task environment must be relied upon to provide resource support – even though the amount of resource dependence of an organization is not a given, but may change over time as the organization becomes more or less self-contained (Cook 1994: 365; Levine and White 1961: 120; Pfeffer 1981: 101; Pfeffer and Salancik 2003: 43–4). This implies that organizations are typically oriented to the acquisition (and defense) of an adequate and secure supply of crucial resources from external parties (Benson 1994: 106; Cook 1994: 365–6; Edele 2006: 44–5;

Oliver 1990: 249–50; Yuchtman and Seashore 1967). Note that, in a long-term view, dependence on resources presumably controlled by an organization will only continue to shape actors' behavior when these organizations show their ability to perform the provision of crucial resources to the organization. In the longer run, if organizations have an important and critical function, but fail at it, other organizations will not rely on them as potential resource providers (Pfeffer 1981: 98, 101).

Resource dependence and the establishment of interorganizational relationships

Both resource dependence theory and resource exchange theory posit that organizations which, for the accomplishment of their organizational goals, depend on scarce resources controlled by another organization will be prone to establish relationships with this external organization. Thus, resource dependence is the main driver for the development of interorganizational relationships (Oliver 1990: 249; Pfeffer and Salancik 2003: 2, 43–4). In order to get access to external sources of resources crucial for organizational goal attainment, organizations establish relationships with other organizations (Aldrich 1979; Edele 2006: 46; Jansen 1993: 96–100; Levine and White 1961: 587–92; Pfeffer and Salancik 2003; Scharpf 1978: 350–8; Schmidt and Kochan 1977; Van de Ven and Walker 1984: 25–32; Van de Ven et al. 1975: 22). A wide range of symmetrical and asymmetrical, hierarchical and nonhierarchical, tightly and loosely integrated types of interorganizational relationships[7] can be explained on the basis of this (one-way or mutual) resource dependence argument (Nölke 2000: 337; Oliver 1990: 241–8; Pfeffer and Salancik 2003: 144). In other words, resource dependence theory and resource exchange theory remain unspecific as to the *type* of relationship organizations will seek to establish in order to make use of external resources (Theiner 2008).

Now, what are the main propositions of resource exchange theory and resource dependence theory, and what is the difference between resource exchange theory and resource dependence theory? I first outline the main propositions of resource exchange theory, many of which are also held by resource dependence theory, and then introduce resource dependence theory by pointing out the differences from resource exchange theory.

Resource exchange theory is based on an exchange model of interorganizational relationships (Edele 2006: 44–5; see also Brühl 2003: 201–29). Levine and White (1961: 588) define interorganizational exchange as 'any voluntary activity between two organizations which has consequences, actual or anticipated, for the realization of their respective goals or objectives' (Levine and White 1961: 588). Similarly, Cook (1994: 363) notes that an exchange relation 'consists of voluntary transactions involving the transfer of resources between two or more actors...for mutual benefit'. The exchange model contends that all voluntary relationships among organizations can be conceptualized as involving interorganizational exchange of resources. The definition of exchange as a *voluntary* activity between organizations excludes interorganizational relationships based on coercion. Resource exchange theory assumes that the formation of interorganizational relationships is the result of an interaction based on mutual resource dependencies. Interorganizational relationships are only established if and when the interaction helps all involved organizations to achieve their goals (Jansen 1993: 97; see also Cook 1994: 365). However, the exchange model of interorganizational relationships does not necessarily imply equality or symmetry of exchange (Edele 2006: 44; Scharpf 1978: 350–8). In fact, the level and rate of exchange can vary along a continuum ranging from relative exploitation (which still benefits the exploited party in terms of absolute resource gains) through symmetrical reciprocity to benefaction (Jessop 1994: 122–3). At any rate, according to the exchange model, the formation of interorganizational relationships is a reciprocal, interactive process that occurs when two or more organizations exchange resources among each other (Cook 1994: 363; Cook et al. 1994: 389; Jacobs 1974; Levine and White 1961: 587–92; Oliver 1990: 244–5; Van de Ven 1976: 25).

Based on the general exchange model, resource exchange theory more specifically posits that two explanatory factors account for the formation of cooperative interorganizational relationships: *domain consensus* and *resource interdependence* (Edele 2006: 44–5; Jansen 1993: 96–100; Levine and White 1961: 587–92; Litwak and Hylton 1962: 400; Oliver 1990: 244–5, 250; Scharpf 1978: 356–9; Van de Ven 1976: 32; Van de Ven and Walker 1984; Van de Ven et al. 1975). *Domain consensus* is an antecedent condition (or condition variable) in resource exchange theory. Domain consensus refers to 'whether an organization's specific goals and functions are regarded by other actors as supporting their own objectives' (Edele 2006: 45). It is not sufficient for organizations to be informed about the objectives pursued and the resources controlled by external actors; they also have to consider the actors' goals and activities as compatible with or even complementary to their own objectives (Van de Ven 1976: 31). Domain consensus is a prerequisite for resource exchange, and hence for the establishment of cooperative interorganizational relationships (Aldrich 1976: 424; 1979: 120; Edele 2006: 45; Jansen 1993: 97; Levine and White 1961: 587; Oliver 1990: 250; Sydow 1992: 194).

Under the condition of domain consensus, the establishment of cooperative interorganizational relationships is explained with recourse to the degree of *resource interdependence* between organizations. Generally speaking, in social systems and social interactions, interdependence exists whenever one actor does not entirely control all of the conditions necessary for the achievement of its objectives. A situation of resource interdependence between organizations is characterized by two or more organizations that must each acquire access to resources controlled by the other if they want to attain their goals (Pfeffer and Salancik 2003: 40). The probability of cooperative interorganizational relationships is particularly high when there is so-called 'symbiotic' resource interdependence between organizations, which refers to organizations pursuing different goals (or the same goals, but each lacking some means necessary to achieve these goals) and being characterized by a complementary need for resources. In cases of a high degree of symbiotic resource interdependence, two or more organizations can simultaneously achieve their objectives by establishing relationships which allow them to exchange resources (Aldrich 1979: 266; Edele 2006: 46–7; Pfeffer and Nowak 1976: 402; Pfeffer and Salancik 2003: 41). Resource exchange theory postulates that, under the condition of domain consensus, the higher the degree of resource interdependence between organizations, the greater is the likelihood that they will establish cooperative relationships with one another (Edele 2006: 49).

In contrast to resource exchange theory, which is a theory of interaction, resource dependence theory – at least as it is conceived in this book[8] – is a theory of action. It builds on the same basic assumptions as resource exchange theory regarding the rationales for establishing ties to external organizations. However, while resource exchange theory refers to *mutual* resource dependence between at least two organizations, an *exchange* of resources that happens only if and when it benefits all involved organizations, and an *inter*active establishment of interorganizational relationships, resource dependence theory deals with the *resource dependence of an organization* on one (or several) other organizations (Emerson 1994: 349) and an organization's seeking to get access to resources controlled by another organization by establishing (stable) relationships with it (Pfeffer and Salancik 2003: 52). Again, resource dependence theory can, of necessity, only explain the *action* of an organization. Generally speaking, this action consists of efforts to establish relationships with another organization. This implies that, when the objective of a study is to explain the *actual* establishment of relationships with another organization rather than merely an organization's seeking to do so, resource dependence theory is only helpful in situations where a (focal) organization dependent on the resources of another organization for the achievement of its organizational goals is in the power position, either formal–hierarchical or de facto, to effectively force the other organization(s) into a relationship which provides access to the needed resources (Jansen 1993: 98). Note that this does not necessarily imply that external organizations are harmed by this establishment of an interorganizational relationship, but rather that their active consent is not a necessary condition for the establishment of the interorganizational relationship.

The most direct method for controlling dependence is to get possession of the source of that dependence; however, one is not always in a position to achieve control over dependence through acquisition and ownership. In general terms, there are several ways (which characterize different interorganizational relationships) to guarantee access to a resource (Pfeffer and Salancik 2003: 143–4, 182–5). Besides getting *possession* of a resource (i.e. direct and absolute control over the resource), using one's *ability to make rules or otherwise regulate* the possession, allocation and use of resources and to enforce the regulations is another way to gain access to needed resources (Pfeffer and Salancik 2003: 48–9).

At this point it is important to remember that the dependent variable of this study, 'use of private credit ratings by public regulators' – also when it is conceptualized in more abstract terms of delegation of governance tasks and regulatory authority from principals to agents – designates an *action* rather than an *interaction*. The theoretical argument can, therefore, only be one of resource *dependence* rather than one of resource *exchange*. Thus, I rely on a resource dependence theory explanation. For the same reason that the *explanandum* of this study refers to the action of public regulators rather than the interactive establishment of a public–private partnership, I do not include the variable 'domain consensus', referring to a consensus between potential partners in a cooperative relationship that their goals and strategies are at least compatible, in my explanatory framework.

To be sure, the use of credit ratings in financial regulation may well serve the business interests of credit rating agencies, which, contrary to what credit rating agencies overtly claim (Cantor 2001), would make the potential resource 'recognition by public regulators as de facto regulators' seem attractive to credit rating agencies. From this point of view, it might appear worthwhile to model the relationship between public regulators and credit rating agencies as a resource exchange relation, involving an exchange of the public resource 'recognition as publicly sanctioned regulators' and the private resource 'analytical resources'. However, this conception fails to recognize that the crucial element of agency that is bringing about the specific mode of public–private governance we witness when credit ratings are used for regulatory purposes stems *solely* from public regulators. Other than the formation of public–private partnerships (see Edele 2006) or inclusive, public–private institutions (Rittberger et al. 2008), the emergence of the institutional mode of public–private governance in the case at hand does not involve an interactive 'coming together' and 'joining forces' *initiated by both* public and private actors, but an essentially top-down decision by public regulators. This implies that the explanation of this mode of governance warrants a theory of action rather than interaction.

For an empirically testable explanation derived from resource dependence theory, it is crucial to adequately conceptualize and operationalize the independent variable 'resource dependence'. In order to determine the resource dependence of an organization, it is first of all necessary to identify its objectives, since its objectives determine the resources required for goal attainment (Edele 2006: 47). In addition, resource dependence theory refers to two dimensions which have to be taken into account when determining an organization's dependence on resources of any other organization: *essentiality* and *substitutability* (Edele 2006: 48). In other words, dependence is seen to be a function of the importance of what one organization gets from the other and an inverse function of the availability of this resource (outcome or performance) in other places or from other sources (Pfeffer 1981: 99; Pfeffer and Salancik 2003: 46; see also Cook 1994: 367; Emerson 1994: 349; Hickson et al. 1994: 202; Jacobs 1974; Thompson 1967: 29–30).

Essentiality describes the extent to which an organization requires resources controlled by an external organization to attain its goals. It refers to how important the resources are to the organization. There are two indicators for the essentiality of a resource: the *relative magnitude of resource needs* and the *criticality* of the resource. The *relative magnitude of resource needs* is a quantitative indicator that is measurable by determining the total amount of a specific resource required by an organization to achieve its objectives, and by subsequently assessing how much is lacking within the organization (Edele 2006: 46–7; Pfeffer and Salancik 2003: 46). *Criticality* measures the ability of the organization to continue functioning in the absence of the resource (Pfeffer and Salancik 2003: 46–7). As the criticality of a resource in the functioning of an organization is a qualitative factor, it is usually more difficult to determine than the relative magnitude of resource needs (Edele 2006: 47; Pfeffer 1981: 109; Scharpf 1978: 354–5; Thompson 1967: 31; Yuchtman and Seashore 1967: 900–1). The criticality of a resource for an organization may vary from time to time as conditions in the organization's environment change. As the environmental contingencies change, what is a crucial resource may also change (Pfeffer and Salancik 2003: 46–7).

Substitutability denotes the extent to which resources provided by an external organization can be replaced from other sources. In other words, it refers to the concentration of resource control by external organizations, or the extent to which essential resources are possessed by relatively few organizations. Substitutability is contingent upon the ability of other external organizations to provide the same resources. The important thing is whether the focal organization has access to the resource from additional sources (Edele 2006: 48; Pfeffer and Salancik 2003: 50).

Both essentiality and substitutability of the resources determine the focal organization's dependence on any other organization

(Pfeffer and Salancik 2003: 51). A high degree of resource dependence exists when the resources demanded by an organization are characterized by high essentiality and low substitutability. '[I]f an organization cannot achieve its goals without the resources controlled by an external actor, and if it is not able to obtain them elsewhere, it is highly dependent on the resources of the external organization' (Edele 2006: 48).

In a nutshell, resource dependence theory predicts that organizations will seek to establish relationships with other organizations if, for the attainment of their goals, they are dependent on essential resources which those organizations control and which are hard to obtain elsewhere. The higher the essentiality of the resource and the lower its substitutability, the more likely it becomes that an organization will seek to establish relationships with other organizations. If the (focal) organization, due to either formal–hierarchical or de facto power, is in the position to establish resource-providing relationships with other (external) organizations without their active consent, a high degree of resource dependence of the (focal) organization is not only a necessary, but also a sufficient, condition for the actual establishment of the interorganizational relationship.

A resource dependence view on the delegation of regulatory authority to credit rating agencies

Having presented the explanatory framework of resource exchange and resource dependence theory in general terms, the next step consists of adapting resource dependence theory to the study of delegation of regulatory authority from public regulators to transnational expert standard-setters, namely credit rating agencies. Essentially, the adaptation process consists of embedding the concepts and causal assumptions of resource dependence theory into a principal–agent framework of delegation to specialized agents that are assumed to enhance the effectiveness, efficiency and thus the overall quality of regulation because of their superior professional expertise and policy-relevant information.

As outlined in Chapter 1, concepts from interorganizational research have already been applied to analyze the evolution of a rather broad range of public–private modes of governance (Börzel and Risse 2005; Brühl 2003; Edele 2006; Liese 2009; Nölke 2000; Rittberger 2008; Schäferhoff et al. 2007). This gives us reason to suppose that resource dependence theory is applicable to a particular mode of public–private governance that involves the delegation of regulatory authority to transnational expert standard-setters. In particular, it has been shown that public actors (state actors and intergovernmental organizations) as well as private actors (nongovernmental organizations and business actors) can be conceived as organizations, in the sense of interorganizational analysis, whose (mutual) resource dependencies lead them to establish public–private interorganizational relationships (Edele 2006: 50). This conception of public and private actors as organizations in the sense of interorganizational analysis represents a major advantage, since it enables us to include resource dependence theory in our theoretical framework, which seeks to explain public actors' (i.e. public regulators') delegation of regulatory authority to private actors (i.e. credit rating agencies). National and international regulatory bodies, as well as credit rating agencies, can be regarded as organized entities with the objective of achieving specific goals; in the case of regulatory bodies, the main organizational goal is ensuring the stability and efficiency of the public goods financial market (Dieter 2004; Griffith-Jones 2003). As private business enterprises, credit rating agencies are first and foremost oriented toward making profits (Gras 2003: 30). However, the assumption by credit rating agencies, other market participants and regulators is that the economic goals and incentives of credit rating agencies will make them act in ways conducive to the achievement of the public goal of financial market stability (ibid.: 16, 30).

Scholars making (explicit or implicit) use of arguments derived from resource dependence or resource exchange theory have identified a number of material and immaterial resources, controlled by private actors, which are frequently sought after by public actors and thus drive the establishment of relatively stable relationships with nonstate actors: funds, legitimacy-enhancing moral authority,[9] specialized issue knowledge, information, technical expertise and analytical capacities (Brühl 2003: 204–8; Edele 2006: 63; Nölke 2000: 336). Quite obviously, it is the latter analytical resources (comprising expert knowledge and information collection and processing capacities) that appear relevant to this study. Studies have found that the capacity to collect, process and provide policy-relevant information can be a scarce resource that is purposefully sought after by social actors in certain issue areas. Public actors have been found to be in need of information that can be provided by private actors (Pappi and König 1993: 111). What is more, it is assumed that the demand for analytical resources controlled by private actors will vary due to the issue area-specific uncertainty of public actors, which in turn depends on the complexity of the major issues public actors have to deal with. It is in these areas that public actors should be particularly prone to establishing relationships with private actors controlling analytical resources (such as specialized knowledge about cause-and-effect relations and (technical) expertise in describing and defining causes of problems and identifying potential solutions), since access to and making use of these resources would reduce organizational uncertainty (Brühl 2003: 205–8).

Furthermore, resource dependence theory has already been applied to analyze dependencies that exist both between credit rating agencies and investors, and between credit rating agencies and the companies whose debts are rated. Investors depend on the analytical resources of credit rating agencies for their investment decisions; rated companies depend on the legitimacy of these agencies for their access to capital (Nölke and Perry 2007: 130). Credit rating agencies' analytical resources are crucial in contemporary global finance. Their legitimacy is derived from the expert character of these analytical resources as perceived by market participants and regulators. 'The demand for the analytical output of rating agencies stems from the overwhelming quantity of information available to market actors' (ibid.: 129; Nölke 2004).

If we now transfer these insights to the relationship between regulators and credit rating agencies and apply a combined principal–agent theory and resource dependence theory perspective to the relationship between public regulators and credit rating agencies in financial market governance, the following theoretical argument can be made. Public regulators are organizations which, for the attainment of their main organizational goals (financial market stability and efficiency), are dependent on resources controlled by external organizations. As they lack essential analytical resources for measuring credit risks themselves, public regulators delegate governance tasks and regulatory authority to specialized risk-measuring agents, namely credit rating agencies conceived as transnational expert standard-setters.

Quite evidently, the independent variable 'dependence on credit rating agencies' analytical resources' is still formulated in rather broad terms and is not measurable as such. However, a broad conceptualization is useful at this point, because one of the aims of this book is to develop a theoretical framework for analysis which is, as far as possible, framed in general rather than case-specific terms in order to allow the framework to be tested against other cases of delegation of regulatory authority to private actors. The variable 'dependence on analytical resources' might be relevant for a broad range of transnational standard-setters and other kinds of private expert actors. The independent variable 'dependence on credit rating agencies' analytical resources' will be operationalized by taking recourse to the proxy variable 'uncertainty coping capabilities' taken from strategic contingencies theory, which is a specific variant of resource dependence theory (see below).

Before further elaborating on the theoretical framework for analysis and turning to its proposed causal mechanism and condition variable, it should be noted that several scholarly findings in the global governance and standardization literature strengthen belief in the potential validity of this resource dependence argument. While the following remarks do not prove the validity of the above argument and should not be regarded as a test of the theory, they do suggest that the proposed resource dependence argument possesses enough plausibility that it may be further built on and finally tested.

Hutter (2006: 75–6), for instance, argues that 'economic nonstate regulators' may have high levels of expertise and technical know-how which allow them to create forms of regulation that are more flexible and sensitive to the market and/or technical innovations than public regulators' directives. These nonstate analytical resources stand in contrast to the major difficulties encountered by state regulators in marshaling adequate regulatory capacities, not only in terms of financial resources, but also with regard to knowledge and training, most essentially in relation to many business actors they seek to regulate. As well as the assumed willingness of firms to provide more accurate information to third parties (rather than public regulators), private actors taking on a regulatory role may be able 'to provide more accurate risk assessments and advice because of their specialist training and knowledge' (Hutter 2006: 76) while sparing the state the costs of regulatory activity. In sum, 'these [non-state] sources may act as a supplement or even alternative to limited or absent state resources' (ibid.: 76–7).

In a similar vein, and with a view specifically to financial market governance, Tsingou (2008: 64) claims that the complexity and speed of financial innovation have put private market actors in a privileged position as knowledge holders, with public authorities lagging behind in terms of expertise: 'If regulators and supervisors cannot keep up (and cannot afford to keep up) with the development of financial products that are complex, often tailor-made and used by a variety of institutions and firms, they cannot regulate nor supervise effectively. As a result, private initiatives gradually take over important functions and promote standards based on private expertise' (Tsingou 2008: 64).

Scholars of standardization have found ample evidence that demand for private expert standards has increased in modern societies, that knowledge resources underlying standardization have become more important, and that it is increasingly considered acceptable by public actors to allow experts to govern, in particular if the issue area is highly complex (Jacobsson 2002: 40–1; see also Brunsson and Jacobsson 2002a: 16). Addressing the proliferation of standards in global finance, Kerwer (2006: 95) cites as reason for the expansion of standards 'the expectation ... that flexible standards might target complex rapidly changing problems better and adapt faster to changing circumstances than international directives'. This reflects a widespread belief that regulation is better adapted to the needs of the market if performed by standardizers rather than by bureaucracies (Jacobsson 2002: 47).

In this book, I argue that the consequence of public regulators' dependence on credit rating agencies' analytical resources has been to make standards based on private expertise binding and thus to transfer regulatory authority. Similarly, King and Sinclair (2003: 349) consider the tendency 'to devolve state activities onto nominally private institutions, such as the rating agencies, ... [as] a way for the formal political system to distance itself from the increasing uncertainty of globalized markets' (King and Sinclair 2003: 349).

Against the background of these findings, there are good reasons to believe in the plausibility of the combined principal–agent/resource dependence theory framework. In the following, the causal framework is further refined by proposing a causal mechanism linking the independent variable 'dependence of public regulators on credit rating agencies' analytical resources' and the dependent variable 'use of credit ratings in financial regulation'.

Bounded rationality, cost–benefit analysis and the decision for delegation

From the rationalist point of view of both principal–agent theory and resource dependence theory, delegation of governance tasks and authority to credit rating agencies will be based on a cost–benefit analysis. Principal–agent theory assumes that the likelihood of delegation increases with the size of gains that principals expect to reap from delegation. In other words, 'the larger the (expected) gains from delegation, the more likely it becomes that principals will opt for delegation' (Hawkins et al. 2006b: 23). However, delegation does not only offer potentially significant advantages to principals; delegation also creates the potential for losses, in so far as the agents thus empowered might possess policy preferences distinct from those of the principals and use their delegated powers to pursue those preferences (Pollack 2003: 4). Thus, delegation involves both costs and benefits for the delegating party. The assumption of principal–agent theory is that, in a world of rational actors, the relative attractiveness of alternative governance structures is determined by the balance between costs and benefits (Tallberg 2002: 25–6; Thatcher 2002: 129; see also Koenig-Archibugi 2006: 6–7). More precisely, the decision to delegate governance tasks and authority to agents implies a trade-off between benefits from delegation and agency costs (Mutschler 2007: 26–7). Principals incur agency costs when agents engage in undesired action (agency slack) or when they themselves expend resources to contract with or monitor and control those agents. Principals always incur some costs in contracting with or supervising agents – even with the most 'sincere' types of agents. Furthermore, it is virtually impossible to devise contract rules that will completely preclude the possibility of agency slack without foregoing significant gains from delegation.

Therefore, there is a certain costly loss of control implied in any act of delegation. Should the principal want to wholly overcome the problem of asymmetric distribution of information inherent in any principal–agent relationship – and most clearly prevalent in relations between a principal and a *specialized agent* – it would itself have to acquire specialized knowledge and expertise that would enable it to adequately monitor and assess the adequacy of the agent's behavior. This, in turn, would create enormous costs and thus reduce the net gains from delegation (Mutschler 2007: 26–7; see also Hawkins et al. 2006b: 23–4; Pollack 2003: 26–7). In sum, there are always agency losses associated with delegation. In choosing whether to delegate, principals must therefore weigh the benefits of delegation against expected agency losses (Hawkins et al. 2006b: 9).

This reasoning of principal–agent theory on actors' cost–benefit analysis can be complemented by resource dependence theory's assumption that cost–benefit analysis is the causal link between resource dependence and the establishment of relationships with another organization (Edele 2006: 49). The decision of organizations, conceived as subjectively and boundedly rational actors, to establish relationships with another organization is based on a cost–benefit analysis. Organizations expect to reap benefits from the creation of interorganizational relationships by acquiring resources needed for organizational goal attainment. The higher the degree of resource dependence, the greater these benefits will be. Unlike resource exchange theory, resource dependence theory does not presuppose the notion of reciprocity (i.e. resource exchange for the formation of interorganizational relationships). According to resource dependence theory, organizations that are in the position to force other organizations into relationships for the provision of essential and concentrated resources do not incur direct costs in terms of organizations demanding certain actions in exchange for providing resources. However, it is crucial to note from the perspective of resource dependence theory that, when the external world is brought into the organization, for instance by giving authority to some other organization, external influence over the organization is increased and its own discretion is simultaneously constrained even as taking up relationships with the other organization increases the certainty of its environment. However, organizations are willing to bear the costs of restricted discretion for the benefits of predictable and assured resource flows (Pfeffer and Salancik 2003: 183). Organizations will only establish relationships with others if the benefits from receiving valued resources are equal to or greater than the costs of giving up their own discretion; that is, organizations will seek to establish relationships with other organizations if they reap a net benefit (Edele 2006: 49; see also Brühl 2003: 200–1; Oliver 1990: 256–8; Pfeffer and Salancik 2003: 183; Scharpf 1978: 350–8; Schmidt and Kochan 1977: 220; Sydow 1992: 193).

As outlined above, the underlying concept of rationality is one of 'bounded and intentional' and subjective rather than perfect 'classical' rationality. Public regulators make choices for or against delegation under conditions of imperfect information and cognitive biases. Thus, their decisions are based on a subjective and informationally incomplete cost–benefit analysis. With uncertainty increasing in their task environment (in financial markets), public regulators will rely more heavily on 'rules of thumb' in their decisions for or against reliance on credit rating agencies. An important rule of thumb is 'look for what peers in financial regulation in other countries do'. This implies that there is considerable space for imitation and diffusion of the policy practice of ratings-dependent regulation once it is adopted by a critical mass of states.

If we apply the arguments of principal–agent theory and resource dependence theory to the decision of public regulators on whether to delegate regulatory authority to credit rating agencies, the following causal mechanism can be formulated. Delegation does not come for free for public regulators. Delegation may be costly, because regulators lose part of their control over the regulated entities. In fact, whenever financial regulators use credit rating agencies in regulation, they relinquish some control over the regulated entities to credit rating agencies (Kerwer 2005: 463). The Basel provisions may serve as an example, illustrating how public regulators' reliance on credit rating agencies involves some loss of control for regulators. Under Basel I, public regulators set a uniform 8 percent minimum capital requirement for claims on corporate firms which were not risk-weighted (see Chapter 2). This was a rather crude measure of credit risk; nonetheless, *all* the parameters that finally determined the capital requirement were set by public regulators. Under the Basel II standardized approach, the asset base on the basis of which the 8 percent capital requirement is calculated is risk-weighted according to the credit ratings of the debtors. This implies that a crucial parameter for credit risk, the risk-weighted asset base of a bank, is no longer determined by public regulators but by credit rating agencies through their ratings. In other words, regulators have given up control over some regulatory parameters to a private agent.

Therefore, one should expect that some (costly) control mechanisms for the raters would be established. Indeed, over time public regulators have intensified selection and screening as well as administrative procedures and (to a far more modest extent) oversight mechanisms. When public regulators refrained from setting up extensive administrative and oversight procedures (as in fact most public regulators did, until at least the turn of the century), this was because they relied on market forces to do the control job for them (Kerwer 2006: 92–3). Thus, they saved on costs arising from setting up and maintaining public control mechanisms but increased their vulnerability to agency losses from agency slack. Even granted that public regulators in earlier days (i.e. at the beginnings of the use of credit ratings in US regulation) might not have been aware of the potential for losses, later regulators at least (from the 1970s and 1980s onwards) can be assumed to have noticed the potential for undesired behavior on the part of credit rating agencies – otherwise the introduction of the NRSRO concept in the US (1975) does not make sense. Despite this apparent awareness of agency risks and costs, the use of ratings in regulation expanded in the US and in other regulatory systems until the US subprime and global financial crisis (2007–10).

Thus, when the use of credit ratings in financial regulation entails (agency) costs, rational public regulators must be assumed to be trading control for gains in terms of effectiveness and efficiency of regulation. Using credit ratings for regulatory purposes makes risk regulation more flexible and thus more likely to adequately address risks. Given the dynamics of modern finance, adaptation to risk can only be achieved in a rather crude way within fixed regulatory categories (such as the distinction between OECD and non-OECD debtors in Basel I). A better way to make risk regulation sensitive to financial market risk is to use credit ratings instead. They offer a more fine-grained risk estimate, and also an estimate that varies over time (Kerwer 2005: 464). Furthermore, using private credit ratings in risk-sensitive regulation is far more cost-efficient for regulators than building up adequate risk-measuring capacities themselves.

In sum, delegation of governance tasks and regulatory authority to credit rating agencies will be based on a cost–benefit analysis. Public regulators will only delegate if the perceived benefits, in terms of organizational goal attainment, from making use of credit rating agencies' analytical resources through the reliance on credit ratings in financial market regulation are larger than expected (agency) losses.

The macro-institutional conditions for resource dependence

Good, 'complete' theories that satisfy our curiosity strike a balance between individualism and structuralism; they take into account both individual interests, preferences and actions (the agency level) and social structures constraining and framing actors' behavior (McAnulla 2002; Schimmelfennig 1995: 254–5). The combined principal–agent / resource dependence theory framework outlined so far is an individualistic approach which accounts for the delegation of regulatory authority on the basis of actors' interests and motivations (Edele 2006: 84). While it is certainly defensible for scholars to focus on individualistic, agency-centered explanations when this is their genuine research interest, these explanations nonetheless remain incomplete in that they fail to take into account the fact that actors' behavior is significantly constrained by structural conditions (Schimmelfennig 1995: 254–5). Resource dependence theory's explanation of public actors' delegation of regulatory authority to transnational expert standard-setters almost inevitably raises the question of where the resource dependence actually comes from. I argue that public regulators' resource dependence should not be conceived as something exogenously given that appears out of the blue to exert causal effects. Rather, I work towards pinpointing structural macro-institutional contexts that operate as condition variables. Macro-institutions can be defined as sets of broader rules and regularities, formal or informal, which actors generally follow, no matter for what reasons. They are mechanisms which structure and stabilize behavioral expectations of social actors through routines, regularities, norms and consistent patterns of organization and association. (Macro-) institutions embed and frame utilitarian action, such as actors' cost–benefit analysis (Hoffmann 2003: 124). In this book, I seek to specify under what conditions dependence of public regulators on private expert actors' analytical resources is more (or less) likely to be high. This would allow us to significantly refine the otherwise somewhat underdetermined argument of resource dependence.

Structural environmental approaches in organization theory

In this context, it is fortunate that resource dependence theory and resource exchange theory, which take an open systems perspective on organizations, can be situated in the broader category of environmental approaches in organization theory. Environmental approaches claim that, in order to explain the behavior of an organization, we must take into account the context of that behavior, i.e. 'the ecology of the organization' (Pfeffer and Salancik 2003: 1), since the forms which organizational adaptations take are contingent on the organizational environment (ibid.: 5, 108). The environment is thus identified as a force in its own right – as a source of resources *and* structural constraints profoundly shaping the activities, problems, forms and outputs of organizations (Scott 1981: 115; Salancik and Pfeffer 1994: 230).

The ecology of an organization consists of both other organizations and structural environmental conditions (Blau 1987; Thompson 1967). While resource dependence theory focuses on the microprocesses arising from organizations' (mutual) resource dependencies (Hamilton and Woolsey Biggart 1994: 150–1), structural context-oriented approaches acknowledge the macro-institutional social context of microprocesses driven by resource dependencies (Benson 1994: 104, 113; Blau 1987: 83–4; Cook 1994: 364; Galbraith 1973; 1977; Hamilton and Woolsey Biggart 1994: 150–1). From that perspective, the best way to organize, both internally and in relation to other organizations, is contingent upon the nature of the macrostructural environment of the organization(s) (Scott 1981: 114). Macro-institutional contexts shape the means–end calculations of organizational actors and, consequently, their activities, their organizational forms and their relations with one another (Hamilton and Woolsey Biggart 1994: 157).

The basic pattern of a macro-institutionally embedded resource dependence argument would thus be that properties of the relationship between two or more organizations are explained with reference to the way in which the relevant organizations deal with resource dependencies, which in turn is marked by macro-institutional context variables (Benson 1994: 103; Jansen 1993: 99). While this argument seems plausible on an intuitive level, it raises some issues. When the resource dependencies of organizations are significantly affected by macro-institutional environmental conditions providing a social context for the establishment of interorganizational relationships, the obvious difficulty with the idea of the macro-institutional environment is that of sorting out those aspects of the larger social world which are most relevant, in order to prevent 'macro-institutional environment' becoming a residual category in which diverse factors and conditions may be indiscriminately grouped (Benson 1994: 113).

Proponents of environmental approaches in organization theory have singled out the uncertainty a macro-institutional environment poses as crucial organizational context variable. Lawrence and Lorsch (1967) argue that environments characterized by uncertainty and rapid rates of change (e.g. in market conditions or technologies) make different demands – both constraints and opportunities – on organizations than do placid and stable environments. Organizations tend to match or co-align with these environments (Scott 1981: 114). They will seek to establish stable resource flows which contribute to reducing the uncertainty of their environment. Similarly, in Galbraith's studies (1973, 1977), the organizational environment is characterized by the amount of uncertainty it poses for the organization. Uncertainty enters the organization by affecting the work or tasks that organizations perform, and 'the greater the task uncertainty, the greater the amount of information that must be processed among decision makers during task execution in order to achieve a given level of performance' (Galbraith 1977: 36). The organizational design challenge is to select an (intra- and/or inter-)organizational arrangement appropriate for the environmentally conditioned information processing requirements of the tasks to be performed (Scott 1981: 115).

If we now try to integrate the reasoning of environmental approaches in organization theory into the theoretical framework of this book, it seems, first of all, reasonable to assume that the relevant structural environment shaping and framing public regulators' resource dependence on the analytical resources of transnational expert standard-setters is made up by macro-institutional socioeconomic conditions, since the relevant issue area is economic or, more precisely, financial governance. These macro-institutional socioeconomic conditions are assumed to set incentives for or against delegation of authority to transnational expert standard-setters in the regulation and supervision of financial markets by determining public regulators' dependence on private analytical resources.

The (rather abstract) organization theory reasoning on the impact of structural environmental conditions on interorganizational relations offers several points of contact for *more specified* macro-institutional context conditions, both for public actors' propensity to delegate regulatory authority *and*, even more importantly, for the significance of credit rating agencies in financial governance systems. These conditions, which have been identified in more recent political science literature, can be conceived as particular manifestations of the very broad organization theory variable 'macro-institutional context', which as such is not very helpful for a reasonably specific, falsifiable explanatory framework.

First of all, the 'macro-institutional environment' argument of organization theory is in line with scholarly findings on the context conditions for delegation of regulatory tasks from governments and legislators to national 'independent regulatory authorities' conceived as non-majoritarian bodies (Thatcher 2002: 136). Thatcher (2002: 136) argues that contextual factors mediated pressures for delegation to national independent regulatory authorities (such as the German Federal Cartel Office) in Western European countries. Cross-national variation in delegation suggests that there is no automatic link between functional advantages of delegation and the creation of independent regulatory authorities. Instead, the choice of delegation must be analyzed in its macro-institutional context. Thatcher found in his study (2002) that the broader socioeconomic institutional setting of different West European states was one of the key context variables (apart from entrenched traditions and structures in regulation). While this finding strengthens our belief in the general plausibility of the argument that macro-institutional context matters to the likelihood of delegation of regulatory authority, and demonstrates that the 'macro-institutional environment' argument can complement not only resource dependence theory but also principal–agent theory, it does not go far towards helping us *specify* the theoretical argument in a way that is both plausible and conceptualized specifically enough to allow empirical observation and falsification. This specification can be achieved, though, when we consider which kinds of macro-institutional contexts might have an effect on public regulators' dependence on credit rating agencies' analytical resources. In the following I argue that relevant macro-institutional contexts conditioning public actors' dependence on credit rating agencies' analytical resources are to be found on both global and national/regional levels.

Global and national/regional macro-institutional conditions for resource dependence

The main structural argument I propose is that variations in global and national/regional macro-institutional contexts have an impact on public regulators' demand for credit ratings in financial regulation. Changes in the global financial architecture from embedded to disembedded liberalism and variations across countries and over time in types of capitalism (Rhenish coordinated market economy or Anglo-Saxon liberal market economy) are assumed to be relevant for understanding different degrees of resource dependence and thus different degrees of reliance on credit rating agencies in financial regulation. I first explicate the argument on variations in the global financial architecture (embedded vs. disembedded liberalism) and then elaborate on the regional varieties-of-capitalism approach.

It seems highly plausible to suggest that variations over time in the macro-institutional context of the *global* financial architecture affect the dependence of public regulators around the world on the analytical resources of credit rating agencies. From this perspective, which focuses on global macro-institutional contexts and their transformation over time, changes in the global financial architecture from embedded liberalism to disembedded liberalism in the past three decades (Ruggie 1982; Rittberger et al. 2010: 137–44) would lead us to expect a growing demand for the regulatory use of credit ratings by public authorities and the diffusion of ratings-dependent regulation beyond the US. This is because the essentiality of credit rating agencies' analytical resources for public regulators will be higher in a global financial system of disembedded liberalism. At the same time, we would not expect an increase in the substitutability of credit rating agencies' analytical resources. As a result, dependence of public authorities on credit rating agencies should be higher in a system of disembedded liberalism than in one of embedded liberalism. In the following, I elaborate in more detail why this is a reasonable proposition.

First of all, it is important to have a clear conception of embedded and disembedded liberalism. The distinction between embedded and disembedded economic orders goes back to Karl Polanyi's seminal work *The Great Transformation*. Polanyi (1944: 71) argued that 'normally, the economic order is merely a function of the social, in which it is contained.' In that conception, embedded economic and financial systems are politically created, shaped and guided orders. By contrast, disembedded orders refer to economic and financial systems that are decoupled from political and social systems and left on their own as separate economic systems in society. John G. Ruggie picked up Polanyi's distinction in order to characterize the international post-World War II economic and monetary order built around the Bretton Woods institutions and the General Agreement on Tariffs and Trade (Ruggie 1982). For Ruggie, 'embedded liberalism' designates an international compromise between economic liberalism advocating free movement of goods and capital on the one hand and state interventionism in markets for socially and politically defined goals on the other hand (Ruggie 1982: 393).

This embedded liberalism was reflected in the global financial order that was established by the Bretton Woods Agreement of 1944 and lasted into the 1970s. In this embedded order, states were committed to fixed, but adaptable, exchange rates for their currencies (Kahler 1995: 48–64). They had to guarantee the free convertibility of their currencies and to maintain a stable exchange rate with the US dollar, which was itself tied to a gold standard (Rittberger and Zangl 2006: 43–4; see also Eichengreen 1996; Helleiner 1994; Kapstein 1994). In a global financial system of embedded liberalism, the relevant norms and rules did not force states to renounce controls over capital movements. States were able to use controls over capital movements to finance domestic measures through their taxation system or debt policy without fear of a flight of capital (Gilpin 2000: 139–40). In addition, it was hoped that a restricted movement of capital would strengthen the system of fixed exchange rates because it limited the possibility of speculative foreign exchange movements and the resulting attacks on one or the other currency (Rittberger and Zangl 2006: 160–3; see also Helleiner 1994: 25–72; Pauly 1997: 79–97). However, the Bretton Woods system was only effective as long as the movement of capital could really be limited. Yet this became less and less feasible with the creation of the eurodollar markets that arose in the late 1950s and early 1960s and allowed banks to circumvent controls on the movement of capital for their international financial business[10] (Rittberger and Zangl 2006: 162; see also Eichengreen 1996: 93–152; Helleiner 1994: 81–122). The freer movement of capital enabled speculative attacks on individual currencies, making it more and more difficult to maintain the fixed exchange-rate parities.[11] Eventually, it proved impossible to maintain the dollar–gold parity in the long term (see Helleiner 1994: 81–122). The US finally gave up gold parity with the dollar in 1971 and the fixed rates became untenable. After a futile attempt to revive the fixed rates in the Smithsonian Agreement of 1971, exchange rates were finally set free in 1973 (Gilpin 2000: 124–5). The passage from fixed to flexible exchange rates reflected and fundamentally drove the emergence of a disembedded liberal financial and currency order that was largely devoid of controls on capital movements (Rittberger and Zangl 2006: 162–3). From the mid-1970s through the 1990s, the global financial systems continuously and progressively moved away from embedded liberalism to disembedded liberalism.

The turn towards disembedded liberalism was also furthered by the oil price shock in the 1970s and 1980s and a widespread debt crisis at the beginning of the 1980s. Neoliberal monetarists argued that the failure of the state, that is, the failure of Keynesian economic policies, in preventing these crises had led to 'stagflation', little or no economic growth coupled with rising inflation rates. In this situation of economic crisis, monetarists advocated for a reduction in political interference with economic affairs (Rittberger et al. 2010: 142). State interference was considered a part of the problem rather than the solution to economic crises. The role of the state should be limited to being a guardian of austerity, shunning public spending, limiting liquidity on the markets and preserving monetary stability. In the 1980s and 1990s principles of economic and financial deregulation, liberalization and privatization shaped the policy programs of not only national governments but also international financial institutions (Biersteker 1992: 118). Promoted by the leading financial powers (the UK and the US), neoliberalism, the ideological foundation of a disembedded liberal economic order, achieved hegemonic status in the global system (Rittberger et al. 2010: 143). Leading financial powers (the US and the UK), the financial industry and international financial institutions (the IMF and the World Bank) together propagated and contributed to bringing about open and integrated capital markets, devoid of state controls over capital movement, and new complex financial instruments (Higgott 2001: 134; Stiglitz 2002: 27–8; Williamson 2000). The crucial point for this book is that the transformation of the global (material and ideological) financial infrastructure from embedded liberalism to disembedded liberalism would be expected to increase public regulators' demand for credit ratings.

There are a number of reasons why the dependence of public regulators on credit rating agencies and the demand for credit ratings in financial regulation can be expected to be systematically higher in a global financial system of disembedded liberalism. First of all, the liberalization and deregulation of capital transfers in a global system of disembedded liberalism, as well as the transnational integration of financial markets, have made public authorities more dependent on credit rating agencies' analytical resources. The transition to a system of floating exchange rates after the breakdown of the Bretton Woods system paved the way for an increasingly unrestricted transfer of capital around the world, led to a dramatic increase in the volume of transnational flows of capital, and thus spurred not only private but also public demand for credit ratings. An increasing number of diverse public and private market actors offering and seeking capital, a trend towards transnationalization of portfolios, and the emergence of new complex financial instruments created higher market complexity and a growing need for reliable information and risk assessment. In sum, the greater volatility and higher complexity of disembedded, transnationally integrated financial markets creates a greater demand for expert knowledge and rapid adjustment of risk assessments to changing market circumstances. Credit agencies are one of the few sources for supply of these resources, which public regulators striving for effective regulation under these market conditions will of necessity seek.

Global deregulation of capital markets has also opened up opportunities for disintermediation and transnational securitization, that is, a shift from banks to global financial markets (also see below in the discussion of different varieties of capitalism). This obviously creates incentives for investors and borrowers to use the services of credit rating agencies (see Chapter 2); but it also pushes public regulators into increasingly relying on credit rating agencies. In the process of transnational securitization, banks, which have been traditional targets and partners of public authorities in financial market supervision, grow relatively weaker in comparison to capital market actors; therefore, new partners in regulation need to be found for public authorities. This increases public regulators' propensity to turn to credit rating agencies and to bolster their authority in financial market governance.

Moreover, direct public interference through bureaucratic command-and-control regulation becomes more or less politically banned in disembedded liberalism. Deregulation and hands-off economic policies are the norm that international financial institutions and private capital markets teach 'responsible' policymakers and supervisory bodies to follow. Therefore, direct interference of state regulators in financial markets becomes more and more politically and economically costly. But, in a situation where public authorities shun direct regulation and supervision but still do not want to wholly abandon the steering and oversight of financial markets, relying on indirect financial governance through the use of credit rating agencies appears to be a promising strategy. This tendency is reinforced by the partial assimilation of market conditions and transfer to the global capital market of market practices predominant in the leading US capital market, which accompany deregulation and transnational integration of financial markets (Gras 2003: 12–13). This diffusion process should entail an expansion of the acceptance of the regulatory use of credit ratings. Thus, public authorities' dependence on credit rating agencies, their analytical resources and their risk assessment increases around the world as the global financial architecture moves from embedded to disembedded liberalism, because this shift increasingly forecloses direct state interference and makes reliance on private regulators in tune with financial markets appear more essential as well as more appropriate and 'normal'.

Finally, transnational integration of financial markets without concomitant international political (supervisory) integration, which is a characterizing feature of disembedded liberalism, poses a severe problem for national supervisory authorities. Their competencies remain by and large limited to national territories and markets. The more transnational integration progresses, the more inadequate national regulation and supervision become. At the same time, effective international supervisory mechanisms have been hard to devise, since states fear sovereignty losses and reductions in their freedom to attract and foster financial industries through financial-market-friendly policies. Having recourse to transnationally operating credit rating agencies that are able to assess credit risk across borders and do not face comparable obstacles of state sovereignty and territorial restrictions on their 'supervisory' competencies seems like an attractive policy option under these circumstances.

All these factors would lead us to expect that public regulators will be more dependent on credit rating agencies' analytical resources in a global financial system characterized by disembedded liberalism than in one of embedded liberalism. Thus, the regulatory use of credit ratings should be expected to become more extensive in terms of regulatory scope and geographical reach if and when the global financial architecture moves from embedded to disembedded liberalism.

In a similar vein, I argue that, on the national/regional level, differences between *varieties of capitalism* (Anglo-Saxon liberal market economies vs. Rhenish coordinated market economies) have an impact on whether public authorities use private credit ratings for regulatory purposes. From this point of view, variations in types of capitalism across countries, but also over time – such as when a country moves from a coordinated market economy to a more liberal market economy – are an important source of variation in public regulators' need for credit rating agencies' analytical resources. This in turn explains varying degrees of public reliance on private credit rating agencies across countries and also over time.

Relying on the varieties-of-capitalism approach, Nölke (2004) and Nölke and Perry (2007) have already found that the overall significance of credit rating agencies and accounting firms (both belonging to the broader category of transnational standard-setters) in economic governance varies in different varieties of capitalism. Drawing on these studies, the resource dependence argument on the delegation of governance tasks and regulatory authority to credit rating agencies can be embedded into a macro-institutional varieties-of-capitalism argument. It can be hypothesized that the essentiality and substitutability of analytical resources controlled by credit rating agencies are conditioned by prevailing national or regional varieties of capitalism (Hall and Soskice 2001b; Lütz and Eberle 2007).[12] In the following, I develop the line of argument that links different varieties of capitalism with varying degrees of public regulators' dependence on credit rating agencies' analytical resources. For that purpose, I mainly rely on Nölke and Perry's (2007) reasoning, but adapt and transfer it to the relationship between public regulators and credit rating agencies.

Nölke and Perry (2007) link different varieties of capitalism with varying degrees of overall impact of coordination service firms such as credit rating agencies and accounting firms. They do not elaborate on potential linkages between varieties of capitalism and *public regulators'* reliance on credit rating agencies in financial regulation, though. One of their main arguments is that a strong position of credit rating agencies in financial market governance is not all-pervasive, but, rather, dependent on certain circumstances. From an intertemporal perspective, credit rating agencies are linked to a phase in the development of capitalism in which financial markets are increasingly influential even in countries which belong to the category of coordinated market economies. Many coordinated market economies have moved closer to the Anglo-Saxon model of finance. From an interregional perspective, not all varieties of capitalism are equally conducive to a strong role for credit rating agencies in financial market governance, since the activities of credit rating agencies fit more easily with the Anglo-Saxon variety of capitalism than with the Rhenish variety (Nölke and Perry 2007: 122).

These insights are based on a recognition that has become widely accepted in mainstream political economy: capitalism is not a homogeneous whole (Gourevitch 2007; Hall and Soskice 2001a). Scholars of comparative politics, who might be grouped together as proponents of the varieties-of-capitalism approach, have shown that there are national and regional variations in the operations of capitalism (Busch 2000; 2005; Coates 2005; Crouch and Streeck 1997a; Dunlavy and Welskopp 2007; Dyson and Padgett 2005; Hall and Gingerich 2004; Hall and Soskice 2001a; Hoffmann 2003; Lütz 2000; 2004; Lütz and Eberle 2007; Schmidt 2002). The varieties-of-capitalism approach provides a framework for capturing institutional similarities and differences among economies and for studying how 'behavior [of business and political actors] is affected by the institutions of the political economy' (Hall and Soskice 2001b: 4–5). Both economic policies and business activities are assumed to be shaped by existing macro-institutional socioeconomic arrangements such as systems of social security, structures of trade unions and employers' associations, industrial relations, education and training systems and corporate financing modes (Busch 2000: 61). Differences in the macro-institutional framework of the political economy set incentives and constraints for the behavior of individual and corporate actors in a capitalist system, and thus generate systematic differences in business actors' and politicians' strategies across different varieties of capitalism (Busch 2000: 61; Hall and Soskice 2001b: 15–16; see also Hoffmann 2003; Naschold 1997).

We can broadly distinguish conceptually between the Rhenish variety of capitalism, which has also been termed 'coordinated market economy' and is characterized by a long-term investment horizon, and the Anglo-Saxon variety of capitalism, which is sometimes referred to as 'liberal market economy' and features a short-term investment horizon (Hall and Soskice 2001b: 8). A dichotomous categorization of economies as either liberal market economies or coordinated market economies necessarily implies a significant degree of simplification of empirical variations. Hall and Soskice (2001b: 8) therefore argue that 'pure' liberal market economies and 'pure' coordinated market economies should, rather, be conceived as extreme poles of a spectrum along which many countries can be arrayed.[13]

When in the following the core features of the Rhenish as opposed to the Anglo-Saxon variety of capitalism are outlined, I focus mainly on those macro-institutional features of liberal market economies and coordinated market economies that are relevant for financial market governance. However, it would be misleading to completely neglect other spheres of the economy, since one of the key tenets of the varieties-of-capitalism approach is that countries 'with a particular type of [institutional] coordination in one sphere of the economy should tend to develop complementary practices in other spheres as well' (Hall and Soskice 2001b: 18). Institutions in different spheres of the political economy can be said to be complementary if the presence of one increases the returns from the other. Labor market arrangements that permit shedding labor in a downturn ('hire and fire') are complementary to financial markets that render a firm's access to funds dependent on current profitability ('shareholder value, because firms can easily release labor when facing pressure from financial markets (Hall and Soskice 2001b: 30–2; see Busch 2000; Hoffmann 2003: 125)).

Core features of the *Rhenish coordinated market economy* model are a fairly balanced and consensual relationship between labor and capital (Hall and Soskice 2001b: 24–5). Usually, in coordinated market economies management has to make an arrangement with well-organized representatives of both labor and capital that often participate directly in the corporate governance decision-making process. Decision-making may take a long time, but implementation of the resulting consensus is relatively smooth (Nölke and Perry 2007: 127). Firms rely on 'patient' capital being provided by major banks ('Hausbanken') and, to a more limited extent, internally generated funds and retained earnings (Nölke and Perry 2007: 127). This makes firms less vulnerable to short-term fluctuations of profitability (Hall and Soskice 2001b: 23–4). The financial system in coordinated market economies typically provides companies with access to finance that is both 'patient' and not entirely dependent on publicly available financial data or current returns (Hall and Soskice 2001b: 22–3). The coordinated market economy model of corporate finance leads to a comparatively long-term perspective with regard to the economic well-being of firms (Hoffmann 2003: 125). 'Hausbanken' entertaining close relationships with firms are less interested in short-term price movements on the stock markets than in the long-term solvency of their loans, which makes it possible for firms to retain a skilled workforce through economic downturns and to invest in projects generating returns only in the long run. The same long-term perspective applies to other sources of investment capital, such as large investors in a company. All these factors support long-term investment in human resource development, which is crucial for coordinated market economies' specialization in high-skill and high-quality products (Nölke and Perry 2007: 127; see also Busch 2000; Fioretos 2001; Hall and Soskice 2001b: 25–6; Hoffmann 2003: 125; Naschold 1997: 28–30; Streeck 1997; Vitols 2001).

The structure of financial markets in an *Anglo-Saxon liberal market economy* links firms' access to capital and ability to resist takeover to their current profitability. The more fluid financial markets of liberal market economies provide economic actors with greater opportunities to move their resources around in search of higher returns (Hall and Soskice 2001b: 16–7). The financial system of liberal market economies encourages firms to be attentive to current profitability and the price of their shares on equity markets (Hall and Soskice 2001b: 28). This focus on current profitability is complemented by labor market arrangements allowing labor to be easily released in times of economic downturn, which in turn favors education and training systems that focus on the development of general rather than industry/firm-specific skills (Busch 2000; Hoffmann 2003: 125). Firms in liberal market economies tend to rely more heavily on capital (bond and equity) markets for financing than those in coordinated market economies (Hoffmann 2003: 125). Access to risk capital is crucial for investment opportunities in product innovations. The terms on which large firms can secure finance are heavily dependent on their valuation in equity markets; investors must process large amounts of dispersed information to value the creditworthiness of companies. Lacking the facilities to monitor the creditworthiness of a company closely, distant investors usually need other sources of information (Hall and Soskice 2001b: 60). Banks (particularly investment banks) are themselves deeply engaged in short-term capital market investments. In sum, in all major spheres of economic governance (financial system, labor markets, education and training, etc.), there is a preference for deregulated competitive markets and market-based solutions for the coordination of economic activities, for instance through market-based technical and professional standards (Busch 2000: 62; Hall and Soskice 2001b: 27–9; Hoffmann 2003: 125; Fioretos 2001; Vitols 2001).

Credit rating agencies are a characteristic component of the Anglo-Saxon variety of capitalism. Due to the different intensities of financial disintermediation and the varying complexity and uncertainty of financial markets, the activities of credit rating agencies fit better with – and are more important in – liberal market economies than coordinated market economies. Quite obviously, the argument on national/regional variations in the operation of capitalism largely mirrors, and in part also converges with, the reasoning on the impact of changes over time in the global financial architecture (see above). This indicates that the distinction between global and national/regional macro-institutional contexts is a heuristic–conceptual one; in empirical terms these different levels are heavily interlinked.

In a system of disintermediated finance, users and suppliers of capital increasingly come to an agreement without the intermediation of banks via capital markets. In this situation, credit rating agencies take over the crucial task of collecting dispersed information on the financial situation of borrowers and condensing it into a single measure of creditworthiness (King and Sinclair 2001: 5–8; Nölke and Perry 2007: 129). Credit rating agencies are more important in liberal market economies, since the number and diversity of actors in financial markets and the scope of financial products are larger than in a coordinated market economy system of intermediated finance where long-term financing through banks is prevalent, the range of financial products is more limited and overall financial market volatility is less pronounced. In other words, credit rating agencies are empowered by deregulated, liberalized and disintermediated financial markets, which are characteristic of liberal market economies, because they are more complex and pose higher uncertainty to both private investors *and* public regulators, due to larger volatility and because borrowers depend more heavily on an external certification of their creditworthiness in order to get to capital markets than in a system of intermediated financing (Nölke and Perry 2007: 126–7; see also Nölke 2004, 2008). At the same time, credit rating agencies have contributed to financial disintermediation in the Rhenish model, thereby furthering tendencies towards the Anglo-Saxon variety of capitalism. Credit rating agencies aid the deterritorialization of capital by providing basic analytical services for mobile trans-border investors, and thus spread preconditions for the operation of transnational financialized capitalism. It should be kept in mind, though, that there is nothing inevitable about the processes of financial market liberalization, deregulation and ensuing disintermediation. In fact, they were initiated or at the very least supported by governments (Nölke and Perry 2007: 127, 135).

While the argument of the greater importance of credit rating agencies in liberal market economies for investors (dependent on information on the creditworthiness of borrowers) and borrowers (dependent on a seal of approval of their creditworthiness for access to capital markets) is pretty straightforward, the linkage with greater dependence of public regulators on credit rating agencies' analytical resources is somewhat more subtle. Nonetheless, it can be assumed that, in a macro-institutional environment marked by a higher degree of market uncertainty due to the short-term investment horizon of many investors, greater volatility of the financial system, and a lack of control of creditworthiness through long-term, close bank–borrower relationships, public regulators will depend more heavily on the analytical resources of credit rating agencies. Making use of credit rating agencies' analytical resources contributes to containing systemic uncertainty, which tends to be higher in the more complex and volatile financial markets of liberal market economies, without much (direct) public interference with market processes. The context conditions of Anglo-Saxon liberal market economies would thus make credit rating agencies' analytical resources appear essential for public regulators pursuing the goals of financial market stability and efficiency through risk-sensitive regulation.

Summary of the theoretical argument and hypotheses

The main line of argument and the general hypotheses developed so far can be summarized as follows. Public regulators, conceived as rational organizations aiming at producing the public goods of financial market stability and efficiency, lack essential analytical resources for the attainment of these organizational goals. External analytical resources are more essential for the attainment of these goals in situations of higher uncertainty and complexity of organizational task achievement, which are in turn conditioned by different macro-institutional socioeconomic contexts, namely different varieties of capitalism. Public regulators seek to establish relationships with credit rating agencies (conceived as transnational expert standard-setters) in order to make use of analytical resources which are essential for their goal attainment and hard to obtain (i.e. difficult to substitute) from other sources. The relationship that public regulators establish, pursuant to their formal–hierarchical authority, can be conceived as a principal–agent relationship with a specialized agent. Thus, public regulators delegate governance tasks and regulatory authority to credit rating agencies in order to enhance regulatory effectiveness and efficiency by making use of essential analytical resources. Delegation of regulatory authority necessarily involves some agency costs, in this case mainly some loss of control over regulated entities and (still rather modest) costs for control mechanisms to avoid agency slack. Public regulators will delegate regulatory authority if the perceived benefits, in terms of organizational goal attainment, from making use of credit rating agencies' analytical resources are larger than expected (agency) costs.

General hypothesis

In a nutshell, we can hypothesize that the higher the (*degree* of) public regulators' dependence on credit rating agencies' analytical resources, the higher will be the (*degree* of) public regulators' use of credit ratings

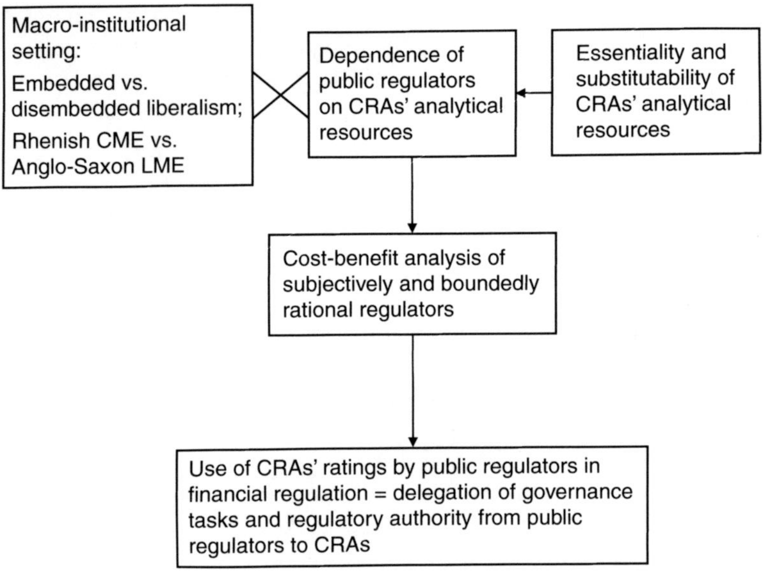

Figure 3.1 Theoretical model: explaining public regulators' use of credit ratings

in regulation. The dependence of public regulators on credit rating agencies, that is, the essentiality and the substitutability of credit rating agencies' analytical resources, will be conditioned by the macro-institutional socioeconomic contexts prevailing on both global and national/regional levels. Disembedded liberalism in the global financial architecture leads to a higher overall degree of dependence on credit rating agencies than embedded liberalism, and an Anglo-Saxon variety of capitalism (LME) is linked to a considerably higher degree of dependence on credit rating agencies' analytical resources than a Rhenish variety of capitalism (CME). See also Figure 3.1.

Operationalization of key variables

The *dependent variable* 'use of private credit ratings by public regulators' is operationalized in such a way that it can take three values: absent, modest and extensive. 'Absent' refers to a regulatory system in which credit ratings are not used. If credit ratings *are* used in a regulatory system, the following dimensions are to be taken into account in order to determine whether the value of the dependent variable is 'modest' or 'extensive'.

A first indicator is the *absolute number of regulations* that reference credit ratings. A second, related but not identical, indicator is the *relative scope of the use of credit ratings* for regulatory purposes, which refers to the question of how many distinct regulatory purposes credit ratings are used for within a given regulatory system (e.g. only for banking regulation; for banking and securities regulation; for banking regulation, securities regulation and further financial regulation such as insurance regulation etc.). A final indicator is the *compulsory character of the use of credit ratings for addressees* of financial regulation in the fulfillment of the regulatory duties imposed by the regulation. In other words, can the addressees of regulation (e.g. banks, insurances, institutional investors etc.), at least according to the letter of the regulation, meet the requirements of the financial regulation without relying on the credit rating agencies' risk assessment, so that reference to a (good) credit rating would be a bonus but not a must for fulfilling regulatory duties? Or is reference to a (good) rating compulsory in the sense that addressees of rules can meet regulatory requirements *only* when obtaining a certain rating?

The degree of public regulators' dependence on credit rating agencies' analytical resources is determined by the essentiality and substitutability of analytical resources. Therefore, I operationalize the independent variable in such a way that it comprises three values: low, medium and high resource dependence. The value 'low' refers to a situation marked by either low essentiality and high substitutability of analytical resources or high essentiality and high substitutability of analytical resources. This is because a need for a resource that is highly essential but easily available from many other sources cannot constitute any meaningful dependence relation. The value 'high' refers to a situation of high essentiality and low substitutability of analytical resources; the value 'medium' refers to a situation of high *or* medium essentiality of analytical resources and medium substitutability; medium substitutability means that, although there is clearly more than one source for the resource, the range of alternatives is still not abundant but limited to a rather small number of *accessible* sources.

Thus, the degree of *substitutability* of analytical resources varies depending on their availability from other sources. It is necessary to explore whether there are potential sources of analytical resources other than credit rating agencies, how many of them there are, and whether they can be easily accessed by public regulators (see Edele 2006: 62–3; Hickson et al. 1994: 202).

Useful indicators to measure the *essentiality* of analytical resources are hard to find. While the essentiality of material resources (such as funds) can be measured pretty easily, things are more difficult with immaterial resources (Edele 2006: 62). *Relative magnitude* of resource needs as a quantitative indicator cannot be applied. Instead, we can use the *criticality* of analytical resources as an indicator. Unlike relative magnitude, however, a clear-cut measurement of criticality is not possible. The criticality of immaterial resources such as analytical resources depends on the objectives of the organization at hand. In the case of public regulators, these goals are financial market stability and efficiency. The criticality of analytical resources for public regulators varies according to the complexity of the regulatory tasks. If appropriate means to design financial market regulation that is effective in achieving public regulators' organizational goals are readily available within public regulatory agencies, and if they are already used effectively, the degree of criticality is low (Edele 2006: 62). Yet, if public regulators lack the analytical resources for effective financial market regulation, external analytical resources are highly critical.

However, this operationalization of 'essentiality of analytical resources' is still too vague. To allow empirical observation and measurement, it might therefore be helpful to measure the proxy variable 'capabilities to cope with financial market uncertainty', which is taken from a specific variant of resource dependence theory, namely, strategic contingencies theory. Strategic contingencies theory holds that relationships of dependence *within* an organization result from the distribution of subunits' capabilities to cope with uncertainty (Hickson et al. 1994: 196–9; Pfeffer 1981: 109–12; Pfeffer and Salancik 2003: 45; Scott 1981: 267–8; see also Cyert and March 1963; Thompson 1967). Dependence on uncertainty coping capabilities is determined by both the essentiality and the substitutability of uncertainty coping capabilities (Pfeffer 1981: 110–11). While strategic contingencies theory was initially used to analyze the impact dependencies on uncertainty coping capabilities had on intraorganizational relations (Hickson et al. 1994; Lawrence and

Lorsch 1967), it was later also applied to analyze interorganizational dependence relations (Benson 1994: 123–4; Wamsley and Zald 1973a, b). Strategic contingency theory claims that organizations or organizational units in a social system are most heavily dependent on those units that are able to reduce organizational uncertainty in the system (Hickson et al. 1994; Pfeffer 1981: 109–11; Salancik and Pfeffer 1994). Uncertainty, in this context, refers to a lack of information about future events, so that alternatives and outcomes relevant to organizational goal attainment are unpredictable. In general terms, organizations deal with environmentally derived uncertainties in the sources, composition and quality of inputs, with uncertainties in the processing of throughputs, and again with environmental uncertainties in effective disposal of outputs. 'Organizations ... are forever seeking to reduce uncertainty' (Scott 1981: 304). Organizations must acquire means to deal with these uncertainties to enable adequate task performance (Hickson et al. 1994: 198). This capability is called uncertainty coping capability (Hickson et al. 1994: 200–1).

By uncertainty coping, the subunit or organization provides (sometimes only the impression of) certainty for the other subunits or organizations by controlling what are otherwise contingencies for other activities (Hickson et al. 1994: 201–4). In this context, the categorial distinction between 'uncertainty' and 'risk' advanced by Knight (1921) in his seminal work *Risk, Uncertainty, and Profit* is still very useful. Knight (1921: 19) refers to uncertainty as

> ... in a sense radically distinct from the familiar notion of risk. ... The essential fact is that 'risk' [in everyday language, A.K.] means in some cases a quantity susceptible of measurement, while at other times it is something distinctly not of this character; and there are far-reaching and crucial differences in the bearings of the phenomenon depending on which of the two is really present and operating. ... It will appear that a measurable uncertainty, or 'risk' proper, as we shall use the term, is so far different from an unmeasurable one that it is not in effect an uncertainty at all.

The term 'uncertainty' is thus restricted to cases of the nonmeasurable type. From that perspective, uncertainty coping organizations absorb incalculable uncertainty by transforming it into calculable risk, and thus control contingencies and enhance the predictability of organizational work processes aimed at organizational goal attainment (Hickson et al. 1994: 204). Hickson et al. (1994: 198; see also Scott 1981: 268) insist that it is not the presence of uncertainty alone, but the *successful coping with uncertainty*, that produces continued dependence on the subunit or organization. Only if the subunit or organization can effectively manage the uncertainty confronted, and in doing so protect the other units or organizations from disturbing effects, does uncertainty create the basis of continued dependence relations. Credit rating agencies' analytical resources can be conceived as capabilities to cope with financial market uncertainty. Note that the operationalization of analytical resources as uncertainty coping capabilities also establishes a more explicit link to the condition variable 'macro-institutional socioeconomic contexts', since it can be assumed that in a financial system of disembedded liberalism, and in an Anglo-Saxon variety of capitalism, financial market uncertainty will be higher than in an embedded liberal financial architecture and in a Rhenish coordinated market economy.

The *substitutability* of credit rating agencies' uncertainty coping capabilities can be determined pretty straightforwardly by answering the question: how many actors are capable of coping with financial market uncertainty in such a way that they are able to transform incalculable uncertainty into calculable risk? If the answer is 'many', the substitutability of the analytical resource 'uncertainty coping capabilities' is high. This implies that the dependence of regulatory bodies on credit rating agencies' analytical resources should be limited.

The *essentiality* of credit rating agencies' uncertainty coping capabilities is determined, first, by *the total number and the diversity (i.e. the qualitative scope) of borrowers* that are covered by financial market regulatory requirements within a given regulatory system; second, by *the average complexity of the prevalent financial products* in a certain market; and, third, by *the relative volatility* of a certain financial market. The higher the values of these indicators, the more essential are credit rating agencies' uncertainty coping capabilities for public regulators.

Specification of the test design and formulation of specific hypotheses

In the *intertemporal analysis* of the global use of private credit ratings in financial market regulation (see Chapter 4), this study undertakes an intertemporal comparison of the condition variable, the independent variable and the dependent variable of the proposed framework.

The time span that is examined ranges from the post-World War II financial order (before the breakdown of the Bretton Woods System, when the use of credit ratings was limited to the US and there were no international regulatory bodies using credit ratings in financial market regulation), through the 1990s (when credit rating agencies expanded their business activities in terms of geographical reach and scope of rated products, and national governments in developed countries increasingly resorted to the services of credit rating agencies in financial market regulation) until the year 2006 (when the Basel II Accord of 2004 was implemented within the EU). I analyze, first, whether there are indicators that the global financial architecture has become 'disembedded' and financial markets around the world have moved closer to the Anglo-Saxon liberal market economy model; second, whether we can find indicators that in this time span the dependence on credit rating agencies' analytical resources, conceived as uncertainty coping capabilities, has increased worldwide; and, third, whether public regulators beyond the US have also increasingly come to use credit ratings in financial regulation. If all these questions could be answered with 'yes', this would lend further plausibility to the proposed theoretical argument.

In the *interregional analysis* (see Chapter 4), I determine the socioeconomic macro-institutional context (Anglo-Saxon liberal vs. Rhenish coordinated market economy), the degree of dependence on credit rating agencies' analytical resources, operationalized in terms of essentiality and substitutability of their uncertainty coping capabilities, and the degree of public regulators' delegation of governance tasks and regulatory authority to credit rating agencies that could be observed in 2006 (i.e. before the beginning of the US mortgage crisis in 2007) in the *US* and in *Continental Europe*. For Continental Europe, not only national financial market authorities, but also the EU regulators and legislators that have transformed the Basel II Accord into binding EU law (see European Parliament and Council of the European Union 2006a, b), are relevant 'public regulators'. I test whether the independent, dependent and condition variables – as they were operationalized above – covary in a pattern consistent with the predictions of the theoretical framework.

We should expect that the degree to which US regulators (primarily the SEC, but also the FDIC, OCC, OTS, etc.) and EU legislators and regulators (implementing the international compromise formulae of the Basel II Accord) use credit ratings for regulatory purposes (*absent, modest or extensive*) will correspond to a variance in the degree of dependence on credit rating agencies' analytical resources (*low, medium or high*) in the US and the Continental European financial markets. These differences in dependence on credit rating agencies' analytical resources, which will be measured in terms of the degree of essentiality and substitutability of credit rating agencies' uncertainty coping capabilities, should in turn mirror variance in the condition variable 'macro-institutional socioeconomic settings' (*Anglo-Saxon liberal market economy* vs. *Rhenish coordinated market economy*).

Finally, in *process-tracing* the road to Basel II (in Chapter 5), I analyze commonalities and differences in the positions of the German and the US negotiators in the Basel II process and examine whether their negotiating positions reflect expectations derived from the theoretical framework. We would expect the US, which can be assigned to the category of the Anglo-Saxon variety of capitalism, to be more dependent on credit rating agencies' analytical resources and thus to be in favor of extensive use of credit ratings in the Basel II provisions, while Germany, which can be assigned to the category of the Rhenish variety of capitalism, should be less dependent on credit rating agencies' analytical resources and thus be more cautious as far as extensive use of credit ratings in the Basel II provisions is concerned. In the national positions of the US and Germany in the Basel II negotiations, we would further expect to find evidence for the proposed causal mechanism 'cost–benefit analysis', that is, for public regulators' calculation of expected gains (in terms of better attainment of the goals of financial market stability and effectiveness) and potential costs of delegation of regulatory authority to credit rating agencies (in terms of a partial loss of control over banking regulation).

4
Explaining Trend and Variation in the Regulatory Use of Credit Ratings

Having outlined an explanatory framework for the regulatory use of credit ratings, the next step is to check whether the proposed theoretical model holds any water when it is confronted with empirical evidence. This chapter examines how far the theoretical model introduced in Chapter 3 is able to account for both the common trend and cross-country variations in the use of credit ratings for regulatory purposes. An intertemporal and interregional congruence analysis is performed as an initial test of the empirical tenability of the theoretical model. The analysis checks whether the condition variable (macro-institutional context), the independent variable (public regulators' dependence on credit rating agencies' analytical resources) and the dependent variable (public regulators' use of credit ratings in regulation) of the proposed theoretical model covary over time and across world regions in line with the predictions of the theoretical framework.

Intertemporal analysis: accounting for a common trend

As outlined above, the breakdown of the Bretton Woods System (1973) as well as the liberalization and deregulation of capital transfers in the US and in the UK have promoted the transnational integration of financial markets. The transition to a system of floating exchange rates paved the way for an increasingly unrestricted transfer of capital around the world and led to a dramatic increase in the volume of transnational flows of capital. There can be no doubt that the global financial architecture has moved from embedded liberalism to disembedded liberalism over the past few decades.

Moreover, in the 1990s, many researchers claimed that economic globalization had already led to a partial convergence of national economic policies and, what is more, would continue to erase macro-institutional differences between capitalist systems (Crouch and Streeck 1997b; Hoffmann 2003; Hollingsworth et al. 1994). Political scientists diagnosed a loss of the steering capacity of the state due to globalization (Strange 1996) and an increasing pressure for competitive deregulation in economic policies which would necessarily and quasi-automatically lead to an adaptation of macro-institutional socioeconomic contexts in countries around the world to the deregulated Anglo-Saxon variety of capitalism (Hoffmann 2003: 126).

Later analysts have rightly made the criticism that these deterministic assumptions about the convergence of national economic policies and polities were premature and not adequately supported by empirical facts (Busch 2000: 60; Hoffmann 2003: 130; Schirm 2004b; Schirm et al. 2007). Not only does the hypothesis of a general convergence of economic systems under the pressure of economic globalization fail to recognize the importance of deliberate political choices even in the design of polity-level, broader macro-institutional economic arrangements (Helleiner 1994; Schirm 2004a: 75);[1] as far as the policy level is concerned, it can also be observed that, despite the global transformation from embedded to disembedded liberalism, no complete global convergence of national economic governance has taken place; that is, there are still quite different national approaches to specific economic policies (Schirm 2004b; Schirm et al. 2007). In brief, globalization does not seem to be the 'great leveler'; there is still room for distinct national economic policies, and a general convergence of macro-institutional socioeconomic contexts has not taken place (Hoffmann 2003: 130). The pressures of globalization seem to play out differently in different macro-institutional contexts (Hall and Soskice 2001b: 56–8).

Notwithstanding these important qualifications, there seems to be one sphere of the economy where a certainly incomplete, but nonetheless significant, adaptation of national macro-institutional contexts has indeed taken place: (internationalized) finance. There have been significant changes in most financial systems around the world in the past three decades. The financial innovation of floating exchange rates, which was, among several other factors, based on a belief in the efficiency of competitive, self-regulating financial markets, marked the beginning of a new era in financial relations which has been characterized by widespread deregulation of financial markets (Filc 2008: 5). The breakdown of the Bretton Woods system of fixed exchange rates (1973) and the ensuing deregulation and globalization of financial markets have thus not only led to an exponential growth of the volume of transnational flows of capital and to a global integration of money, currency and capital markets which has made national financial markets more vulnerable to external shocks and contagion in the case of financial crises. Macro-institutional arrangements in coordinated market economies have also come under increasing pressure, to the extent that there has been a tendency in most developed (and some emerging) economies at least to move closer to the Anglo-Saxon finance model (Gras 2003: 3; Hall and Soskice 2001b: 60–3; Kerwer 2006: 88, 95; Lütz 2000).

Deep 'infrastructural' changes could be observed in the financial systems of numerous coordinated market economies. The relationship between banks and industry has changed profoundly under the conditions of globalization. Tendencies of securitization and disintermediation in the credit business have gained momentum in coordinated market economies also (Everling 1991: 67–9; Peters 2001: 23–5). Banks got rid of firms' shares in order to free up resources for international investment business (Hoffmann 2003: 130; Lütz 2000). Some of the large banks in coordinated market economies that once cultivated close relations with manufacturing firms have been disengaging from them in order to enhance their global competitiveness through more flexibility in investment decisions (Hall and Soskice 2001b: 61–2). These developments threaten traditional practices in coordinated market economies by reducing the access of firms to capital that is not tied to current profitability. This could force firms to become more attentive to shareholders and rates of return at the detriment of other stakeholders, including employees (Hall and Soskice 2001b: 61; see also Busch 2000). These changes are important enough for many people in terms of real-world impact. For the purposes of this book, another consequence of the shift towards disembedded liberalism on the global level and the growing prevalence of an Anglo-Saxon model of finance in national/regional polities is even more significant.

There is ample evidence that, around the world, the degree of uncertainty posed by financial markets has increased tremendously in terms of a larger number and a broader scope of financial market actors, growing average complexity of the prevalent financial products, and increasing volatility of financial markets (Filc 2008: 5–7; Gras 2003: 11–14; Hishow 2007: 1–3; Speyer 2006: 103, 109; Wahl 2008: 34–38). Thus, in accordance with the operationalization of the independent variable, the *essentiality* of the uncertainty coping capabilities of credit rating agencies has increased around the world.

Since the 1970s, the *number of financial market actors* offering and seeking capital has risen significantly; in addition to that, the scope of financial market actors has become much broader, with large institutional investors (i.e. transnationally operating insurance companies, pension and investment funds, state-owned investment funds, hedge funds, etc.) becoming crucial capital market actors (Gras 2003: 11). In 2005, around 70 percent of all global financial assets were administered by institutional investors, which are usually staffed with highly specialized professionals seeking the highest possible returns on equity capital (Wahl 2008: 37). While, certainly, not all institutional investors are engaged in speculative transactions, the relative share of investors striving for short-term maximum profits resulting from speculative financial transactions has increased around the world (Filc 2008: 5). This leads to volatile capital flows across borders and a higher level of systemic uncertainty (Filc 2008: 5). This volatility is further increased by the large amount of liquidity in the markets. In developed economies, the sum of all foreign claims and foreign debts relative to gross domestic product has increased in the past 30 years from around 50 percent to more than 300 percent (Filc 2008: 5–6). The consequence is that there is a lot of liquidity 'out there' looking for short-term investment opportunities around the globe. At the same time, 'borrower diversity' (Cantor and Packer 1994: 1) has also increased. The number and range of both private and public actors seeking capital in transnational financial markets have expanded, making it more difficult for investors to keep track of the creditworthiness of potential borrowers (Gras 2003: 11–12).

In combination with the increasing number of market actors, the creation of *new complex financial instruments* due to financial innovation and modern communication technology, which makes it possible to instantaneously manage large volumes of short-term financial products, has led to a growing complexity and uncertainty in global financial markets (Gras 2003: 11). Investors have diversified and internationalized their portfolios. These qualitative changes have created a growing gap in regulators' capacity to collect and process information, design adequate regulation and conduct reliable risk assessments of products and issuers. The liberalization and deregulation of global flows of capital have opened up new opportunities for the financial industry: there has been a proliferation of new, ever more complex financial market instruments (e.g. derivatives such as futures, forwards, options, swaps and CDOs[2]) which account for both the growth of the financial sector in most countries and an increase in financial market uncertainty (Hishow 2007: 1; Osman 2007; Wahl 2008: 38). This development was in no way limited to the US and the UK, though it played out at a slower pace and with weaker intensity in Continental European economies. For instance, the European Commission and the European Council have propagated for years to open up the European financial sector for global competition (Hishow 2007: 1). This has also affected the business of European banks, which for a long time had been considered rather 'conservative' in their investment strategies. Financial market deregulation has *enabled*, and intensified global competition has *'forced'*, banks to create and trade in ever more complex financial products whose construction is hard to comprehend even for the originators of the products (Filc 2008: 3). Even smaller European banks have started to manage their own investment funds. Banks must increasingly compete in the capital market and feel forced to diversify their portfolios. This has led to a higher propensity of banks to take risks in transnational trade in financial products; at the same time, the degree of mutual dependence of banks has increased (Hishow 2007: 1). This has transformed the character of financial crises, specifically banking crises. Banks' increasing interlinkages with each other, and their direct and indirect linkages to capital markets, entail that the repercussions of problems in any one institution are quickly transferred to the rest of the financial system (Speyer 2006: 109). It is not difficult to see that these developments increase systemic uncertainty and make risk assessment more difficult, not only for investors but also for public regulators.

The increase in transnational flows of capital and the rise of short-term investments by a variety of market actors have led to *higher average market volatility* (Filc 2008: 3; Gras 2003: 12–13; Wahl 2008: 34). The shift to floating exchange rates and the deregulation of financial markets have entailed a loss of the institutional precautions limiting the volatility of financial markets. In recent decades the volatility of prices and interest rates on global financial markets has grown significantly. This has contributed to systemic uncertainty and favored the more frequent occurrence of financial crises (Filc 2008: 5).

In sum, changes in the global and national/regional macro-institutional context which amounted to a transformation from embedded to disembedded liberalism and from the Rhenish to the Anglo-Saxon model of finance have favored the rise of market actor constellations, financial products, and process features of financial markets that increase systemic uncertainty. Even in the absence of major crises, the complexity, the lack of transparency and the degree of volatility of financial systems have become hard to handle for supervisory authorities around the world (Wahl 2008: 34). Financial markets, not only in the US and the UK, but also in Continental Europe, have become highly uncertain territory for all those who depend on a stable environment and reliable expectations for the attainment of their goals.

Thus, the value to public regulators of all indicators of the *essentiality* of the uncertainty coping capabilities of credit rating agencies has risen in the past three decades on a global scale. This suggests that the uncertainty coping capabilities of credit rating agencies have become ever more significant for both investors and regulators around the world.

This diagnosis is further corroborated by the findings of numerous scholars that public regulators are indeed increasingly overwhelmed by the sheer quantity of information on the credit risk of diverse financial market actors, by the complexity of the information to be processed and by the speed of financial market changes. These developments make fixed bureaucratic rules neglecting (temporal) variation in credit risk increasingly inadequate, while private actors' analytical resources become more crucial for risk assessment

(Filc 2008; Gras 2003; Hishow 2007; Speyer 2006; Tsingou 2008; Wahl 2008).

Globalization and financial product innovation have rendered public financial market supervision and bureaucratic regulatory efforts around the world less effective – the EU is no exception to this rule (Hishow 2007: 1–2). Regulators have acknowledged that fixed bureaucratic rules are increasingly inappropriate in light of the fast pace of evolution of financial markets:

> Financial markets are marked by a high degree of innovativeness. Institutional structures of financial markets, the kind of instruments preferred by actors on financial markets as well as the structure and volume of international capital flows can and do change quickly.... The important thing to note is that those changes simultaneously alter the scope, nature and distribution of risk within the financial system. (Speyer 2006: 103)

Creating regulation that is not risk-sensitive is inappropriate, since rules and supervisory structures would quickly be out of line with the actual risk situation. Similarly, public regulators are plagued by growing deficits in their capability to adequately guide and oversee complex financial activities that transcend national regulatory and legal boundaries. This has made them increasingly reliant on private sector (e.g. credit rating agencies') know-how (Tsingou 2008: 58).

As far as the development of the *substitutability* of credit rating agencies' analytical resources over time is concerned, it is more difficult to make reasonably safe, generalizable statements. However, there are strong indications in the literature that, while the essentiality of external private expertise for designing and implementing risk-sensitive financial market regulation has increased significantly over time (Osman 2007; Speyer 2006; Tsingou 2008), the number of accessible and functionally adequate private sources for analytical resources has in fact remained limited (Estrella et al. 2000: 55–8; Kerwer 2005: 469). One option for public regulators is to rely on investors' or banks' publicly approved procedures for (self-)assessment of the risk implied in the investments they make or the credits they issue. However, this always implies strong incentives for underestimating risk and creates a potential for moral hazard. In other words, entrusting private financial institutions involved in financial deals with assessing the risks of these very deals requires public regulators to set detailed and 'intelligent' framework provisions on how the internal rating procedures must be designed to avoid moral hazard. It will necessarily require a considerable amount of trust on the part of public regulators in the reliability and integrity of financial institutions' self-assessment of risk exposure. As these conditions will not always be met, relying on independent external risk assessment will in many cases be an attractive option for public regulators. While, particularly within the EU, there are a limited number of alternative sources of credit risk information apart from credit rating agencies (see above and Estrella et al. 2000: 55–8), the analytical resources these institutions offer tend to become less adequate for public regulators' goal attainment when the entities whose risk exposure they are to measure are operating more transnationally. This is because at least some of these other credit risk assessment institutions only operate within national jurisdictional boundaries (Estrella et al. 2000: 57). In brief, if public regulators do not want to rely on internal ratings-based procedures, the range of alternatives to credit rating agencies is limited, and the usefulness of these other sources decreases with the increasing transnationalization of financial markets.

Thus, we can state, in rather general terms, that for the past two to three decades the substitutability of credit rating agencies' analytical resources has, at the very least, not increased. In fact, there are good reasons to argue that it has decreased. In combination with the earlier finding that the essentiality of credit rating agencies' analytical resources has increased considerably around the world, this means that dependence on credit rating agencies' analytical resources has increased in the past three decades – not only in the US but also in Continental Europe. We should thus expect to be able to observe an expansion and an increase of the use of credit ratings in regulation over time.

The actual intertemporal development of the use of credit ratings by national and international public regulators corresponds to this expectation. As outlined in Chapter 2, the use of credit ratings in financial regulation was initially limited to the US. However, since the late 1980s and early 1990s, the use of credit ratings for regulatory purposes has expanded to other developed economies (i.e. most EU member states, Switzerland, Australia, Canada and New Zealand) and emerging markets, particularly in the Latin American and Asian areas (Adams et al. 1999: 160–1; Gonzalez et al. 2004: 9; Gras 2003: 13–4; King and Sinclair 2001: 14–17; 2003: 348; Kerwer 2002: 304–6; 2005: 463; Nicholls 2005: 15–6, 28–30; Sinclair 2005: 46). Thus, the regulatory use of credit ratings has spread geographically and can now be found in most countries in the developed world: 'In fact, the regulatory use of rating agencies has become an accepted best practice world wide' (Kerwer 2005: 463). The use of credit ratings in regulation has gone global. Not only the geographical reach but also the number and scope of regulations that reference credit rating agencies have increased significantly, as evidenced, for instance, by the boom of ratings-dependent regulation in the US in the 1980s and 1990s (see Table 2.3).

Thus, the intertemporal covariation analysis has demonstrated covariation of the condition variable, the independent variable and the dependent variable over time. The result of the longitudinal analysis corroborates the plausibility of the proposed theoretical framework.

Interregional analysis: explaining differences across regulatory systems

For the interregional covariation analysis, I determine the values of the condition variable (Rhenish coordinated market economy vs. Anglo-Saxon liberal market economy), the independent variable and the dependent variable in the US and in Continental Europe and check whether they covary according to the predictions of the theoretical framework.

First of all, it is pretty straightforward to designate the values of the condition variable 'macro-institutional socioeconomic context'. While the US clearly belongs to the category of Anglo-Saxon liberal market economies (Hall and Soskice 2001b: 20–1), all Continental European states still share many of the features of coordinated market economies. Recent studies have confirmed the original categorization into coordinated market economies and liberal market economies by Hall and Soskice (Botzem 2008: 48; see also Hall and Soskice 2001b; Schmidt 2002). While, in the particular sphere of financial relations, significant changes in coordinated market economies have taken place in the past decades, moving them closer to the Anglo-Saxon model of finance, there are still differences in the corporate financing modes and the banking industry structures between the US and

Continental Europe which are pronounced enough to warrant the categorization of Continental European countries as coordinated market economies (Lütz 2000; Lütz and Eberle 2007).

In order to gauge the dependence of public regulators on the analytical resources of credit rating agencies, I have suggested measuring the essentiality and substitutability of the proxy variable 'uncertainty coping capabilities'. As far as the *essentiality* of the uncertainty coping capabilities of credit rating agencies is concerned, we can summarize the following scholarly findings (Dieter 2008: 14; Gras 2003: 11–3; Hishow 2007: 1–3; Osman 2007; Rosenbaum 2004: 20). First, the total number and the diversity (i.e. the qualitative scope) of borrowers that are covered by financial market regulatory requirements within the US regulatory system are larger than in Continental European regulatory systems.[3] There is a much broader range of different types of institutional investors engaged in US financial markets, since the financial system is far more disintermediated; the SEC, the US securities market watchdog, thus faces a more complex range of regulated entities with broader variation in their risk profiles than its European counterparts. The still considerable overall importance of bank lending limits the number and scope of financial market actors in Continental Europe; however, European banks themselves are increasingly invested in risky capital market products, contributing to an increase in systemic uncertainty in Continental European regulatory systems as well.

Second, the average complexity of the prevalent financial products in the US financial markets is considerably higher than in the Continental European markets. This is not just because most of the recent financial innovations have been designed in the US; trade in derivatives is larger in volume and more diverse in terms of different types of derivatives than in Continental Europe. The general rule is that the more complex and the less transparent the products, the more important uncertainty coping capabilities become (Osman 2007).

Third, the relative volatility of US financial markets is larger than that of Continental European markets; that is, prices and interest rates fluctuate more extensively in US markets (World Federation of Exchanges 2008). This increases systemic uncertainty and favors regulation that is risk-sensitive and thus adjusts to credit risk exposure that varies over time.

In sum, these indicators suggest that the essentiality of the uncertainty coping capabilities of credit rating agencies is high for US public regulators, whereas it is only medium for Continental European public regulators. Thus, while the dependence on the uncertainty coping capabilities of credit rating agencies is lower for Continental European regulators, it is by no means negligible. This finding is nicely illustrated, for instance, by statements from European politicians such as the finance policy spokesman for the parliamentary group of the German Christian Democrats (CDU), who claimed that '[a] world without rating agencies is no longer conceivable. Banks, private investors and even supervisory authorities depend on the views of the [rating] evaluators' (Bernhardt, quoted in Reuters 2007).

As to the *substitutability* of the uncertainty coping capabilities of credit rating agencies in the US and in Continental Europe, clear differences can be identified. The number of alternative sources of credit risk information in Europe is limited, and some of these alternative sources are plagued with shortcomings; but the substitutability of the uncertainty coping capabilities of credit rating agencies is clearly higher than in the US (Estrella 2000: 55–8). Renouncing the use of credit ratings in regulation would put US regulators in the 'awkward position of having to find a substitute', which was in fact hard to do (Kerwer 2005: 469), and would basically lead to relying on institutional investors' and banks' internal risk assessment procedures. However, many American banks are not at all keen on being 'allowed' to conduct their own credit risk assessments (Becker 2007: 85–6, 90; see also Chapter 5). On the contrary, they have advocated the use of credit ratings in regulation. Thus, for US regulators, the substitutability of the uncertainty coping capabilities of credit rating agencies is low.

European regulators have at least some alternatives, such as central credit registers (CCRs) and scoring based on central financial statements databases (CFSDs). Central credit registers and central financial statements databases are services provided by several European central banks, frequently operating jointly with the banking sector. The central credit registers service involves collecting, processing, managing and releasing information on banks' credit exposures, while central financial statements databases do the same for the credit quality of counterparties to which banks are exposed (Estrella et al. 2000: 55). These systems have been implemented for a long time; they were established in 1946 in France, 1963 in Spain, 1964 in Italy and 1967 in Belgium (Estrella et al. 2000: 57). Seven European countries have implemented central credit registers and central financial statements databases. The countries covered are Austria, Belgium, France, Germany, Italy, Portugal and Spain. It is important to note that central credit registers and central financial statements databases are national databases: a country's coverage does not extend beyond its national borders. This puts them at a disadvantage compared with transnationally operating credit rating agencies and makes their uncertainty coping capabilities somewhat less attractive than those of credit rating agencies. Furthermore, adaptation of ratings from private credit rating agencies to changes in credit risk exposure is usually quicker. Thus, their ratings are more appropriate for risk-sensitive regulation. Credit assessment agencies (CAAs) are another source of credit risk assessment. Credit assessment agencies have much in common with central financial statements databases and credit rating agencies, in that their business is based on collecting financial information on companies. Credit assessment agencies are private businesses that sell information or provide consultancy services regarding credit management. Generally, they assign ratings based on proprietary methods. Unlike credit rating agencies, credit assessment agencies only rely on public data which can be bought on the market. They do not have access to nonpublic data, which puts them at a disadvantage (Estrella 2000: 57). In sum, we can conclude that the substitutability of the uncertainty coping capabilities of credit rating agencies for Continental European regulators is medium.

Thus, the dependence of US public regulators on the uncertainty coping capabilities of credit rating agencies is high, while the value of the independent variable for Continental European public regulators is medium.

For the purpose of determining the values of the dependent variable, we can make use of the detailed description of the regulatory use of credit ratings in the US, in other national regulatory systems, including Continental European states, and in the Basel II provisions which now form the common basis of European banking supervision (see Chapter 2). The value of the dependent variable for the US is clearly 'extensive'. First, a large absolute number of US financial market regulations issued by a variety of public regulators reference

NRSROs' ratings (see Table 2.3). Second, the scope of the use of credit ratings for regulatory purposes is broad, comprising a large number of distinct regulatory purposes in banking regulation, securities regulation, insurance regulation, and further specific issue areas of financial regulation. Third, there are several US rules which strictly *mandate* credit ratings in such a way that addressees can only fulfill the regulatory duties imposed by the regulation through a (good) rating. Reference to a (good) rating is compulsory in the sense that addressees of rules can meet regulatory requirements *only* when obtaining a certain rating.

In contrast to that, the value of the dependent variable for Continental Europe is 'modest'. There is regulation referring to private credit ratings, namely the 2006 Banking Directive and Capital Adequacy Directive, and, even earlier, the 1993 Capital Adequacy Directive on market risk assessment of banks, which did not apply to Germany. However, both the absolute number and the scope of regulations referencing credit ratings are limited. There might be additional minor and therefore less salient ratings-dependent regulations in some Continental European national regulatory systems apart from the European-level banking regulation directives. However, there can be no doubt that the Basel II provisions implemented by the Banking Directive and the Capital Adequacy Directive are the only *major* set of rules referencing credit ratings in Continental European financial market regulation. Even these rules do not make reference to a credit rating compulsory for banks in their calculation of minimum capital requirements. Banks may opt for an internal ratings-based procedure (which must be recognized by the competent national authority) or even renounce any rating. Under the standardized approach of Basel II, unrated credit claims receive a risk weight of 100 percent (see Table 2.7). Thus, renouncing the use of any rating procedure will cost the banks capital reserve discounts that are possible in the case of good (external and internal) ratings; however, banks are still able to fulfill regulatory requirements imposed by European legislators and regulators without being compelled to make use of ratings. In combination, these indicators display a modest use of credit ratings for regulatory purposes in Continental Europe.

Thus, the interregional analysis has indeed demonstrated that the condition variable, the independent variable and the dependent variable covary systematically across countries or world regions. US regulators, under the macro-institutional conditions of an Anglo-Saxon liberal market economy, display a high degree of dependence on credit rating agencies' analytical resources (measured in terms of uncertainty coping capabilities). The use of credit ratings in US financial market regulation is extensive. Continental European regulators, under the macro-institutional conditions of a coordinated market economy, face a medium degree of dependence on credit rating agencies' analytical resources. The use of credit ratings in Continental European financial market regulation is modest.

5 Making Sense of the Role of External Ratings in Basel II

The intertemporal and interregional analysis of the regulatory use of credit ratings has provided empirical support for the theoretical framework proposed in Chapter 3. In a next step, I examine more closely the decision to include the option of external ratings-based credit-risk assessment into the Basel II provisions. This should provide a more accurate picture of the causal factors underlying decisions for or against the use of credit ratings in regulation. In particular, it should serve to retrace and, if need be, specify the causal mechanism connecting the independent variable and the dependent variable.

The Basel II Accord highlights the increased role that nonstate actors (both credit institutions and, which is particularly relevant for this book, credit rating agencies) play in the design and implementation of rules governing global financial markets (Speyer 2006: 101). On the following pages, I take a closer look at commonalities and differences in the positions of the US negotiators (i.e. representatives from the Board of Governors of the Federal Reserve System, the Federal Reserve Bank of New York, OCC, FDIC and OTS) and the German negotiators (German Central Bank and BaFin) in the Basel II negotiations (1998–2004).[1] I examine to what extent the national positions of the US and Germany in the Basel II process and the final provisions in the Basel II Accord correspond to the causal arguments and hypotheses of the theoretical framework developed in this book.

Commonalities and differences in the positions of Basel II negotiators

As outlined in Chapter 2, Basel II was supposed to address regulatory issues left open by Basel I, to correct wrong incentives set by uniform capital requirements which did not take into account the creditworthiness of borrowers, and, more broadly speaking, to adapt banking supervision procedures to changed conditions in financial markets. There was broad agreement in the BCBS on these general objectives, and both US and German representatives were in favor of a revision of the Basel I standards (Becker 2007: 82). In 1999, the US Department of the Treasury stressed it was 'very important that the Basel Committee work quickly to complete its updating of the Basel Capital Accord, by expanding the number of credit-risk categories and revising the current all-or-nothing system for classifying loans to sovereign borrowers' (US Department of the Treasury, quoted in Becker 2007: 82). The German Federal Bank agreed on the need for an overhaul of banking supervision procedures and a revision of capital requirements with a view to making them more risk-sensitive.

Furthermore, there was a consensus among negotiators on some major necessities and the general regulatory approach to be taken in banking supervision. Negotiators saw a need for closer alignment of the regulatory framework and market practice in order to promote market stability and efficiency. For that purpose, more flexibility and risk-sensitivity in regulation and thus more sophisticated rules were necessary (Speyer 2006: 111–12; Tsingou 2008: 58–60).

In 2000, the then Federal Reserve Board Governor, Laurence Meyer, aptly summarized the US preference for designing supervisory solutions which are in tune with markets:

> [W]e have limited public policy choices for large and complex organisations. Choice 1: we can accept systemic risk as a cost of having large, global organisations in the marketplace. Choice 2: in order to limit systemic risk, we can adopt very detailed regulation and supervision programmes that include a growing list of prohibitions. Choice 3: we can rely more on market discipline to supplement capital reforms and can maintain a level of supervision similar to the one we have today. Given the choices, we simply must try market discipline. (Meyer, quoted in Tsingou 2008: 59)

This preference for flexible regulation that would be in tune with the market and make use of the disciplining forces of the market was by no means a singular US position, but was, to slightly varying degrees, common to all BCBS members (including Germany). There was also agreement that nonstate actors (i.e. banks and/or credit rating agencies) should not have a consultative role in the drafting of the Basel II Accord. An important feature of the Basel II negotiations, which differed from Basel I, was the broad participation of private-sector actors (including credit rating agencies) in the negotiations. Private actors were involved in several rounds of consultations and ongoing dialogue between industry and supervisors (Speyer 2006: 111; Tsingou 2008: 60). Moreover, there was a general consensus that private actors would be significantly involved in the application and implementation of Basel II (Speyer 2006: 111–12). In the late 1990s, a consensus in the international and transnational financial policy community (including public regulators) emerged in favor of an increased private-sector involvement in banking supervision (Tsingou 2008: 61–2). For instance, a 1997 report by the Group of Thirty (G-30)[2] formulated a set of guidelines for the design of an enhanced regulatory and supervisory framework for banks. The G-30 proposals, which can be conceived as an exercise in testing the waters and a useful start to the revision of the Basel accord, betrayed a 'high comfort level with the principle that the private sector needs to be more involved' in banking supervision and that 'traditional supervisors should no longer have the lead' (Tsingou 2008: 61; see also Institute of International Finance 1997).

Banking regulators' shared preferences for market-generated standards and market-based oversight solutions have become manifest in the Basel process (Tsingou 2008: 62). They can be traced back to financial market developments that make private actors' expertise, that is, their analytical resources, appear more essential to public authorities for accomplishing the goals of financial market stability and efficiency (see Chapter 4). From that perspective, the involvement of nonstate actors in global governance structures for financial markets has been a 'demand-pull process' to a significant extent (Speyer 2006: 107). Regulators became increasingly convinced that state-of-the-art expertise on risk measurement and management was to be found in the financial industry (i.e. in the credit institutions and in credit rating agencies) (Speyer 2006: 108).

The complexity and speed of financial innovation over the past two decades seemed to put banks in a privileged position as knowledge holders. Public authorities themselves believed that they lagged behind in terms of technical capabilities and analytical expertise. Their feeling was that they could not (afford to) keep up – in terms of expertise and sheer volume constraints on their oversight capacities – with the development of financial products that are complex, often tailor-made and used by a variety of institutions and firms. As a result, BCBS members became increasingly prepared to accept public reliance on private-sector know-how and the recognition of market-based standards based on private expertise, involving a transfer of regulatory authority to private sources. In fact, this approach to designing and implementing banking regulation became widely accepted because it was intended to fit new regulatory challenges under changed market circumstances. The turn to private expertise was further encouraged by the reputation of global finance as being increasingly complicated, technical and best left 'to the experts' (Tsingou 2008: 64). In the absence of major financial crises, financial market regulatory issues attract limited attention among the wider public, as evidenced by the 'low domestic visibility of the issue of financial liberalisation among politicians and the general public' (Helleiner 1994: 14). This has favored private 'expertocracy'.

In sum, the BCBS members shared a general inclination to make use of private actors' capacities in banking supervision in order to mitigate systemic risk. It is important to stress that both US and German regulators seemed willing to delegate (quasi-)regulatory tasks to private actors. However, the degree to which German and US regulators were willing to rely on *credit rating agencies* as a specific type of private actor taking on (quasi-)regulatory tasks clearly diverged. Germany's position, that internal rating procedures of banks should be regarded as equivalent to external ratings by credit rating agencies, is, therefore, not so much a position against delegation of public tasks to private actors as a position that is in favor of delegation to another type of private actor. I will argue below that this German preference for internal ratings conducted by banks themselves can largely be explained with reference to the macro-institutional context, namely the Rhenish type of capitalism in Germany: credit rating agencies' analytical resources were somewhat less essential, and more substitutable, for German regulators. Moreover, extensive reliance on external ratings in Basel II would have been at odds with the German model of capitalism. This explains why Germany pushed for a lesser role for credit rating agencies in the final Basel II Accord.

Before analyzing the divergent US and German positions in the Basel II negotiations in some detail, it should be noted that the Basel II Accord 'was explicitly a joint G-10 effort' (Speyer 2006: 111). In addition to the G-10, representatives from non-G-10 countries were informally consulted, which reflected the fact that the Basel provisions had acquired applicability far beyond the members of the BCBS. On the one hand, due to their strong position in the global financial system, the consent of the US (and the UK) was still necessary for effective international rules for financial market governance in general and for effective international banking standards in particular. This implied that the Basel II standards needed to be acceptable to the US. On the other hand, it could also be observed that the US was no longer as dominant in international banking as it had been in the 1980s. Thus, the outcome of the Basel II negotiations was not a US dictate, but reflected a 'true' compromise between the national positions of the BCBS members (Tsingou 2008: 60). Financial institutions with their home base in the EU, but with extensive operations in the US, prodded their national regulatory authorities to participate actively from the very beginning in the negotiations on the reform of the Basel Accord (Speyer 2006: 105; Tsingou 2008: 60).

Essentially, there were four main areas of disagreement between US and German negotiators. These referred to the scope of applicability of Basel II, the timetable for the implementation of Basel II, preferential treatment provisions for credits for small and medium-sized enterprises, and the rating procedure for the assessment of credit risk under the First Pillar of Basel II (Becker 2007: 84–91).

As far as the *scope of applicability* is concerned, in the later stages of the drafting of the Basel II accord, US regulators announced a reduced applicability of the accord in the US. In a somewhat surprising turn, the OCC and the Federal Reserve System argued that, due to the high complexity of the standards, which were challenging enough to implement even for internationally active banks (Becker 2007: 85, 88–9), only the largest, internationally active banks should be legally required to adopt the relevant requirements and practices (Becker 2007: 84–5). This change in the US position was mainly the result of divisions between the US regulatory community, where at a technical level the emphasis was on safety and soundness, and the political level, where the focus shifted to competition and competitive advantages (Tsingou 2008: 62–3). Thus, the US negotiators argued that Basel II should apply only to around 20 large and internationally active US banks. However, it should be noted that the 10 largest US banks alone hold a 95 percent share of the volume of all international business transactions of US banks (Becker 2007: 84). In line with the common EU position, German negotiators argued that the Basel II provisions should be applicable to all financial institutes, including smaller banks, because otherwise the goal of achieving an 'international level playing field' (Macht 2007) would not be achieved.[3] As to the *timetable for implementation*, Germany called for timely implementation so that the main Basel II provisions would be in force at the beginning of 2007. In the US, implementation was to be postponed due to difficulties of banks in shifting to the more complex procedures required by the Basel II provisions, for which many banks were not prepared, the US Department of Treasury and regulatory bodies claimed (Becker 2007: 85). Thus, before the global financial crisis (2007–10), the US, despite being among those initiating negotiations on Basel II, lagged behind in the implementation of Basel II (Becker 2007: 86).

The Basel II negotiations became politicized on the issue of *treatment of loans to small and medium-sized enterprises* (Speyer 2006: 113–14). According to initial proposals, loans to small and medium-sized enterprises would have, on average, to be backed by more capital than was the case under Basel I rules. This reflected the empirical fact that probabilities of default are, on average, higher for loans to small and medium-sized enterprises than for other corporate loans. Furthermore, small and medium-sized enterprises frequently have a (relatively) low equity capital base, which also makes bank credits more risky (Becker 2007: 90). The consequence would have been higher credit interest rates on loans to small and medium-sized enterprises due to higher capital requirements for banks giving credits to small and medium-sized enterprises. Thus, German industry associations warned of a significant deterioration of the business environment of the 'Mittelstand' with a concomitant negative effect on jobs. This in turn called politicians onto the scene. The German Government interfered with the negotiations, threatening to veto the Accord, and Parliament passed a cross-party resolution on Basel II in June 2000 (Speyer 2006: 114). Both German regulatory authorities negotiating in Basel and politicians in Berlin called for more favorable treatment of loans to small and medium-sized enterprises in order to avoid disadvantages for the 'Mittelstand' in Basel II. The US was opposed to special clauses for small and medium-sized enterprises (Becker 2007: 87). In the US, small and medium-sized enterprises are less dependent on bank credits; they rely, rather, on other sources of (capital market) financing or higher equity capital rates. Furthermore, US small and medium-sized enterprises are less well organized than the German 'Mittelstand', which implies that they have less political influence (Becker 2007: 90–1). Eventually, the BCBS accommodated the German demands in order to find a consensus, and Germany managed to insert special provisions on favorable treatment for loans to small and medium-sized enterprises into the final accord. Thus, banks may put aside lower capital reserves for credits to small and medium-sized enterprises than for credits to larger companies (Speyer 2006: 114).

The most critical issue contested between German and US negotiators referred to the *use of internal rating procedures* (done by banks themselves) or *external rating procedures* (done by approved credit rating agencies) in the measurement of banks' exposure to credit risk (Becker 2007: 86–7; Hishow 2007: 4; King and Sinclair 2003; Nölke and Perry 2007: 131; Sinclair 2005: 46). US regulatory agencies pushed for 'considering greater use of external ratings for determining capital requirements for a *broad range* of exposure' (US Department of the Treasury 2005, quoted in Becker 2007: 86; my emphasis). German representatives were unfamiliar with the use of credit ratings in regulation, and feared that accepting external ratings as the only major procedure for credit-risk assessment would entail a competitive advantage for US banks and firms. They therefore pushed for the introduction of an alternative internal ratings-based approach. German negotiators made a strong case that, at least, sophisticated credit institutions with extensive analytical capacities should be allowed 'to assess all ... risk parameters themselves. The risk evaluation system developed by the bank must be approved by the BaFin' (German Ministry of Finance, quoted in Becker 2007: 87). The German negotiators pushed strongly for a capital requirements framework that would acknowledge that different financial firms require different treatment in terms of sophistication of rules;

reward banks' advanced risk management capabilities; and make use of more sophisticated banks' own analytical resources for measuring the exposure to credit risk (Tsingou 2008: 60).

Theoretical expectations and the Basel II provisions

Thus, it seems that one reason for insisting on the possibility of internal ratings-based procedures was indeed the belief of German regulators in the adequacy of banks' own analytical resources, that is, banks' capabilities of coping with financial market uncertainty. Again, the German position that internal rating procedures of banks should be regarded as equivalent to external rating by credit rating agencies was not so much a position against delegation of public tasks to private actors. Rather, in contrast to US negotiators, German regulators were convinced that banks could do the job just as well as credit rating agencies. In other words, the analytical resources of credit rating agencies were more substitutable (through reliance on banks) for German regulators than for US public authorities. Remember that US authorities justified the late implementation of the Basel II provisions by reference to US banks' inability to quickly install the more complex requirements and procedures of Basel II. Interestingly, some US banking associations themselves favored the use of external ratings rather than pleading to be allowed to use their own internal ratings in the calculation of capital requirements: 'ICBA [Independent Community Bankers of America, A.K.] also agrees with the concept of using external credit ratings to enhance the risk sensitivity of the Basel I risk-based capital rules' (ICBA, quoted in Becker 2007: 90). Thus, while the essentiality of private analytical resources seems to have been high for both US and German regulators, the substitutability of these resources varied. There was, at least, a stronger belief on the part of German regulators that, as well as credit rating agencies, banks would be another reliable source of the uncertainty coping capabilities needed for the attainment of financial market stability and efficiency. Thus, credit rating agencies' uncertainty coping capabilities were more easily substitutable for German regulators; credit rating agencies' uncertainty coping capabilities would only be difficult to substitute in the case of less sophisticated, smaller banks. Given a high essentiality of uncertainty coping capabilities and a medium substitutability for German regulators, we would designate

German regulators' dependence on credit rating agencies' analytical resources as 'medium'. The medium value of the independent variable 'dependence on credit rating agencies' analytical resources' thus corresponds to Germany's position that internal ratings-based procedures for sophisticated banks should be included in the Basel II Accord as an alternative to credit rating agencies' external ratings. This is in line with the main hypothesis of the theoretical framework.

However, another important factor which influenced the German negotiators' position on the issue of appropriate rating procedures needs to be taken into account: the fear that exclusive reliance on private credit ratings would disadvantage small and medium-sized enterprises. In the German debate on Basel II, the issues of appropriate rating procedures and the impact of Basel II on small and medium-sized enterprises were closely linked. Due to their lower equity capital ratio, small and medium-sized enterprises usually obtain worse ratings than do other corporate firms (Hishow 2007: 4). Moreover, German small and medium-sized enterprises are not used to publicly disclosing their balance sheets. In contrast to most US firms, many German small and medium-sized enterprises simply do not have a credit rating, which would have been a clear disadvantage in a regulatory framework based exclusively on external ratings, since being 'unrated' would mean higher interest rates for small and medium-sized enterprises because of higher capital requirements for banks (Becker 2007: 90). Representatives of German small and medium-sized enterprises were opposed to provisions for credit-risk assessment based exclusively on credit ratings. They argued that German enterprises would be disadvantaged internationally, and German regulatory agencies and politicians (even German Chancellor Schröder) adopted this argument (Becker 2007: 89–91).

So, it is pretty clear that the cost–benefit calculation of German negotiators was influenced by concerns that the use of credit ratings in regulation would harm the competitiveness of economically and politically important actors ('Mittelstand' companies) of the German economy (Becker 2007: 92). What does this finding mean for the validity of the theoretical framework of this book? First of all, it seems that the causal mechanism proposed in Chapter 3 *correctly* conceives the decision to delegate (quasi-)regulatory authority to credit rating agencies as a cost–benefit calculation. However, at least as far as the Basel II process is concerned, it seems that negotiators feared that using credit ratings in regulation would harm important national economic players (small and medium-sized enterprises) and might even reduce international competitiveness. That was considered a more important 'cost' in German regulators' calculations than the potential for agency/control losses, which were identified in Chapter 3 as the major costs arising from delegation to credit rating agencies. In other words, there was another important determinant of German regulators' position in the Basel II negotiations that is not adequately captured by the proposed theoretical framework.

Yet, it is interesting to see that the fear of disadvantages for small and medium-sized enterprises, which seemed to play a crucial role in public regulators' cost–benefit analysis, is closely related to another key variable of this study, namely the condition variable 'variety-of-capitalism'. This implies that the theoretical framework could easily be modified to enhance its explanatory reach. The degree to which the use of credit ratings in regulation fits (or tends to run counter to) the macro-institutional financing structures in an economy seems to be an important determinant of the causal mechanism 'public regulators' cost–benefit analysis'. In the Basel II negotiations, there were (legitimate) concerns that extensive reliance on credit ratings in Basel II could undermine a core feature of the Rhenish variety of capitalism, namely small and medium-sized enterprises' access to 'patient' capital at reasonable cost. Exclusive reliance on credit ratings in Basel II would have changed the financing structure of many 'Mittelstand' companies significantly, since an expanded role of credit rating agencies would have led to a steep increase in small and medium-sized enterprises' credit costs (due to their 'problematic' credit-risk profile in the eyes of credit rating agencies) and thus made financing more difficult. Thus, a greater role for credit rating agencies in Basel II would have threatened a core component of the Rhenish variety of capitalism (Nölke and Perry 2007: 131).

6
Conclusion and Outlook: After the Crisis

Findings and implications of the book

This book has sought a theory-based explanation for the use of credit ratings in financial market regulation. For that purpose, a macro-institutionally embedded resource dependence perspective on the delegation of regulatory authority from public regulators private to credit rating agencies has been proposed: public regulators have delegated regulatory authority to credit rating agencies (in varying degrees) because (to varying extents) they have perceived themselves as dependent upon, and have sought to make use of, credit rating agencies' analytical resources. The dependence of public regulators on credit rating agencies' analytical resources is in turn conditioned by the prevailing global and national/regional macro-institutional socioeconomic contexts, that is, the global transformation of the financial architecture from embedded to disembedded liberalism and different national/regional varieties of capitalism.

The results of an intertemporal and interregional congruence analysis and a process-tracing exercise underlined the plausibility of the proposed theoretical framework. The core hypothesis, that the higher the degree of public regulators' dependence on credit rating agencies' analytical resources, the higher will be the degree of public regulators' use of credit ratings in regulation, has been corroborated. There has also been empirical evidence that public regulators' dependence on credit rating agencies' analytical resources is contingent on macro-institutional socioeconomic contexts on both global and national/regional levels. In particular, dependence on credit rating agencies' analytical resources and thus the use of ratings in financial market regulation seem to be systematically higher in the Anglo-Saxon variety of capitalism (liberal market economy) than in the Rhenish variety (coordinated market economy).

The main findings of this book also give rise to some open questions which call for further research. While the examination of the US and German positions in the Basel II negotiations has confirmed the core hypothesis of the proposed theoretical framework, it has also revealed that a slight modification (or supplementation) of the proposed theoretical framework might be in order: The decision whether or not to use credit ratings in financial regulation does indeed seem to be based on a (subjective) cost–benefit calculation: public regulators delegated regulatory authority to credit rating agencies if the perceived benefits were larger than the costs. However, there was no publicly available evidence that the loss of control over parts of financial regulation, or costs of control mechanisms to avoid agency slack on the part of credit rating agencies, played a significant role in public regulators' cost–benefit analysis. At least, the German position in the Basel II process seems to suggest that the degree to which the use of credit ratings in regulation fits or undermines prevalent macro-institutional modes of financing that are supported by both influential economic interest groups and public actors is an important determinant of the decision for or against the use of credit ratings in regulation. This is in line with the general argument that the condition variable 'macro-institutional socioeconomic context' affects public regulators' behavior when it comes to decisions for or against delegation of public tasks to private actors and when *specific types* of private actors are chosen. However, it might be that the variable 'macro-institutional socioeconomic context' does not only function as a condition variable affecting the independent variable 'dependence on credit rating agencies' analytical resources'. Rather, the degree to which the use of credit ratings fits the broader macro-institutional financing modes in an economy might directly influence public regulators' cost–benefit analysis. Quite obviously, more empirical research is needed on the interplay between macro-institutional settings and (micro-)behavior of public regulators – not only in the issue area of financial policies.

Further studies on the delegation of public tasks to credit rating agencies, and also to other private actors in different issue areas, could more extensively assess the explanatory merit of the proposed theoretical framework relative to alternative (critical neo-institutionalist or constructivist) approaches which conceive of privatization as a strategy to reduce political costs or as an ideology- and discourse-driven phenomenon (see Kruck 2010a, b). In a competitive test design, hypotheses from different theoretical perspectives could be taken into consideration. A research design which also tests alternative approaches would contribute to further specifying the explanatory value of the proposed theoretical framework and advancing our understanding of the transformation of governance.

Moreover, further research could systematically compare different types of principal–agent relationships between public and private actors. For example, as pointed out in Chapter 2, credit rating agencies have their own sources of genuinely private authority. The social fact that credit rating agencies are private authorities – not only by the grace of the state but also in their own right – differentiates them from other subordinate regulatory agencies which are created and funded by a public principal and whose political authority is *solely* delegated authority. This difference raises conceptual, theoretical and policy-related issues which merit closer comparative consideration.

Moreover, while principal–agent relationships always imply a hierarchy between principals and agents, in the empirical world there seem to exist different degrees of hierarchy between principals and agents. Relationships between public principals and private agents, in which public actors support and bolster the authority and governance capacities of private actors, can be more or less hierarchical (in a 'master–servant' way) on the one hand or horizontal (in a 'supporter and empowerer – helpful ally' way) on the other. The regulatory endorsement of private credit rating agencies by public actors seems to constitute a more horizontal type of principal–agent relationship than is usually assumed when the principal–agent framework is applied to phenomena of international and transnational politics. Further application of principal–agent theory to cases in which public tasks have been delegated to private actors seems worthwhile.

Regulatory change after the global financial crisis: preliminary assessment and tentative outlook

This book cannot conclude without a theoretically and empirically informed preliminary assessment and tentative outlook on regulatory changes after the US subprime and global financial crises (2007–10). In the search for the culprits for the financial market turmoil which started out as a US mortgage crisis in 2007 and evolved into the most severe global financial and economic crisis since the Second World War, credit rating agencies have become one of the main targets of criticism by both politicians and media. Indeed, credit rating agencies have contributed to the market turmoil by greatly underestimating the credit risk of complex structured finance products. Mortgage-backed collateralized debt obligations (CDOs) had been rated AAA despite poor underlying credit quality. Investors around the world relied on the very good credit ratings for these packaged securities and bought the mortgage-backed CDOs without being aware of the credit risks implied in those complex structured finance products. Credit rating agencies have been blamed for downgrading mortgage-backed securities far too late and for failing to develop adequate risk models to identify risks and value those products properly (*The Economist* 2007a). In fact, it is safe to argue that, by failing to evaluate these structured finance products properly and giving them the 'stamp of approval' concerning adequate protection against default risks, credit rating agencies have contributed to both the intensity and the geographical reach of the current financial crisis. This has raised (or rather revived) more general doubts about the factual and interpretive reliability of credit ratings and led to accusations that credit rating agencies faced a conflict of interest, because they earned fees for providing ratings for financial instruments from the originators of the packaged securities. Moreover, credit rating agencies have been criticized for an organizational overlap of their rating advisory and rating assessment units. The accusation was that sometimes analysts who advised issuers of a CDO on how to construct the structured finance product were also involved in rating the final product (Taylor 2008: 20; see also *The Economist* 2007a, b; Financial Times Deutschland 2007; Lowenstein 2008; Norris 2007, 2008; Osman 2007; Tomlinson and Evans 2007).

It is still difficult to make reliable statements on the long-term consequences of the financial crisis for both regulation *by* credit rating agencies and regulation *of* credit rating agencies. However, some recent regulatory developments in the US and the EU, and their implications for the validity of the theoretical framework proposed in this book, should be highlighted and assessed, even though the conclusions suggested here are necessarily tentative.

Financial market regulators are in the formal position to withdraw the (quasi-)regulatory authority they have bestowed upon credit rating agencies in the relevant regulations (e.g. national laws and regulations, supranational directives or the Basel II Accord) and thus to effect a partial 're-statification' of financial governance. Indeed, the involvement of credit rating agencies in the global financial crisis has led public regulators around the world to initiate stricter regulation *of* CRAs (Bohsem and Schieritz 2007) and propose rules amendments curbing regulation *by* credit ratings.

In reaction to the failures and shortcomings of credit rating agencies displayed in the financial crisis, the SEC proposed a set of interrelated rules (SEC 2008, 2009b) which aimed at limiting the influence of credit rating agencies in US financial market regulation, more precisely in securities regulation. This reflects the SEC's new position since the US subprime and global financial crisis (2007–10) that '[t]he official recognition of credit ratings for a variety of securities regulatory purposes may have played a role in investors' overreliance on CRAs' (SEC chairman Christopher Cox, quoted in Ackerman 2008). The SEC is not the only US supervisory body using credit ratings for regulatory purposes, and so far other bodies have not expressed any intent to change regulations relying on credit ratings. Nonetheless, the new SEC rule, passed as 'final rule' in October 2009 (SEC 2009b) significantly curbs the publicly sanctioned use of ratings for regulatory purposes in the US by stripping references to NRSROs from a number of SEC rules (Ackerman 2008; SEC 2008, 2009b). Stripping references to NRSROs from SEC rules entails a significant shift in terms of formal attribution of responsibility and an attempt to prod investors to conduct more credit analysis on their own. Since financial market actors are no longer *obliged* to rely on credit ratings to the same extent as before the crisis, responsibility for incorrect assessment of investment quality can formally be attributed more clearly to investors, rather than to credit rating agencies, whose legal liability is limited, or even to the SEC, which sanctioned the use of ratings but failed to clearly define responsibilities for grave failures in risk assessment. However, US regulators are well aware that the rule changes might not change much in terms of investors' actual reliance on NRSROs' ratings. In that vein, Erik Sirri, the SEC's director of trading and markets, said that the SEC rules provided investment firms with two paths – they could either continue to rely heavily on NRSROs or they could craft their own mechanisms to analyze investment quality: 'As a practical matter, I think the large number of broker-dealers ... will continue to make use of NRSRO ratings. But they *need not*' (Sirri, quoted in Ackerman 2008; my emphasis). The issue of ratings-dependent regulation has also been picked up in US President Barack Obama's initial 2009 plan for a general overhaul of the US financial system, which included a brief appeal to regulators to 'reduce' the regulatory use of ratings, and the final US Financial Market Reform Act of July 2010. Thus, despite considerable delays and initial hesitation, there has developed a tendency to reduce the regulatory use of credit ratings in the US financial system.

The option to stop or reduce using credit ratings for regulatory purposes was not only raised in the US. German financial policymakers threatened as early as summer 2007 that German supervisory authorities 'would either stop using the assessments of rating agencies, or we'll fold the rating agencies' voluntary [IOSCO] code of conduct into a reform by law', but also added that '[a] world without rating agencies is no longer conceivable. Banks, private investors and even supervisory authorities depend on the views of the [rating] evaluators' (Bernhardt, quoted in Reuters 2007). Stopping the use of ratings in national regulatory systems within the EU would be politically costly, since the regulatory use of credit ratings in Germany and other EU countries is based on the supranational Banking and Capital Adequacy Directives, which in turn incorporate the main Basel II provisions into EU law. Thus, a withdrawal from the use of credit ratings in one European country would require a number of difficult regulatory revisions on different political levels. In other words, the regulatory use of credit ratings has been institutionalized in a way that makes it hard, though certainly not impossible, to reverse the decision on the use of credit ratings. In September 2010 the core components of a new Basel III Accord, which reflects lessons learnt from the global financial crisis and demands higher core capital quotas from banks, were agreed. There was no decision to completely renounce the use of external ratings in the calculation of banks' capital reserve requirements. But note that Basel II already included internal rating procedures of banks as an alternative to the external rating of banks' credit risk exposure. It would be interesting to pursue the further development of the ratio between external and internal rating in banks' calculation of capital reserve requirements.

Regulatory initiatives for stronger oversight and control of the activities of credit rating agencies have been taken in both the US and the EU. The SEC has devised additional disclosure, transparency and reporting requirements for NRSROs (SEC 2009a) which go beyond the previous requirements of the Credit Agencies Reform Act 2006 and the concretizing 2007 SEC rules. On the EU level, even more stringent regulations were devised after European policymakers had come to the conclusion that the voluntary Code of Conduct issued by IOSCO (2004, revised in 2008) had not had the desired effects of ensuring the reliability and integrity of the rating business. Thus, a European Commission regulatory initiative, approved by the European Parliament in April 2009, put in place a European registration and external oversight regime for credit rating agencies whereby European regulators will supervise the policies and procedures followed by credit rating agencies active in Europe. Besides procedural provisions on the new mandatory registration process coordinated by the Committee of European Securities Regulators (CESR), the Regulation also imposed further regulatory requirements on credit rating agencies, including measures to prevent conflicts of interests through in-house rotation, disclosure requirements concerning the risks models of credit rating agencies, their rating methods and basic assumptions, a ban on rating consultancy services for companies that are to be rated, and the issuance of transparency reports that list major customers and outline the measures taken by the agency to ensure the quality of its ratings.

Even more fundamentally, in the wake of the global financial crisis the Anglo-Saxon financial market governance model has come under fire. There has been growing disenchantment in Europe with the US financial system, which includes criticism of both particular financial market policies and, in a broader sense, the Anglo-Saxon model of financial market governance (Dieter 2008: 13–14). For some European politicians, the US assumption that an increasing securitization of credits and a growing use of financial derivatives should lead to a better assessment of risk by private financial market actors who are most competent and have the right incentives to handle the risks properly has proven dubious. Rather, some European policymakers have concluded that financial markets have become less transparent and thus more prone to crises, that financial innovations have led to a growing confusion among market participants, and that many investors no longer understand the risks inherent in complex financial products (Dieter 2008: 14). In this context, European politicians such as German Chancellor Angela Merkel have pointed to weaknesses of the US Anglo-Saxon financial market model and argued that Continental Europe should actively work towards devising new rules for financial markets because 'the Anglo-Saxon model of regulation has failed' (Merkel, in Barber et al. 2008; Süddeutsche Zeitung 2008).

It will certainly take more time before the depth and pervasiveness of regulatory reform of financial markets on national or even international levels can be evaluated. What seems clear now is that regulatory measures to ensure stricter public oversight and control of credit rating agencies have been passed and will be implemented in the foreseeable future. In the wake of the global financial crisis, public regulation of credit rating agencies' activities has increased in the EU and in the US. As far as the future use of credit ratings in financial regulation is concerned, the picture is less clear. Nonetheless, the SEC rules curbing the use of credit ratings in securities regulation (SEC 2009b) seem to suggest that there is a tendency to reduce, rather than maintain or even expand, the regulatory use of credit ratings after the global crisis.

These policy responses to credit rating agencies' role in the crisis call for a theoretically informed analysis of the future use of credit ratings in financial regulation. On the following pages I examine to what extent the theoretical model developed in this book can help to make sense of observable developments, and engage in some theoretically and empirically informed speculation on the future role of CRAs in financial governance after the crisis (see Kruck 2010b).

From the perspective of the theoretical model, the establishment of stricter registration and control mechanisms for credit rating agencies appears as a logical and likely policy response. It corresponds to principal–agent theory's assumption that principals will design and implement control mechanisms to prevent agency slack. It also fits in with the trend to (modestly) tighten selection criteria and procedures for the recognition of credit rating agencies for regulatory purposes which had started even before the 2007 US mortgage crisis. The US Credit Rating Agencies Reform Act of 2006 and the 2006 EU and German implementation of Basel II are cases in point. As credit rating agencies have obviously displayed behavior undesired by public regulators, regulators have corrected their erroneous assumption that market discipline and reputational concerns would render tight public oversight of credit rating agencies' behavior unnecessary. From that perspective, introducing a control regime for credit rating agencies is merely the correction of a previous failure to design adequate administrative and oversight procedures, given the impact credit rating agencies make, due partly to their status as holders of state-sanctioned regulatory authority.

The propositions of the model are more complicated when it comes to stripping references to credit ratings from financial regulations. Assuming that neither the essentiality nor the substitutability of credit rating agencies' analytical resources for public regulators should have changed significantly, we should not expect substantial cuts in the use of credit ratings in financial regulation. Decisions to curb the use of credit ratings in US financial regulation as taken by the SEC (2009b) would therefore appear puzzling from the perspective of resource dependence theory. However, things are more nuanced than that. There are several lines of argument which help us to make sense of a reduction of the use of credit ratings in regulation from the perspective of the proposed theoretical model.

The analytical resources of credit rating agencies are less stable than material resources, 'since they may be severely affected by perceived rating miscalls. Thus, the reputation as global experts for debt quality, which has been accumulated by rating agencies over decades, may be eroded quickly' (Nölke 2004: 167). In consequence, relationships based on dependence on credit rating agencies' analytical resources should also be less stable and more vulnerable to interruption or even termination when the belief of public regulators in the quality of credit rating agencies' expertise is eroded by their failure to adequately assess credit risk. In the terms of (inter-) organizational research, public regulators, which are conceived as rational organizations, may decide to terminate their reliance on other, external, organizations, in this case credit rating agencies, when the resources which these external organizations control prove inadequate for organizational goal attainment (financial market stability through adequate credit risk assessment). This may occur even though the kind of analytical resources these external organizations were presumed to offer are still important for public regulators and difficult to get elsewhere. As outlined in Chapter 3, this argument reflects assumptions of earlier organization theorists (Hickson et al. 1994: 198): Only if an organization can *effectively* manage the uncertainty that confronts another organization, and in doing so protect the other organization from disturbing effects in organizational task achievement, will the external organization's resources for coping with uncertainty become the basis of a continued dependence relation. Once an interorganizational relationship has been established, *the ongoing performance* of an external organization in the provision of crucial and hardly substitutable (analytical) resources must be considered another determinant of resource dependence in general and of public regulators' use of credit ratings in particular.

Moreover, the essentiality of credit rating agencies' analytical resources depends on the regulatory objectives of public agencies. In the case of public regulators, these goals were assumed to be both financial market stability and efficiency. Now, it is not self-evident that financial market stability and efficiency necessarily go hand in hand, even though proponents of financial market liberalization would like to have it that way. After a major financial crisis such as the current one, public regulators might well focus on designing more rigorous rules that seek to ensure, first and foremost, financial market stability, even if that would entail some losses in terms of financial market efficiency by imposing higher capital costs on financial market actors. While the use of credit ratings was intended to serve the purpose of designing risk-sensitive, sophisticated and thus efficient regulation, public regulators might intentionally opt for a less flexible and less market-friendly, but more restrictive, regulatory approach that deliberately foregoes some of the efficiency gains from flexible regulation in favor of more stability (i.e. protection against major crises). In this case, the essentiality of credit rating agencies' analytical resources and thus the propensity to use credit ratings in financial regulation might be reduced.

Thus, the theoretical model proposed in this book would lead us to expect that public regulators will prefer to impose stricter registration and control mechanisms for credit rating agencies rather than completely renounce the regulatory use of credit ratings. However, the latter option cannot be ruled out if regulators hold the firm conviction that credit rating agencies' analytical resources are of little help and/or no longer necessary to achieve their (changed) regulatory goals. While at first sight one might expect that this conviction should indeed have taken ground among regulators after credit rating agencies' dismal performance in the financial crisis, the empirical evidence is less conclusive so far. In the midst of the crisis, some politicians have continued to claim that not only banks and private investors, but also supervisory authorities, depend on the views of the private evaluators. However, there are indications that disillusionment with credit rating agencies' reliability and integrity has grown over time in the US Administration and in the European Commission (see Taylor 2008). This corresponds to the slow and rather hesitant advancement of US regulatory initiatives to reduce the regulatory use of credit ratings.

Of necessity, these concluding thoughts are still somewhat speculative. It will certainly take more time for a clearer picture of the regulatory consequences of the global financial crisis to emerge. While stricter public oversight of credit rating agencies seems certain, the future extent of the use of credit ratings in regulation is doubtful. Besides the growing salience of Asian varieties of capitalism, even a (partial) reversal of the global macro-institutional trend towards an Anglo-Saxon model of finance seems possible right now, which, according to the theoretical argument of this book, would imply a decrease, or at least no further increase, in the use of credit ratings as regulatory tools.

In this very fluid situation, this book has offered a synthetic theoretical model of ratings-dependent regulation. This model should not only help to account for intertemporal and interregional variations in the regulatory use of credit ratings. Perhaps even more significantly, the macro-institutionally embedded resource dependence perspective on delegation to private actors advanced in this book could be useful for a wide range of situations in which public actors have transferred political authority to private actors. It could thus contribute to a better, theoretically grounded understanding of the ongoing transformation of governance and the advanced western OECD state.

Notes

1 Introduction: Private Ratings and Public Purposes

1. Broadly speaking, the term 'governance' refers to purposive mechanisms steering social systems towards their goals and can thus be understood as a process of intentional creation (and implementation) of political order, that is, of rule systems that facilitate the coordination and cooperation of social actors and determine the distribution of the costs and benefits of collective action (Koenig-Archibugi 2006: 3; Rosenau 1992: 3; Trebesch 2008: 8). According to Rittberger (2008: 1–2), 'governance' can be more precisely defined as collective action which claims authority and is aimed at dealing with common problems and producing public goods. Governance refers to identifying promising and sustainable approaches to solve societal problems, translating these approaches into rules of conduct, ensuring adherence to these rules and, where necessary, adjusting these rules to changing circumstances (see also Rittberger 2004: 247–9). *Global* governance refers to governance aimed at dealing with transsovereign, (potentially) *global* problems and producing *global* public goods.
2. The terms 'nonstate actors' and 'private actors' are used interchangeably in this book. 'Transnational actors' denotes private actors that operate across borders. The term 'public actors' refers to states such as the US and specific state institutions such as national financial market regulatory authorities, as well as to intergovernmental organizations (such as the International Monetary Fund) and international committees of national regulatory bodies (e.g. the Basel Committee on Banking Supervision). The Basel Committee on Banking Supervision (BCBS) is, strictly speaking, not an intergovernmental organization in its own right, since it is embedded in the institutional framework, and supported by the secretariat, of the Bank for International Settlements (BIS). Nevertheless, the BCBS is treated as a collective public actor in this book (Macht 2007: 28–30, 54–6; Schwarcz 2001b: 6).
3. Note that the term 'public regulator' is used here in a broad sense that also includes the international standard-setter BCBS, which does not issue immediately binding rules but, rather, international standards that are supposed to guide the creation and implementation of binding national rules.
4. Collateralized debt obligations (CDOs) can be conceived of as funds in which large numbers of credits of different qualities are pooled and sold on (global) capital markets as a package. Technically speaking, CDOs are securities that are backed by a portfolio of diverse assets (e.g. mortgages). These assets are divided into different tranches with varying degrees of

default risk ('senior', 'mezzanine', 'junior', 'first-loss piece'). Credit rating agencies rate those tranches and offer assessments of the default risk of CDOs. The complexity and lack of transparency of CDOs have been considered to be one of the main reasons for the global repercussions of the US mortgage crisis (*The Economist* 2007a, b; Norris 2007; Tomlinson and Evans 2007).

5. Apart from some early seminal studies on credit rating agencies' activities, the credit rating industry structure and credit rating agencies' functions in financial markets, which were published by scholars of economics in the early and mid-1990s (Cantor and Packer 1994; Everling 1991), it was not until the late 1990s that credit rating agencies attracted broader scholarly interest. The controversial role of credit rating agencies in the Asian financial crisis (1997/98) and the Enron bankruptcy (2001) was a catalytic event sparking a scholarly and, to a more limited extent, also a political discussion on the factual and interpretive reliability of credit rating agencies and their role and function in financial markets (Gras 2003: 3–4; Rosenbaum 2004: 10; see also Hunt 2002; Lieberman 2002). Observers argue that credit rating agencies downgraded sovereign ratings of some Asian countries far too late (Fuchs 2005: 125). In the context of the Enron bankruptcy, credit rating agencies assigned excellent credit quality assessments to the company up to the day before it went bankrupt (Gerke and Mager 2005: 203; Wyatt 2002). Research has not only focused on the performance of credit rating agencies in credit risk assessment in the context of specific financial crises (e.g. the Asian crisis, the financial crises in Argentine and Turkey in 2001) and large corporate bankruptcies (e.g. Enron, WorldCom in 2002, Parmalat in 2002). Scholars have also investigated credit rating agencies' more general track record in contributing to a sound and efficient global financial system (see e.g. Adams et al. 1999; Coleman 1999; Estrella et al. 2000; Gerke and Mager 2005; Gonzalez et al. 2004; Levich et al. 2002; Partnoy 1999).
6. These pathologies include the oligopolistic market structure of the rating industry; the business model of credit rating agencies, which provides that in most cases issuers of bonds (i.e. the rated entities) pay for the credit rating; and potential conflicts of interest that might result from this business model, as well as the organizational overlap between rating assessment and rating advisory units in credit rating agencies (Reuters Bloomberg 2008; Zydra 2008).
7. Principal–agent theory was originally developed in economics to illustrate agency problems arising from information asymmetries (Arrow 1985; Richter and Furubotn 2003). In political science, principal–agent theory was first applied to the analysis of the US domestic political system (Hawkins et al. 2006b: 3–4). However, in the past few years, studies have proliferated that transfer principal–agent theory to the realm of international relations and apply it to the analysis of delegation of competences from states to intergovernmental, and in particular supranational, organizations (Hawkins et al. 2006a; Mutschler 2008; Pollack 1997, 2003; Tallberg 2002).

Principal–agent theory can also be used to analyze the delegation of governance tasks to private nonstate actors such as civil society organizations or business firms (Hawkins et al. 2006b: 11). Moreover, principal–agent theory has already been used to illuminate credit rating agencies' deficits of accountability (Kerwer 2005; Smith and Walter 2001). Furthermore, scholars of comparative politics have employed principal–agent theory to analyze transformations of governance in Western European countries induced by 'non-majoritarian institutions', that is, public or private entities 'that a) possess and exercise some grant of specialised public authority, separate from that of other institutions, but b) are neither directly elected by the people, nor directly managed by elected officials' (Thatcher and Stone Sweet 2002: 2; see also Thatcher 2002). They found that, in the past 50 years, states, executives and parliaments have empowered an increasing number of non-majoritarian institutions to make public policy.

8. Ideas from resource dependence theory inform a number of studies on public–private cooperation on both national and transnational levels (Edele 2006: 51–2). Resource exchange theory has been applied to account for the proliferation of public–private partnerships within domestic settings (Börzel 1998: 263–4; Jansen 1993). Benner et al. (2004: 196) describe global public–private partnerships as 'mechanisms that facilitate the transfer and use of... resources of various actors in the global public policy-making process'. Börzel and Risse (2005: 14) explicitly refer to the mutual resource dependence of public and private actors at the international level and state that 'in those areas in which public actors control only limited material and ideational resources, nonstate actors are said to come to the rescue.' Kaul (2006: 229) argues that global public–private partnerships are established because they allow actors involved to 'capitalize on the differences between public and private actors – differences in incentive structures, competencies, and assets. They trade, pool, and match in often innovative ways the comparative advantage that partners offer'. Take (2001: 240) claims that the emergence of more and more private actors endowed with resources relevant for the solution of common problems, and the decreasing governance capacity of states, renders the establishment of alliances between governmental, international and societal actors increasingly likely. Brühl (2003: 186–230) contends that the extended but varying participation rights of civil society organizations in multilateral environment negotiations can be accounted for by the 'situation-specific resource demand' of states. Brühl models the inclusion of civil society organizations in international environmental negotiations as interorganizational resource exchange, arguing that, while civil society organizations provide knowledge, power and values, states offer them participation rights. However, only a few studies (Edele 2006; Liese 2009; Nölke 2000) explicitly refer to resource exchange theory, and they present their theoretical framework in detail in order to subsequently adapt it to the study of the formation of public–private modes of governance.
9. Generally speaking, a model is 'a simplification of, and approximation to, some aspects of the world' (King et al. 1994: 50). It is a simplified abstract

reproduction of the real world that highlights some crucial aspects of the real world (Brühl 2003: 170). A heuristic model can be understood as a 'what-model', since it answers questions like: 'What are the relevant elements of the real world that are to be explained? What are the central concepts for the description of reality? What is the empirical problem in more abstract conceptual terms?' The heuristic conceptual model is pre-theoretic in that it contains no substantial testable hypotheses and no causal relationships. It is the beginning of the analytical scientific process, since it is formed in a reflective way, orders singular empirical observations by providing more abstract concepts and categories, and lays the conceptual basis for further methodologically sound explanatory research (Brühl 2003: 177; Schimmelfennig 1995: 20–2).

10. A causal–theoretical model answers 'why-questions', that is, it provides explanations for *why* the phenomenon described and conceptualized in accordance with a heuristic conceptual model has occurred (Opp 1995; Schimmelfennig 1995: 21–2; Spinner 1974; Wenturius et al. 1992: 369).
11. In fact, there are – so far undiscovered or at least unexplicated – 'points of contact' *inherent* in any one of the theoretical and conceptual approaches to be used in this study (principal–agent theory, resource dependence theory, embedded and disembedded liberalism and varieties-of-capitalism approach) that allow or even call for systematically connecting these approaches. This means that the explanation proposed by principal–agent theorists for the delegation of authority to *specialized agents* is implicitly based on causal assumptions of resource dependence that have been explicated by resource dependence theory. This book makes these underlying hypotheses from resource dependence theory explicit, operationalizable and testable. In a similar way, resource dependence theory, which is a theory taken from (intra- and inter-)organizational research, can easily and theoretically plausibly be linked to structural environmental approaches in organizational theory which claim that resource dependence, and thus the formation of interorganizational relationships, is a function of the macro-institutional context of the relevant organizations (see Chapter 3; Blau 1987). From that vantage point, the argumentative step to introducing different global financial architectures (embedded vs. disembedded liberalism) and different national/regional varieties of capitalism (Rhenish vs. Anglo-Saxon varieties of capitalism) as different macro-institutional contexts, which in turn lead to varying degrees of resource dependence, is a small and plausible one.

2 The Regulatory Use of Credit Ratings: Overview and Conceptualization

1. The scale of symbols used for short-term ratings differs. However, it is long-term ratings that are usually employed in financial regulation, so the short-term rating scale can be neglected in this book.
2. A 'D' with S&P's even indicates that there is already a credit default.

3. In this book, I consistently use S&P's rating scale when referring to regulatory requirements.
4. In particular, operational risk has often been responsible for banking crises. Operational risk refers to the 'danger of losses, which occur due to inadequacy or failure of internal procedures, human beings and systems or because of an external shock' (definition of the BCBS, quoted in Becker 2007: 82). There were no capital reserve requirements for operational risks under Basel I.

3 The Theoretical Model: An Embedded Resource Dependence View on Delegation

1. The dependent variable 'use of private credit ratings by public regulators' – also when it is cast in more abstract terms of delegation of governance tasks and regulatory authority from principals to agents – designates an *action* rather than an *interaction*. This implies that the theoretical argument can only be one of resource *dependence* rather than one of resource *exchange*. (See below for a more detailed discussion on the applicability of resource dependence theory rather than resource exchange theory.)
2. Hawkins et al. (2006b: 4–5) have shown that quite often the causes of delegation to international organizations are remarkably similar to those of delegation in domestic politics. This implies that hypotheses on the reasons for delegation in domestic settings might also apply to delegation in the international realm. This is fortunate, because I seek to explain delegation of quasi-regulatory authority to credit rating agencies on both national and inter-/supranational levels.
3. While Majone (2001) and Alter (2008) hold that principal–trustee relationships refer to qualitatively distinct phenomena that should be kept apart, conceptually also, from principal–agent relationships, Pollack (2003: 29–31) argues that principal–agent theory is broad enough to encompass delegation for both informational (effectiveness-enhancing) *and* credible commitments (legitimacy-enhancing) reasons. Based on the conceptualization of 'trust' and 'trustees' in the legal literature, one might conclude that all trustees are agents but not all agents are trustees: a trustee is an agent and something more (Bogert 1987: 36; Majone 2001: 113). At any rate, what is important is that delegation – and discretion granted to agents (or 'trustees') – might follow very different rationales. In the following, the term 'principal–agent theory' is used in a broad sense as an overarching conception that encompasses Alter's and Majone's principal–trustee theory.
4. The 'classic' rational actor (*homo oeconomicus*) model assumes that actors pursue exogenously given interests and preferences in a utility-maximizing way. Actors follow a logic of consequentiality: in order to attain given goals in a cost-efficient way, actors calculate the costs and

benefits of alternative behavioral options and choose the behavioral option with the most favorable cost–benefit ratio, that is, the one that yields the highest net benefit (Brühl 2003: 195–6; March and Olson 1989: 23, 160).

5. Organizational effectiveness is defined as the organization's ability to create acceptable outcomes and actions, whereas efficiency is measured by the ratio of resources utilized to output produced (Pfeffer and Salancik 2003: 11).
6. Parsons defines an organization as 'a special type of social system organized about the primacy of interests in the attainment of a particular type of system goal' (Parsons 1951: 64).
7. In fact, quite diverse relationships between business enterprises (e.g. mergers, joint ventures and cartels) and between social service organizations (e.g. voluntary agency federations or joint programs) have been analyzed as interorganizational relationships (see Aldrich 1979; Pfeffer and Nowak 1976; Pfeffer and Salancik 2003; Oliver 1990).
8. There is some confusion in interorganizational research over the use of the terms 'resource exchange theory', 'resource dependence theory' and 'power dependence theory'. Some authors explain actual resource exchange processes with recourse to 'resource dependence theory'; many do not conceptually separate resource dependence and resource exchange arguments; others introduce power dependence theory as an alternative explanation for the establishment of interorganizational relationships in contrast to resource exchange theory; some equate resource dependence theory with power dependence theory (see Aldrich 1975; 1979; Cook 1994; Cook et al. 1994; Pfeffer and Salancik 2003; Ulrich and Barney 1984). For an overview of different theoretical approaches in interorganizational research see Jansen (1993: 98). In this book, resource dependence theory is conceived as a theory of action that makes use of the same basic resource dependence argument for the establishment of relationships between organizations, except only that it is cast in one-way rather than mutual dependence terms; the focus is on a situation where the active consent of the external organization is not a prerequisite for the establishment of an interorganizational relationship.
9. The moral authority of civil society organizations is a resource which is increasingly sought after by states. The inclusion of civil society organizations in multilateral negotiations is considered a means to enhance the overall legitimacy of an international institution, due to civil society organizations' moral authority in the eyes of the broader public and the (appearance of) transparency and democracy that is created with their inclusion (Brühl 2003: 205).
10. British and US banks in London attempted to circumvent existing controls on the movement of capital for their international financial business. While British banks began to conduct their international financial affairs in US dollars, American banks transferred their international financial affairs to London. Since British controls on the movement of capital dealt only with deals in sterling and American controls applied only to deals in the US, this created a financial

center in London, allowing a largely unregulated movement of capital (Rittberger and Zangl 2006: 162; Eichengreen 1996: 93–152; Helleiner 1994: 81–122).

11. IMF loans were insufficient to counter these attacks effectively, especially as speculation was directed at the dollar as well. The US faced a dilemma and could do little about it. If it had reduced its balance-of-payments deficits, which began to show up in the 1950s, international trade relations would have suffered lasting damage, since international trade would have lost the liquidity the deficits provided. But, due to the US continuing its policy of balance-of-payments deficits, the US dollar lost its gold-standard-parity credibility (Rittberger and Zangl 2006: 162).
12. The analysis of different national/regional macro-institutional contexts also refers to the debate on the convergence or divergence of global economic governance strategies in the age of economic globalization (see e.g. Schirm 2004b; Schirm et al. 2007; Strange 1996). While there is growing consensus that globalization has not led to a general convergence of economic policies, there are indicators that the global liberalization and deregulation of financial markets has indeed created considerable pressures in favor of adaptation to the 'Anglo-Saxon' capital market model (see Chapter 4 and Lütz 2000; 2004; Lütz and Eberle 2007).
13. The varieties-of-capitalism approach has drawn criticism for being a Western-centric approach that has not so far been applied to Asian countries (Hoffmann 2003: 129). Nonetheless, I think that the varieties-of-capitalism approach is not only useful for the specific purposes of this book, whose focus is mainly on the US and the EU; it can also be adapted and applied to economies other than those of the Western hemisphere (see Nölke and Vliegenthart 2009).

4 Explaining Trend and Variation in the Regulatory Use of Credit Ratings

1. For instance, Gourevitch (1996) has convincingly shown that the US has not always been the prototype of Anglo-Saxon capitalism; rather, there were points in time when the US was close to becoming a coordinated market economy. The clear orientation towards an Anglo-Saxon type of capitalism was a matter of political choice (in particular made in the 1980s).
2. Derivatives are financial instruments whose value changes in response to changes in underlying assets. The diverse range of potential underlying assets and payoff alternatives leads to a wide range of derivatives contracts available to be traded in the market. Derivatives make it possible to diversify and spread risks among a larger number of actors – which can indeed be a desirable thing; however, it also entails considerable risks. Derivatives imply betting on the development of prices; if the bet does not work out the way it was presumed, buyers of derivatives suffer severe losses, which in turn are frequently transmitted to other market participants (Filc 2008: 6).

3. There is in fact no *one* European regulatory system. Banking regulation and supervision in Europe is ultimately a matter of various national supervisory bodies working in conjunction with EU-level supervisory bodies.

5 Making Sense of the Role of External Ratings in Basel II

1. In addition to the official negotiators, representatives from both the US and German governments (e.g. from the Department of the Treasury) occasionally interfered with the negotiations (Becker 2007: 83–4).
2. The G-30 consists of the ministers of finance and the central bank directors of the G-8 and emerging economies (such as Argentina, Brazil, China, India, Mexico, etc.). The G-30 deals with the revision of existing guidelines and standards for financial market supervision and consults on measures for the prevention of financial crises.
3. In Germany, the Basel II provisions (as well as the 2010 Basel III standards) do indeed apply to all banks; it remains to be seen how the US will handle the issue of applicability once implementation of the new Basel III provisions starts in the US.

References

Abbott, Kenneth W. and Duncan Snidal (1998) 'Why States Act Through Formal International Organizations', *Journal of Conflict Resolution* 42: 1, 3–32.

Ackerman, Andrew (2008) 'SEC Votes to Remove NRSRO from 38 Rules', *The Bond Buyer Online*, http://www.bondbuyer.com/article.html?id=20080625YA9RHPDA, date accessed September 15, 2008.

Adams, Charles, Donald J. Mathieson and Garry Schinasi (1999) *International Capital Markets: Developments, Prospects, and Key Policy Issues*, Washington, DC: International Monetary Fund.

Aldrich, Howard E. (1975) 'An Organization-Environment Perspective on Cooperation and Conflict between Organizations in the Manpower Training System', in Anant R. Neghandi (ed.) *Interorganization Theory*, Kent, OH: Kent State University Press, 49–70.

Aldrich, Howard E. (1979) *Organizations and Environments*, Englewood Cliffs, NJ: Prentice Hall.

Aldrich, Howard E. and Jeffrey Pfeffer (1976) 'Environments of Organizations', *Annual Review of Sociology* 2: 79–105.

Alter, Karen J. (2008) 'Agents or Trustees? International Courts in their Political Context', *European Journal of International Relations* 14: 1, 33–63.

Archer, Candace C., Glen Biglaiser and Karl De Rouen (2007) 'Sovereign Bonds and the "Democratic Advantage": Does Regime Type Affect Credit Rating Agency Ratings in the Developing World?' *International Organization* 61: 2, 341–65.

Arrow, Kenneth J. (1985) 'The Economics of Agency', in John W. Pratt and Richard J. Zeckhauser (eds.) *Principals and Agents: The Structure of Business*, Boston, MA: Harvard Business School Press, 37–51.

Asian Development Bank (ADB) (2001) *Development of Credit Rating Agencies*. Background Paper for the Second Workshop on the Development of CRAs in the APEC Region, http://www.adb.org/APEC/cra/cra.pdf, date accessed August 31, 2008.

Asmussen, Jörg (2005) 'Rating-Agenturen und Finanzaufsicht', *Betriebswirtschaftliche Forschung und Praxis (BFuP)* 57: 3, 246–55.

Barber, Lionel, Bertrand Benoit and Hugh Williamson (2008) 'Regulation Model Has Failed, Merkel Says', *Financial Times.com*, June10, http://www.ft.com/cms/s/0/1f436388-371e-11dd-bc1c-0000779fd2ac.html, date accessed June 11, 2008.

Basel Committee on Banking Supervision (BCBS) (1999a) *Capital Requirements and Bank Behaviour: The Impact of the Basel Accord*, Basel: Bank for International Settlements.

Basel Committee on Banking Supervision (BCBS) (1999b) *A New Capital Adequacy Framework: 1st Consultative Paper Issued by the Basel Committee on Banking Supervision*, June, Basel: Bank for International Settlements.

Basel Committee on Banking Supervision (BCBS) (2001) *2nd Consultative Document: Overview of the New Basel Capital Accord*, January, Basel: Bank for International Settlements.

Basel Committee on Banking Supervision (BCBS) (2003) *3rd Consultative Document: Overview of the New Basel Capital Accord*, April, Basel: Bank for International Settlements.

Basel Committee on Banking Supervision (BCBS) (2006) *International Convergence of Capital Measurement and Capital Standards: A Revised Framework – Comprehensive Edition*, Basel: Bank for International Settlements.

Becker, Maren (2007) 'Interessen, Normen und nationale Positionen zu globalen Finanzmärkten: Fallstudie zum Basel II Abkommen über Standards für Banken', in Stefan A. Schirm, Maren Becker and Stephanie John (eds.) *Der Einfluss endogener Interessen und Normen auf nationale Positionen zur Global Economic Governance*, Final Report on the DFG Research Project 'Global Economic Governance', December, Bochum, 80–96.

Benner, Thorsten, Wolfgang H. Reinicke and Jan Martin Witte (2004) 'Multisectoral Networks in Global Governance: Towards a Pluralistic System of Accountability', *Government and Opposition* 39: 1, 191–210.

Bennett, Andrew and Alexander L. George (2005) *Case Studies and Theory Development in the Social Sciences*, Cambridge, MA: MIT Press.

Benson, J. Kenneth (1994) 'The Interorganizational Network as a Political Economy', in John Scott (ed.) *Power: Critical Concepts*, Vol. III, London: Routledge, 103–26.

Bernstein, Steven and Benjamin Cashore (2008) 'The Two-Level Logic of Non-State Market Driven Global Governance', in Volker Rittberger and Martin Nettesheim (eds.) *Authority in the Global Political Economy*, Basingstoke: Palgrave Macmillan, 276–313.

Bieling, Hans-Jürgen (2007) *Internationale Politische Ökonomie: Eine Einführung*, Wiesbaden: VS Verlag für Sozialwissenschaften.

Biersteker, Thomas J. (1992) 'The "Triumph" of Neoclassical Economics in the Developing World: Policy Convergence and Bases of Governance in the International Economic Order', in James Rosenau and Ernst-Otto Czempiel (eds.) *Governance without Government: Order and Change in World Politics*, Cambridge: Cambridge University Press, 102–31.

Blau, Peter M. (1987) 'Microprocess and Macrostructure', in Karen Cook (ed.) *Social Exchange Theory*, London: Sage, 83–100.

Bogert, George T. (1987) *Trusts*, 6th edition, St. Paul, MN: West Publishing.

Bohsem, Guido and Mark Schieritz (2007) 'G7 wollen transparentere Ratings', *Financial Times Deutschland*, October 9, http://www.ftd.de/politik/international/263168.html?mode=print, date accessed July 13, 2008.

Börzel, Tanja (1998) 'Organizing Babylon: On the Different Conceptions of Policy Networks', *Public Administration* 76: 253–73.

Börzel, Tanja and Thomas Risse (2005) 'Public-Private Partnerships: Effective and Legitimate Tools of Transnational Governance?' in Edgar Grande and Louis W. Pauly (eds.) *Complex Sovereignty: On the Reconstitution of Political Authority in the 21st Century*, Toronto, ON: University of Toronto Press, 195–216.

Bottini, Francis A. (1993) 'An Examination of the Current Status of Rating Agencies and Proposals for Limited Oversight of Such Agencies', *San Diego Law Review* 30: 3, 579–620.

Botzem, Sebastian (2008) 'Transnational Expert-Driven Standardisation: Accountancy Governance from a Professional Point of View', in Jean-Christophe Graz and Andreas Nölke (eds.) *Transnational Private Governance and its Limits*, London: Routledge, 44–57.

Brühl, Tanja (2003) *Nichtregierungsorganisationen als Akteure internationaler Umweltverhandlungen: Ein Erklärungsmodell auf der Basis der situationsspezifischen Ressourcennachfrage*, Frankfurt/M.: Campus.

Bruner, Christopher M. and Abdelal Rawi (2005) 'To Judge Leviathan: Sovereign Credit Ratings, National Law, and the World Economy', *Public Policy* 25: 2, 191–217.

Brunsson, Nils (2002a) 'Organizations, Markets and Standardization', in Nils Brunsson and Bengt Jacobsson (eds.) *A World of Standards*, Oxford: Oxford University Press, 21–39.

Brunsson, Nils (2002b) 'Standardization and Uniformity', in Nils Brunsson and Bengt Jacobsson (eds.) *A World of Standards*, Oxford: Oxford University Press, 138–50.

Brunsson, Nils and Bengt Jacobsson (2002a) 'The Contemporary Expansion of Standardization', in Nils Brunsson and Bengt Jacobsson (eds.) *A World of Standards*, Oxford: Oxford University Press, 1–17.

Brunsson, Nils and Bengt Jacobsson (2002b) 'Following Standards', in Nils Brunsson and Bengt Jacobsson (eds.) *A World of Standards*, Oxford: Oxford University Press, 125–37.

Brunsson, Nils and Bengt Jacobsson (2002c) 'The Pros and Cons of Standardization – An Epilogue', in Nils Brunsson and Bengt Jacobsson (eds.) *A World of Standards*, Oxford: Oxford University Press, 169–73.

Buiter, Willem (2007) 'Basel II: Back to the Drawing Board?' *Financial Times.com*, September 21, http://blogs.ft.com/maverecon/2007/09/basel-ii-back-t.html, date accessed June 15, 2008.

Bundgard-Pederson, Torben (1997) *The Europeanization of Standardization: Technical Standards and Multi Level Governance in Europe*, Copenhagen: Copenhagen University.

Busch, Andreas (2000) '"Economic Governance" in angelsächsischen Demokratien', in André Kaiser (ed.) *Regieren in Westminster-Demokratien*, Baden-Baden: Nomos, 59–73.

Busch, Andreas (2005) 'Globalisation and National Varieties of Capitalism: The Contested Viability of the "German Model"', in Kenneth Dyson and Stephen Padgett (eds.) *The Politics of Economic Reform in Germany: Global, Rhineland or Hybrid Capitalism?* Special Issue of *German Politics* 14: 2, 125–39.

Cantor, Richard (2001) 'Moody's Investors Service Response to the Consultative Paper Issued by the Basel Committee on Banking Supervision "A New Capital Adequacy Framework"', *Journal of Banking & Finance* 25: 1, 171–85.

Cantor, Richard and Frank Packer (1994) 'The Credit Rating Industry', *Federal Reserve Bank of New York Quarterly Review* 19: 2, 1–26.

Cerny, Philip G. (1994) 'The Dynamics of Financial Globalization: Technology, Market Structure and Policy Response', *Policy Sciences* 27: 4, 319–42.

Champsaur, Amelie (2005) *The Regulation of Credit Rating Agencies in the U.S. and the EU: Recent Initiatives and Proposals*, LL.M. Paper at Harvard Law School, Cambridge, MA: Harvard Law School.

Coates, David (ed.) (2005) *Varieties of Capitalism, Varieties of Approaches*, Basingstoke: Palgrave Macmillan.

Coleman, William D. (1999) *Private Governance and Democracy in International Finance*, Globalization Working Paper Series 99/3, Hamilton, ON: McMaster University, Institute on Globalization and the Human Condition.

Collier, David (1993) 'The Comparative Method', in Ada W. Finifter (ed.) *Political Science: The State of the Discipline II*, Washington, DC: American Political Science Association, 105–19.

Committee of European Banking Supervisors (CEBS) (2005) *Consultation Paper on the Recognition of External Credit Assessment Institutions*, London: CEBS.

Committee of European Banking Supervisors (CEBS) (2006) *Guidelines on the Recognition of External Credit Assessment Institutions*, London: CEBS.

Cook, Karen S. (1994) 'Exchange and Power in Networks of Interorganizational Relations', in John Scott (ed.) *Power: Critical Concepts*, Vol. I, London: Routledge, 363–87.

Cook, Karen S., Richard M. Emerson, Mary R. Gillmore and Toshio Yamagishi (1994) 'The Distribution of Power in Exchange Networks: Theory and Experimental Results', in John Scott (ed.) *Power: Critical Concepts*, Vol. I, London: Routledge, 388–416.

Cooley, Alexander and James Ron (2002) 'The NGO Scramble: Organizational Insecurity and the Political Economy of Transnational Action', *International Security* 27: 1, 5–39.

Covitz, M. Daniel and Paul Harrison (2003) *Testing Conflicts of Interest at Bond Rating Agencies with Market Anticipation: Evidence that Reputation Incentives Dominate*, Federal Reserve Board Working Paper, Washington, DC: Federal Reserve Board.

Crouch, Colin and Wolfgang Streeck (eds.) (1997a) *The Political Economy of Modern Capitalism: Mapping Convergence and Diversity*, London: Sage.

Crouch, Colin and Wolfgang Streeck (1997b) 'Introduction: The Future of Capitalist Diversity', in Colin Crouch and Wolfgang Streeck (eds.) *The Political Economy of Modern Capitalism: Mapping Convergence and Diversity*, London: Sage, 1–17.

Cusimano, Maryann K. (2000) 'Beyond Sovereignty: The Rise of Transsovereign Problems', in Maryann K. Cusimano (ed.) *Beyond Sovereignty: Issues for a Global Agenda*, Boston, MA: Bedford/St. Martin's, 1–40.

Cutler, A. Claire, Virginia Haufler and Tony Porter (eds.) (1999a) *Private Authority and International Affairs*, Albany, NY: State University of New York Press.

Cutler, A. Claire, Virginia Haufler and Tony Porter (1999b) 'Private Authority and International Affairs', in Claire A. Cutler, Virginia Haufler and Tony

Porter (eds.) *Private Authority and International Affairs*, Albany, NY: State University of New York Press, 2–38.
Cyert, Richard M. and James G. March (1963) *A Behavioral Theory of the Firm*, Englewood Cliffs, NJ: Prentice Hall.
Deutsche Bundesbank (2008a) 'Basel II – The New Capital Accord', http://www.bundesbank.de/bankenaufsicht/bankenaufsicht_basel.en.php, date accessed May 27, 2008.
Deutsche Bundesbank (2008b) 'Basel II – Pillar I: Minimum Capital Requirements', http://www.bundesbank.de/bankenaufsicht/bankenaufsicht_basel_saeule1.en.php, date accessed May 27, 2008.
Deutsche Bundesbank (2008c) 'Basel II – Standardised Approach for Credit Risk: External Rating', http://www.bundesbank.de/bankenaufsicht/bankenaufsicht_basel_kreditrisiko.en.php, date accessed May 25, 2008.
Deutsche Bundesbank (2008d) 'Basel II – Application to Use the IRBA (Internal Rating Based Approach)', http://www.bundesbank.de/bankenaufsicht/bankenaufsicht_basel_irbazulassung.en.php, date accessed May 25, 2008.
Dieter, Heribert (2004) 'The Stability of International Financial Markets: A Global Public Good?' in Stefan A. Schirm (ed.) *New Rules for Global Markets: Public and Private Governance in the World Economy*, Basingstoke: Palgrave Macmillan, 23–43.
Dieter, Heribert (2008) 'Der IWF auf dem Weg in die Bedeutungslosigkeit?' *Aus Politik und Zeitgeschichte (APuZ)* 7: 9–14.
Dittrich, Fabian (2007) *The Credit Rating Industry: Competition and Regulation*, Ph.D. Dissertation, Cologne: University of Cologne, http://kups.ub.uni-koeln.de/volltexte/2007/2045/, date accessed May 30, 2008.
Dunlavy, Colleen and Thomas Welskopp (2007) 'Myths and Peculiarities: Comparing U.S. and German Capitalism', *Bulletin of the German Historical Institute* 41: 2, 33–64.
Dyson, Kenneth and Stephen Padgett (2005) 'Introduction: Global, Rhineland or Hybrid Capitalism?' in Kenneth Dyson and Stephen Padgett (eds.) *The Politics of Economic Reform in Germany: Global, Rhineland or Hybrid Capitalism?* Special Issue of *German Politics* 14: 2, 115–24.
Eckstein, Harry (1975) 'Case Study and Theory in Political Science', in Fred Greenstein and Nelson W. Polsby (eds.) *Handbook of Political Science Vol. 7: Strategies of Inquiry*, Reading, MA: Addison-Wesley, 79–137.
The Economist (1996) 'The Use and Abuse of Reputation', *The Economist* 339 (7960), April 6: 20.
The Economist (1997) 'Risks Beyond Measure', *The Economist* 345 (8047), December 13: 82–3.
The Economist (2001) 'New Interests, New Conflicts', *The Economist* 359 (8217), April 14: 72–3.
The Economist (2002a) 'Badly Overrated', *The Economist* 363 (8273), May 18: 75–6.
The Economist (2002b) 'Free the New York Three', *The Economist* 363 (8273), May 18: 76.

The Economist (2005) 'Who Rates the Raters? – Credit Rating Agencies', *The Economist* 374 (8419), March 26: 65–7.

The Economist (2007a) 'CDOh no! With Trades Scarce and Losses Mounting, It Is Going to Be a Harsh Winter', *The Economist online,* November 8, http://www.economist.com/finance/displaystory.cfm?story_id=10113339, date accessed June 27, 2008.

The Economist (2007b) 'Credit Rating Agencies: Measuring the Measurers', *The Economist online,* May 31, http://www.economist.com/finance/displaystory.cfm?story_id=9267952M, date accessed June 28, 2008.

Edele, Andreas (2006) *All Hands on Deck – The Establishment of Global Public-Private Partnerships for Development from a Resource Exchange Perspective,* unpublished M.A. Thesis, Tübingen: University of Tübingen, Institute of Political Science.

Eichengreen, Barry (1996) *Globalizing Capital: A History of the International Monetary System,* Princeton, NJ: Princeton University Press.

El-Shagi, Makram (2008) 'Weltweite Ansteckung: berechtigte Sorge oder grundlose Panik?' *Aus Politik und Zeitgeschichte (APuZ)* 7: 15–20.

Emerson, Richard M. (1981) 'Social Exchange Theory', in Morris Rosenberg and Ralph H. Turner (eds.) *Social Psychology: Sociological Perspectives,* New York: Basic Books, 30–65.

Emerson, Richard M. (1994) 'Power-Dependence Relations', in John Scott (ed.) *Power: Critical Concepts,* Vol. I, London: Routledge, 348–62.

Epstein, David and Sharyn O'Halloran (1999a) *Delegating Powers: A Transaction Cost Politics Approach to Policy Making under Separate Powers,* Cambridge: Cambridge University Press.

Epstein, David and Sharyn O'Halloran (1999b) 'Asymmetric Information, Delegation, and the Structure of Policy-Making', *Journal of Theoretical Politics* 11: 1, 37–56.

Estrella, Arturo et al. (2000) *Credit Ratings and Complementary Sources of Credit Quality Information,* Basel Committee on Banking Supervision Working Papers No. 3, Basel: Bank for International Settlements.

European Commission (2002) *Responses to the Challenges of Globalisation: A Study on the International Monetary and Financial System and on Financing for Development,* Brussels: European Commission, DG Economic and Financial Affairs.

European Parliament and Council of the European Union (2006a) 'Directive 2006/48/EC of the European Parliament and of the Council of 14 June 2006 relating to the Taking Up and Pursuit of the Business of Credit Institutions (Recast)', *Official Journal of the European Union* (L 177, June 30), Brussels.

European Parliament and Council of the European Union (2006b) 'Directive 2006/49/EC of the European Parliament and of the Council of 14 June 2006 on the Capital Adequacy of Investment Firms and Credit Institutions (Recast)', *Official Journal of the European Union* (L 177, June 30), Brussels.

Everling, Oliver (1991) *Credit Rating durch internationale Agenturen: Eine Untersuchung zu den Komponenten und instrumentalen Funktionen des Rating,* Wiesbaden: Gabler.

Filc, Wolfgang (2008) 'Stabilität des internationalen Finanzsystems', *Aus Politik und Zeitgeschichte (ApuZ)* 7: 3–8.

Financial Times Deutschland (2007) 'Ratingagenturen – Schluss mit den Privilegien', *Financial Times* Deutschland, October 9, http://www.ftd.de/meinung/kommentare/263145.html?mode=print, date accessed May 13, 2008.

Fioretos, Orfeo (2001) 'The Domestic Sources of Multilateral Preferences: Varieties of Capitalism in the European Union', in Peter Hall and David Soskice (eds.) *Varieties of Capitalism: Institutional Foundations of Comparative Advantage*, Cambridge: Cambridge University Press, 213–44.

Fisch, Jacob (2005) 'Rating the Raters: Reflections on Proposals for Regulatory Reform of the Credit Rating Agencies', *U.C. Davis Business Law Journal* 5: 3, http://bizlawjournal.ucdavis.edu/article.asp?id=549, date accessed May 27, 2008.

Freund, Corinna (2002) *Internationale Kooperation zur Prävention von Finanzkrisen: Die Verregelung von Verteilungskonflikten zwischen den Industriestaaten*, Ph.D. Dissertation, Tübingen: University of Tübingen, Institute of Political Science.

Friedman, Thomas L. (1995) 'Don't Mess With Moody's', *New York Times*, February 22, http://query.nytimes.com/gst/fullpage.html?res=990CE5D7163DF931A15751C0A963958260, date accessed May 25, 2008.

Fuchs, Doris (2005) *Understanding Business Power in Global Governance*, Baden-Baden: Nomos.

Galbraith, Jay R. (1973) *Designing Complex Organizations*, Reading, MA: Addison-Wesley.

Galbraith, Jay R. (1977) *Organization Design*, Reading, MA: Addison-Wesley.

Genschel, Philipp and Bernhard Zangl (2007) 'Die Zerfaserung von Staatlichkeit und die Zentralität des Staates', *Aus Politik und Zeitgeschichte (APuZ)* 20–1: 10–16.

Genschel, Philipp and Bernhard Zangl (2008) 'Metamorphosen des Staates: Vom Herrschaftsmonopolist zum Herrschaftsmanager', *Leviathan* 36: 3, 430–54.

Gerke, Wolfgang and Ferdinand Mager (2005) 'Die Macht der Ratingagenturen: Der Fall Thyssen Krupp AG', *Betriebswirtschaftliche Forschung und Praxis (BfuP)* 57: 3, 203–14.

Gilardi, Fabrizio (2008) *Delegation in the Regulatory State: Independent Regulatory Agencies in Western Europe*, Cheltenham: Edward Elgar.

Gilpin, Robert (2000) *The Challenge of Global Capitalism: The World Economy in the 21st Century*, Princeton, NJ: Princeton University Press.

Gonzalez, Fernando, François Haas, Mattias Persson, Liliana Toledo, Roberto Violi, Martin Wieland and Carmen Zins (2004) *Market Dynamics Associated with Credit Ratings: A Literature Review*, ECB Occasional Paper No. 16, Frankfurt/M.: European Central Bank.

Gourevitch, Peter (1996) 'The Macropolitics of Microinstitutional Differences in the Analysis of Comparative Capitalism', in Suzanne Berger and Ronald Dore (eds.) *National Diversity and Global Capitalism*, Ithaca, NY: Cornell University Press, 239–59.

Gourevitch, Peter (2007) 'Explaining Corporate Governance Systems: Alternative Approaches', in Andreas Nölke, Bastiaan van Apeldoorn and Henk Overbeek (eds.) *The Transnational Politics of Corporate Governance Regulation*, London: Routledge, 27–42.

Gras, Isabelle (2003) *The Power to Rate: Eine Untersuchung zur Rolle der Ratingagenturen auf den internationalen Finanzmärkten*, Research Group on Equity Market Regulation (REGEM) Analysis 6, Trier: University of Trier.

Grass, Doris (2007) 'Agenturen sollen für Ratings haften', *Financial Times Deutschland*, September 02, http://www.ftd.de/finanzen/geldanlage/:agenturen-sollen-fuer-ratings-haften/247720.html, date accessed 10 March 2011.

Graz, Jean-Christophe and Andreas Nölke (eds) (2008a) *Transnational Private Governance and its Limits*, London: Routledge.

Graz, Jean-Christophe and Andreas Nölke (2008b) 'Introduction: Beyond the Fragmented Debate on Transnational Private Governance', in Jean-Christophe Graz and Andreas Nölke (eds.) *Transnational Private Governance and its Limits*, London: Routledge, 1–26.

Griffith-Jones, Stephany (2003) 'International Financial Stability and Market Efficieny as a Global Public Good', in Inge Kaul, Pedro Conceiçao, Katell Le Goulven and Ronald U. Mendoza (eds.) *Providing Global Public Goods: Managing Globalization*, Oxford: Oxford University Press, 435–55.

Gündling, Heike and Oliver Everling (1994) 'Rating als Methode der Finanzanalyse', *Die Bank* 12: 727–31.

Hall, Peter and Daniel W. Gingerich (2004) *Varieties of Capitalism and Institutional Complementarities in the Macroeconomy: An Empirical Analysis*, MPIfG Discussion Paper 04/5, Cologne: Max Planck Institute for the Study of Societies.

Hall, Peter and David Soskice (eds.) (2001a) *Varieties of Capitalism: Institutional Foundations of Comparative Advantage*, Cambridge: Cambridge University Press.

Hall, Peter and David Soskice (2001b) 'An Introduction to Varieties of Capitalism', in Peter Hall and David Soskice (eds.) *Varieties of Capitalism: Institutional Foundations of Comparative Advantage*, Cambridge: Cambridge University Press, 1–68.

Hall, Rodney Bruce and Thomas J. Biersteker (eds.) (2002) *The Emergence of Private Authority in Global Governance*, Cambridge: Cambridge University Press.

Hamilton, Gary G. and Nicole Woolsey Biggart (1994) 'Theoretical Observations on Power and Obedience in Complex Organizations', in John Scott (ed.) *Power: Critical Concepts*, Vol. III, London: Routledge, 150–67.

Hartwall, Marcus and Christian Pettersson (2005) *Reformation of the Credit Rating Industry: Is There a Need?* Master Thesis, Lund: Lund University, Institution of Business Studies.

Hawkins, Darren G., David A. Lake, Daniel L. Nielson and Michael J. Tierney (eds.) (2006a) *Delegation and Agency in International Organizations*, Cambridge: Cambridge University Press.

Hawkins, Darren G., David A. Lake, Daniel L. Nielson and Michael J. Tierney (2006b) 'Delegation under Anarchy: States, International

Organizations, and Principal-Agent Theory', in Darren G. Hawkins, David A. Lake, Daniel L. Nielson, Michael J. Tierney (eds.) *Delegation and Agency in International Organizations*, Cambridge: Cambridge University Press, 3–38.

Helleiner, Eric (1994) *States and the Re-Emergence of Global Finance: From Bretton Woods to the 1990s*, Ithaca, NY: Cornell University Press.

Héritier, Adrienne and Christoph Lehmkuhl (2008) 'Introduction: The Shadow of Hierarchy and New Modes of Governance', *Journal of Public Policy* 28: 1, 1–17.

Hickson, David J., Christopher Hinings, Charles A. Lee, Rodney Schneck and Johannes M. Pennings (1994) 'A Strategic Contingencies' Theory of Intraorganizational Power', in John Scott (ed.) *Power: Critical Concepts*, London: Routledge, 196–212.

Higgott, Richard A. (2001) 'Economic Globalization and Global Governance: Towards a Post-Washington Consensus?' in Volker Rittberger (ed.) *Global Governance and the United Nations System*, Tokio: United Nations University Press, 127–57.

Higgott, Richard A., Geoffrey D. Underhill and Andreas Bieler (eds.) (2000) *Non-State Actors and Authority in the Global System*, London: Routledge.

Hillebrand, Ernst (2001) 'Schlüsselstellung im globalisierten Kapitalismus: Der Einfluss privater Rating-Agenturen auf Finanzmärkte und Politik', in Tanja Brühl, Tobias Debiel, Brigitte Hamm, Hartwig Hummel and Jens Martens (eds.) *Die Privatisierung der Weltpolitik: Entstaatlichung und Kommerzialisierung im Globalisierungsprozess*, Bonn: Dietz, 150–73.

Hirsch, Ulrich (1996) 'Rating ist objektiv subjektiv', in Hans E. Büschgen and Oliver Everling (eds) *Handbuch Rating*, Wiesbaden: Gabler, 657–672.

Hishow, Ognian (2007) *Die globalen Finanzmarktturbulenzen: Nicht nur Folge schwacher Regulierung*, SWP-Aktuell 2007/A 46, Berlin: Stiftung Wissenschaft und Politik.

Hoffmann, Catherine (2008) 'Kontrolle für die Türsteher', *sueddeutsche.de*, June 18, http://www.sueddeutsche.de/finanzen/meinung/626/181068/, date accessed June 18, 2008.

Hoffmann, Jürgen (2003) 'Der kleine Unterschied: Varieties of Capitalism', *WSI Mitteilungen* 2: 124–30.

Hollingsworth, J. Rogers, Philippe C. Schmitter and Wolfgang Streeck (1994) 'Capitalism, Sectors, Institutions, and Performance', in J. Rogers Hollingsworth, Philippe C. Schmitter and Wolfgang Streeck (eds.) *Governing Capitalist Economies: Performance and Control of Economic Sectors*, Oxford: Oxford University Press, 3–16.

Hunt, Isaac C. (2002) 'Testimony Concerning the Role of Credit Rating Agencies in the U.S. Securities Markets, Testimony Before the United States Senate Committee on Governmental Affairs, March 20', http://www.sec.gov/news/testimony/032002tsih.htm, date accessed August 19, 2008.

Hurrelmann, Achim, Stephan Leibfried, Kerstin Martens and Peter Mayer (eds.) (2007) *Transforming the Golden-Age Nation State*, Basingstoke: Palgrave Macmillan.

Husisian, Gregory (1990) 'What Standard of Care Should Govern the World's Shortest Editorials? An Analysis of Bond Rating Agency Liability', *Cornell Law Review* 75: 2, 411–61.

Hutter, Bridget M. (2006) 'The Role of Non-State Actors in Regulation', in Gunnar Folke Schuppert (ed.) *Global Governance and the Role of Non-State Actors*, Baden-Baden: Nomos, 63–79.

Institute of International Finance (1997) *Report of the Task Force on Conglomerate Supervision*, Washington, DC: Institute of International Finance.

International Organization of Securities Commissions (IOSCO) (2003a) *Report on the Activities of Credit Rating Agencies*, September, Madrid: IOSCO, Technical Committee.

International Organization of Securities Commissions (IOSCO) (2003b) *IOSCO Statement of Principles Regarding the Activities of Credit Rating Agencies*, September, Madrid: IOSCO, Technical Committee.

International Organization of Securities Commissions (IOSCO) (2004) *Code of Conduct Fundamentals for Credit Rating Agencies*, December, Madrid: IOSCO, Technical Committee.

International Organization of Securities Commissions (IOSCO) (2008a) *General Information on IOSCO: The International Organization of Securities Commissions*, http://www.iosco.org/about/, date accessed September 15, 2008.

International Organization of Securities Commissions (IOSCO) (2008b) *Code of Conduct Fundamentals for Credit Rating Agencies*, Revised May, Madrid: IOSCO, Technical Committee.

Jackson, Howell E. (2001) 'The Role of Rating Agencies in the Establishment of Capital Standards for Financial Institutions in a Global Economy', in Eilis Ferran, Charles A.E. Goodhart (eds.) *Regulating Financial Services and Markets in the Twenty First Century*, Oxford: Hart, 311–22.

Jacobs, David (1974) 'Dependence and Vulnerability: An Exchange Approach to the Control of Organizations', *Administrative Science Quarterly* 19: 1, 45–59.

Jacobsson, Bengt (2002) 'Standardization and Expert Knowledge', in Nils Brunsson and Bengt Jacobsson (eds.) *A World of Standards*, Oxford: Oxford University Press, 40–49.

Jansen, Dorothea (1993) 'Interorganisationsforschung und Politiknetzwerke', in Dorothea Jansen and Klaus Schubert (eds.) *Netzwerke und Politikproduktion: Konzepte, Methoden, Perspektiven*, Marburg: Schüren, 95–110.

Jessop, Robert D. (1994) 'Exchange and Power in Structural Analysis', in John Scott (ed.) *Power: Critical Concepts*, Vol. I, London: Routledge, 112–30.

Joerges, Christian, Harm Schepel and Ellen Vos (1999) *The Law's Problem with the Involvement of Non-Governmental Actors in Europe's Legislative Processes: The Case of Standardization under the 'New Approach'*, San Domenico di Fiesole: European University Institute.

Kahler, Miles (1995) *International Institutions and the Political Economy of Integration*, Washington, DC: Brookings Institution.

Kapstein, Ethan B. (1991) *Supervising International Banks: Origins and Implications of the Basle Accord*, Princeton, NJ: Princeton University Press.

Kapstein, Ethan B. (1994) *Governing the Global Economy: International Finance and the State*, Cambridge, MA: Harvard University Press.

Karacadag, Cem and Michael W. Taylor (2000) *The New Capital Adequacy Framework: Institutional Constraints and Incentive Structures*, IMF Working Paper WP/00/93, Washington, DC: International Monetary Fund.

Kaul, Inge (2006) 'Exploring the Policy Space between Markets and States: Global Public-Private Partnerships', in Inge Kaul and Pedro Conceiçao (eds.) *The New Public Finance: Responding to Global Challenges*, Oxford: Oxford University Press, 219–68.

Kazim, Hasnain (2007) 'Rating-Agenturen: Die böse Macht der Krisen-Katalysatoren', *Spiegel Online*, http://www.spiegelonline.de/wirtschaft/0,1518,druck-499674,00.html, date accessed August 13, 2008.

Keohane, Robert O. (1984) *After Hegemony: Cooperation and Discord in the World Political Economy*, Princeton, NJ: Princeton University Press.

Kerwer, Dieter (2002) 'Standardising as Governance: The Case of Credit Rating Agencies', in Adrienne Héritier (ed.) *Common Goods: Reinventing European and International Governance*, Lanham, MD: Rowman and Littlefield, 293–316.

Kerwer, Dieter (2005) 'Holding Global Regulators Accountable: The Case of Credit Rating Agencies', *Governance* 18: 3, 453–75.

Kerwer, Dieter (2006) 'Governing Financial Markets by International Standards', in Mathias Koenig-Archibugi and Michael Zürn (eds.) *New Modes of Governance in the Global System: Exploring Publicness, Delegation and Inclusiveness*, Basingstoke: Palgrave Macmillan, 77–100.

Kiewiet, D. Roderick and Mathew D. McCubbins (1991) *The Logic of Delegation: Congressional Parties and the Appropriations Process*, Chicago, IL: University of Chicago Press.

King, Gary, Robert O. Keohane and Sidney Verba (1994) *Designing Social Inquiry: Scientific Inference in Qualitative Research*, Princeton, NJ: Princeton University Press.

King, Michael R. and Timothy J. Sinclair (2001) *Grasping at Straws: A Ratings Downgrade for the Emerging International Financial Architecture*, Center for the Study of Globalisation and Regionalisation (CSGR) Working Paper No. 82/01, Coventry: University of Warwick.

King, Michael R. and Timothy J. Sinclair (2003) 'Private Actors and Public Policy: A Requiem for the New Basel Capital Accord', *International Political Science Review* 24: 3, 345–62.

Knight, Frank (1921) *Risk, Uncertainty, and Profit*, Chicago, IL: Houghton Mifflin Company.

Koenig-Archibugi, Mathias (2006) 'Introduction: Institutional Diversity in Global Governance', in Mathias Koenig-Archibugi and Michael Zürn (eds.) *New Modes of Governance in the Global System: Exploring Publicness, Delegation and Inclusiveness*, Basingstoke: Palgrave Macmillan, 1–30.

Koenig-Archibugi, Mathias and Michael Zürn (eds.) (2006) *New Modes of Governance in the Global System: Exploring Publicness, Delegation and Inclusiveness*, Basingstoke: Palgrave Macmillan.

Kröger, Michael (2008) 'Merkel fordert eigene Ratingagentur für Euro-Zone', *Spiegel Online*, June 11, http://www.spiegel.de/wirtschaft/0,1518,558959,00.html, date accessed June 11, 2008.

Kruck, Andreas (2010a) 'From Public to Private and Back Again? Perspectives and Propositions on the Reallocation of Political Authority in Financial Governance', Paper Presented at the SGIR 7th Pan-European International Relations Conference, Stockholm, September 9–11, 2010.

Kruck, Andreas (2010b) 'Privatization Coalitions, Strategic Decisions and Ideational Discourses: The Use of Private Military and Security Companies in Zones of Conflict', Paper Presented at the SGIR 7th Pan-European International Relations Conference, Stockholm, September 9–11, 2010.

Lawrence, Paul R. and Jay W. Lorsch (1967) *Organizations and Environments: Managing Differentiation and Integration*, Boston, MA: Harvard Business School Press.

Leibfried, Stephan and Michael Zürn (eds.) (2005) *Transformations of the State?* Cambridge: Cambridge University Press.

Levich, Richard M., Giovanni Majnoni and Carmen Reinhart (eds.) (2002) *Ratings, Rating Agencies and the Global Financial System*, Norwell, MA, and Dordrecht: Kluwer Academic.

Levine, Sol and Paul E. White (1961) 'Exchange as a Conceptual Framework for the Study of Interorganizational Relationships', *Administrative Science Quarterly* 5: 4, 583–601.

Lieberman, Joe (2002) 'Rating the Raters: Enron and the Credit Rating Agencies, Statement by the Chairmen of the United States Senate Committee on Governmental Affairs, March 20', http://www.senate.gov/~gov_affairs/032002lieberman.htm, date accessed August 19, 2008.

Liese, Andrea (2009) 'Die unterschiedlich starke Öffnung internationaler Organisationen gegenüber nichtstaatlichen Akteuren: Erklärungen der Institutionen- und Organisationstheorie', in Klaus Dingwerth, Dieter Kerwer and Andreas Nölke (eds.) *Die Organisierte Welt: Internationale Beziehungen und Organisationsforschung*, Baden-Baden: Nomos, 189–210.

Lijphart, Arend (1971) 'Comparative Politics and the Comparative Method', *American Political Science Review* 65: 3, 682–93.

Litwak, Eugene and Lydia F. Hylton (1962) 'Interorganizational Analysis: A Hypothesis on Co-ordinating Agencies', *Administrative Science Quarterly* 6: 4, 395–420.

Love, Brian (2008) 'From G-7, Still Just Promises for Global Economy', *International Herald Tribune*, February 11, http://www.iht.com/articles/2008/02/11/business/rtrcol12.php, date accessed March 30, 2008.

Lowenstein, Roger (2008) 'Triple-A Failure', *The New York Times*, April 27, http://www.nytimes.com/2008/04/27/magazine/27Credit-t.html, date accessed August 4, 2008.

Lütz, Susanne (2000) 'From Managed to Market Capitalism?: German Finance in Transition', *German Politics* 9: 2, 149–71.

Lütz, Susanne (2004) 'Convergence Within National Diversity: The Regulatory State in Finance', *Journal of Public Policy* 24: 2, 169–97.

Lütz, Susanne and Dagmar Eberle (2007) *On the Road to Anglo-Saxon Capitalism? German Corporate Governance Regulation between Market and Multilevel Governance*, CLPE Research Paper 4/2007, Toronto: York University, Osgoode Hall Law School.

Lyne, Mona M., Daniel L. Nielson and Michael J. Tierney (2006) 'Who Delegates? Alternative Models of Principals in Development Aid', in Darren G. Hawkins, David A. Lake, Daniel L. Nielson and Michael J. Tierney (eds.) *Delegation and Agency in International Organizations*, Cambridge: Cambridge University Press, 41–76.

McAnulla, Stuart (2002) 'Structure and Agency', in David Marsh and Gerry Stoker (eds.) *Theory and Methods in Political Science*, Basingstoke: Palgrave Macmillan, 271–91.

McCubbins, Mathew D. and Thomas Schwartz (1984) 'Congressional Oversight Overlooked: Police Patrols versus Fire Alarms', *American Journal of Political Science* 28: 1, 165–79.

Macht, Christian (2007) *Der Baseler Ausschuss für Bankenregulierung und Basel II: Bankenregulierung auf einem internationalen* level playing field, Baden-Baden: Nomos.

Majone, Giandomenico (2001) 'Two Logics of Delegation: Agency and Fiduciary Relations in EU Governance', *European Union Politics* 2: 1, 103–22.

March, James G. and Johan P. Olsen (1989) *Rediscovering Institutions: The Organizational Basis of Politics*, New York: Free Press.

Martens, Bertin, Uwe Mummert, Peter Murrell and Paul Seabright (2002) *The Institutional Economics of Foreign Aid*, Cambridge: Cambridge University Press.

Milgrom, John and Paul Roberts (1990) 'Bargaining Costs, Influence Costs, and the Organization of Economic Activity', in James Alt and Kenneth Shepsle (eds.) *Perspectives on Positive Political Economy*, Cambridge: Cambridge University Press, 57–89.

Milgrom, John and Paul Roberts (1992) *Economics, Organization and Management*, Englewood Cliffs, NJ: Prentice Hall.

Moe, Terry M. (1990) 'The Politics of Structural Choice: Toward a Theory of Public Bureaucracy', in Oliver E. Williamson (ed.) *Organization Theory: From Chester Barnard to the Present and Beyond*, Oxford: Oxford University Press.

Moody's Investors Service (1991) *Global Credit Analysis*, London: IFR.

Moody's Investor Service (2008) 'Introduction to Moody's: Moody's Role in Global Capital Markets', http://www.moodys.com/moodys/cust/AboutMoodys/AboutMoodys.aspx?topic=intro, date accessed June 28, 2008.

Murphy, Brendan (2000) *Credit Ratings and Emerging Economies*, Studies on International Financial Architecture No. 3/2000, Bonn: Friedrich-Ebert-Foundation.

Mutschler, Max Markus (2007) *Die Delegation von Agenda-Setting in der Europäischen Sicherheits- und Verteidigungspolitik an den Hohen Vertreter für die Gemeinsame Außen- und Sicherheitspolitik: Eine Analyse aus der Perspektive des*

'Principal-Agent'-Ansatzes, unpublished M.A. Thesis, Tübingen: University of Tübingen, Institute of Political Science.

Mutschler, Max Markus (2008) *The Learning Principals – Die Delegation von Agenda-Setting in der Europäischen Sicherheits- und Verteidigungspolitik*, Tübingen Working Papers on International Politics and Peace and Conflict Studies No. 53, Tübingen: University of Tübingen, Institute of Political Science.

Naschold, Frieder (1997) 'Ökonomische Leistungsfähigkeit und institutionelle Innovation: Das deutsche Produktions- und Politikregime im globalen Wettbewerb', in Frieder Naschold, David Soskice, Bob Hancké and Ulrich Jürgen (eds.) *Ökonomische Leistungsfähigkeit und institutionelle Innovation*, Berlin: Sigma, 19–62.

Nicholls, Christopher C. (2005) *Public and Private Uses of Credit Ratings*, Capital Market Institute Policy Series, Toronto, ON: University of Toronto.

Nölke, Andreas (2000) 'Regieren in transnationalen Politiknetzwerken? Kritik postnationaler Governance-Konzepte aus der Perspektive einer transnationalen (Inter-) Organisationssoziologie', *Zeitschrift für Internationale Beziehungen* 6: 2, 331–58.

Nölke, Andreas (2004) 'Transnational Private Authority and Corporate Governance', in Stefan A. Schirm (ed.) *New Rules for Global Markets: Public and Private Governance in the World Economy*, Basingstoke: Palgrave Macmillan, 155–75.

Nölke, Andreas (2008) *Private Governance in International Affairs and the Erosion of Coordinated Market Economies in the European Union*, Part Three of the Germany in Global Economic Governance Series, Mario Enaudi Center for International Studies Working Paper No. 3-08, Ithaca, NY: Cornell University.

Nölke, Andreas and Arjen Vliegenthart (2009) 'Enlarging the Varieties of Capitalism: The Emergence of Dependent Market Economies in East Central Europe', *World Politics* 61: 4, 670–702.

Nölke, Andreas, Bastiaan van Apeldoorn, Henk Overbeek (eds.) (2007) *The Transnational Politics of Corporate Governance Regulation*, London: Routledge.

Nölke, Andreas and James Perry (2007) 'Coordination Service Firms and the Erosion of Rhenish Capitalism', in Henk Overbeek, Bastiaan van Apeldoorn and Andreas Nölke (eds.) *The Transnational Politics of Corporate Governance Regulation*, London: Routledge, 121–36.

Nölke, Andreas and Jean-Christophe Graz (2008) 'Conclusion: The Limits of Transnational Private Governance', in Jean-Christophe Graz and Andreas Nölke (eds.) *Transnational Private Governance and its Limits*, London: Routledge, 225–42.

Norris, Floyd (2007) 'High and Low Finance: Being Kept in the Dark', *The New York Times*, November 2, http://www.nytimes.com/2007/11/02/business/02norris.html?_r=1&ref=business&oref=slogin, date accessed June 26, 2008.

Norris, Floyd (2008) 'Moody's Admits It Erred in Rating Some Securities', *International Herald Tribune*, January 26–7: 13.

O'Donovan, Martin (2004) 'The Nature of Risk: Credit Agencies and Light Regulation – Building a Market Code', *Balance Sheet* 12: 5, 38–41.

Oliver, Christine (1990) 'Determinants of Interorganizational Relationships: Integration and Future Directions', *Academy of Management Review* 15: 2, 241–65.

Opp, Karl-Dieter (1995) *Methodologie der Sozialwissenschaften: Einführung in Probleme ihrer Theorienbildung und praktischen Anwendung,* Opladen: Westdeutscher Verlag.

Osman, Yasmin (2007) 'Sie meinen ja nur ...', *Financial Times Deutschland,* August 22, http://www.ftd.de/meinung/kommentare/242547.html?mode=print, date accessed May 28, 2008.

Osman, Yasmin and Heike Buchter (2007) 'Wut auf Ratingagenturen', *Financial Times Deutschland,* August 10, http://www.ftd.de/unternehmen/finanzdienstleister/237445.html?mode=print, date accessed February 13, 2008.

Pappi, Franz Urban and Thomas König (1993) 'Informationstausch in politischen Netzwerken', in Dorothea Jansen and Klaus Schubert (eds.) *Netzwerke und Politikproduktion: Konzepte, Methoden, Perspektiven,* Marburg: Schüren, 111–31.

Parsons, Talcott (1951) *The Social System,* New York: Free Press.

Partnoy, Frank (1999) 'The Siskel and Ebert of Financial Markets? Two Thumbs Down for the Credit Rating Agencies', *Washington University Law Review* 77: 3, 619–712.

Partnoy, Frank (2001) *The Paradox of Credit Ratings,* University of San Diego Law and Economics Research Paper No. 20, San Diego, CA: University of San Diego.

Partnoy, Frank (2006) *How and Why Credit Rating Agencies Are Not like Other Gatekeepers,* University of San Diego Law and Economics Research Paper No. 46, San Diego, CA: University of San Diego.

Pattberg, Philipp H. (2007) *Private Institutions and Global Governance: The New Politics of Environmental Sustainability,* Cheltenham: Edward Elgar.

Pattison, John C. (2006) 'International Financial Cooperation and the Number of Adherents: The Basel Committee and Capital Regulation', *Open Economies Review* 17, 443–58.

Paul, Stephan (2006) 'Basel II und Rating: Herausforderungen für Kreditinstitute und Unternehmen', in Thomas Reichmann and Udo Pyszny (eds.) *Rating nach Basel II: Herausforderungen für den Mittelstand,* München, 295–322.

Pauly, Louis W. (1997) *Who Elected the Bankers? Surveillance and Control in the World Economy,* Ithaca, NY: Cornell University Press.

Peters, Andreas C. (2001) *Die Haftung und die Regulierung von Rating-Agenturen,* Baden-Baden: Nomos.

Pfeffer, Jeffrey (1981) *Power in Organizations,* Boston, MA: Pitman.

Pfeffer, Jeffrey and Phillip Nowak (1976) 'Joint Ventures and Interorganizational Interdependence', *Administrative Science Quarterly* 21: 3, 398–418.

Pfeffer, Jeffrey and Gerald R. Salancik (2003) *The External Control of Organizations,* Stanford, CA: Stanford University Press.

Polanyi, Karl (1944) *The Great Transformation: The Political and Economic Origins of Our Time*, Boston, MA: Beacon Press.
Pollack, Mark A. (1997) 'Delegation, Agency, and Agenda-setting in the European Community', *International Organization* 51: 1, 99–134.
Pollack, Mark A. (2003) *The Engines of European Integration: Delegation, Agency, and Agenda Setting in the European Union*, Oxford: Oxford University Press.
Pollack, Mark A. (2006) 'Delegation and Discretion in the European Union', in Darren G. Hawkins, David A. Lake, Daniel L. Nielson and Michael J. Tierney (eds.) *Delegation and Agency in International Organizations*, Cambridge: Cambridge University Press, 165–96.
Porter, Tony (1993) *States, Markets and Regimes in Global Finance*, New York: St. Martin's Press.
Randow, Philipp von (1996) 'Rating und Regulierung', in Hans E. Büschgen and Oliver Everling (eds.) *Handbuch Rating*, Wiesbaden: Gabler, 543–76.
Reisen, Helmut and Julia von Maltzan (1999) *Boom and Bust and Sovereign Ratings*, OECD Development Center Technical Papers 148, Paris: OECD.
Reuters (2007) 'Germany's Ruling Conservatives Want Rating Agency Regulation', *Financial Express Online*, August 23, http://www.financialexpress.com/news/Germanys-ruling-conservatives-want-rating-agency-regulation/212176/, date accessed May 27, 2008.
Reuters (2008) 'Crackdown on Conduct of Rating Agencies', *International Herald Tribune*, May 29: 12.
Reuters Bloomberg (2008) 'Overhaul in S&P's Procedures', *International Herald Tribune*, February 8: 11.
Richter, Rudolf and Eirik G. Furubotn (2003) *Neue Institutionenökonomik: Eine Einführung und kritische Würdigung*, 3rd edition, Tübingen: Mohr Siebeck.
Rittberger, Volker (2004) 'Weltregieren zwischen Anarchie und Hierarchie', in Volker Rittberger (ed.) *Weltpolitik heute: Grundlagen und Perspektiven*, Baden-Baden: Nomos, 245–70.
Rittberger, Volker (2008) *Global Governance: From 'Exclusive' Executive Multilateralism to Inclusive, Multipartite Institutions*, Tübingen Working Papers on International Politics and Peace Research No. 52, Tübingen: Tübingen University, Institute of Political Science.
Rittberger, Volker, Andreas Kruck and Anne Romund (2010) *Grundzüge der Weltpolitik: Theorie und Empirie des Weltregierens*, Wiesbaden: VS Verlag für Sozialwissenschaften.
Rittberger, Volker and Bernhard Zangl (2006) *International Organization: Polity, Politics and Policies*, Basingstoke: Palgrave Macmillan.
Rittberger, Volker, Carmen Huckel, Lothar Rieth and Melanie Zimmer (2008) 'Inclusive Global Institutions for a Global Political Economy', in Volker Rittberger and Martin Nettesheim (eds.) *Authority in the Global Political Economy*, Basingstoke: Palgrave Macmillan, 11–54.
Rittberger, Volker, Martin Nettesheim, Carmen Huckel and Thorsten Göbel (2008) 'Introduction', in Volker Rittberger and Martin Nettesheim (eds.) *Authority in the Global Political Economy*, Basingstoke: Palgrave Macmillan, 1–12.
Rogoff, Kenneth (1985) 'The Optimal Degree of Commitment to an Intermediate Monetary Target', *Quarterly Journal of Economics* 100: 1169–90.

Rosenau, James N. (1992) 'Governance, Order, and Change in World Politics', in James N. Rosenau and Ernst-Otto Czempiel (eds.) *Governance without Government: Order and Change in World Politics*, Cambridge: Cambridge University Press, 1–29.

Rosenbaum, Jens (2004) *Der Einsatz von Rating-Agenturen zur Kapitalmarktregulierung in den USA: Ursachen und Konsequenzen*, Research Group on Equity Market Regulation (REGEM) Analysis 8, Trier: University of Trier.

Rousseau, Stephane (2005) *Enhancing the Accountability of Credit Rating Agencies: The Case for a Disclosure-Based Approach*, Capital Market Institute Policy Series, Toronto, ON: University of Toronto.

Ruggie, John (1982) 'International Regimes, Transactions and Change: Embedded Liberalism in the Postwar Economic Order', *International Organisation* 36: 2, 379–415.

Salancik, Gerald R. and Jeffrey Pfeffer (1994) 'Who Gets Power – And How They Hold on to It: A Strategic Contingency Model of Power', in John Scott (ed.) *Power: Critical Concepts*, London: Routledge, 213–31.

Schäferhoff, Marco, Sabine Campe and Christopher Kaan (2007) *Transnational Public-Private Partnerships in International Relations: Making Sense of Concepts, Research Frameworks and Results*, SFB-Governance Working Paper Series No. 6, Berlin: FU Berlin.

Scharpf, Fritz W. (1978) 'Interorganizational Policy Studies: Issues, Concepts and Perspectives', in Kenneth Hanf and Fritz W. Scharpf (eds.) *Interorganizational Policy Making: Limits to Coordination and Central Control*, London: Sage, 345–70.

Schimmelfennig, Frank (1995) *Debatten zwischen Staaten: Eine Argumentationstheorie internationaler Systemkonflikte*, Opladen: Leske + Budrich.

Schirm, Stefan A. (2004a) *Internationale Politische Ökonomie: Eine Einführung*, Baden-Baden: Nomos.

Schirm, Stefan A. (2004b) 'The Divergence of Global Economic Governance Strategies', in Stefan A. Schirm (ed.) *New Rules for Global Markets: Public and Private Governance in the World Economy*, Basingstoke: Palgrave Macmillan, 3–21.

Schirm, Stefan A., Maren Becker and Stephanie John (eds.) (2007) *Der Einfluss endogener Interessen und Normen auf nationale Positionen zur Global Economic Governance*, Final Report on the DFG Research Project 'Global Economic Governance', December, Bochum.

Schmidt, Vivien (2002) *The Futures of European Capitalism*, Oxford: Oxford University Press.

Schmidt, Stuart M. and Thomas A. Kochan (1977) 'Interorganizational Relationships: Patterns and Motivations', *Administrative Science Quarterly* 22: 2, 220–34.

Schwarcz, Steven L. (2001a) 'The Role of Rating Agencies in Global Market Regulation', in Eilis Ferran and Charles A.E. Goodhart (eds.) *Regulating Financial Services and Markets in the Twenty First Century*, Oxford: Hart, 297–310.

Schwarcz, Steven L. (2001b) *Private Ordering of Public Markets: The Rating Agency Paradox*, Public Law and Legal Theory Working Paper Series No. 18, Duke Law School.

Scott, W. Richard (1981) *Organizations: Rational, Natural, and Open Systems*, Englewood Cliffs, NJ: Prentice Hall.

Securities and Exchange Commission (SEC) (1994) *Nationally Recognized Statistical Rating Organizations: Concept Release*, File No. S7-23–94, Washington, DC: SEC.

Securities and Exchange Commission (SEC) (1997) *Capital Requirements for Brokers or Dealers under the Securities Exchange Act of 1934, Definition of the term "nationally recognized statistical rating organization" (NRSRO): Proposed Rule*, File No. S7-33–97, Washington, DC: SEC.

Securities and Exchange Commission (SEC) (2003a) *Report on the Role and Function of Credit Rating Agencies in the Operation of the Securities Market*, Washington, DC: SEC.

Securities and Exchange Commission (SEC) (2003b) *Concept Release: Rating Agencies and the Use of Credit Ratings under the Federal Securities Laws*, File No. S7-12-03, Washington, DC: SEC.

Securities and Exchange Commission (SEC) (2005) *Proposed Rule: Definition of Nationally Recognized Statistical Rating Organization*, File No. S7-04-05, Washington, DC: SEC.

Securities and Exchange Commission (SEC) (2007a) *Proposed Rule to Implement Provisions of the Credit Rating Agency Reform Act of 2006: Oversight of Credit Rating Agencies Registered as Nationally Recognized Statistical Rating Organizations*, File No. S7-04-07, Washington, DC: SEC.

Securities and Exchange Commission (SEC) (2007b) *Final Rule: Oversight of Credit Rating Agencies Registered as Nationally Recognized Statistical Rating Organizations*, File No. S7-04-07, Washington, DC: SEC.

Securities and Exchange Commission (SEC) (2007c) 'Credit Rating Agencies Apply for Registration as Nationally Recognized Statistical Rating Organizations', Press Release, June 28, Washington, DC: SEC.

Securities and Exchange Commission (SEC) (2008) 'Commission Orders Granting NRSRO Registration: Current NRSROs', http://www.sec.gov/divisions/marketreg/ratingagency.htm, date accessed September 29, 2008.

Securities and Exchange Commission (SEC) (2009a) *Final Rule: Amendments to Rules for Nationally Recognized Statistical Rating Organizations*, Washington, DC: SEC.

Securities and Exchange Commission (SEC) (2009b) *Final Rule: References to Ratings of Nationally Statistical Rating Organizations*, Washington, DC: SEC.

Shepsle, Kenneth A. (1991) 'Discretion, Institutions, and the Problem of Government Commitment', in Pierre Bourdieu and James S. Coleman (eds.) *Social Theory for a Changing Society*, Boulder, CO: Westview Press, 245–65.

Simmons, Beth A. (2001) 'The International Politics of Harmonization: The Case of Capital Market Regulation', *International Organization* 55: 3, 589–620.

Simon, Herbert A. (1982) *Models of Bounded Rationality, Vol. I: Economic Analysis and Public Policy*, Cambridge, MA: MIT Press.

Sinclair, Timothy L. (1994) 'Passing Judgement: Credit Rating Processes as Regulatory Mechanisms of Governance in the Emerging World Order', *Review of International Political Economy* 1: 1, 133–59.

Sinclair, Timothy L. (1999) 'Bond-Rating Agencies and Coordination in the Global Political Economy', in Claire A. Cutler, Virginia Haufler and Tony Porter (eds.) *Private Authority and International Affairs*, Albany, NY: State University of New York Press, 153–68.

Sinclair, Timothy L. (2000) 'Reinventing Authority: Embedded Knowledge Networks and the New Global Finance', *Environment and Planning: Government and Policy* 18: 4, 487–502.

Sinclair, Timothy L. (2001) 'The Infrastructure of Global Governance: Quasi-Regulatory Mechanisms and the New Global Finance', *Global Governance* 7: 4, 441–51.

Sinclair, Timothy L. (2003) 'Global Monitor: Credit Rating Agencies', *New Political Economy* 8: 1, 147–61.

Sinclair, Timothy L. (2005) *The New Masters of Capital: American Bond Rating Agencies and the Politics of Creditworthiness*, Ithaca, NY: Cornell University Press.

Smith, Roy and Ingo Walter (2001) *Rating Agencies: Is There an Agency Issue?* INSEAD Working Paper, Fontainebleau: INSEAD.

Speyer, Bernhard (2006) 'Governing Global Financial Markets – Basel I and II: The Role of Non-state Actors', in Gunnar Folke Schuppert (ed.) *Global Governance and the Role of Non-state Actors*, Baden-Baden: Nomos, 101–16.

Spinner, Helmut F. (1974) 'Theorie', in Hermann Krings, Hans Michael Baumgartner and Christoph Wild (eds.) *Handbuch philosophischer Grundbegriffe*, Band 5, München: Kösel, 1486–513.

Staisch, Matthias (2003) *Reaching Out, or Not: Accounting for the Relative Openness of International Governmental Organizations Towards NGOs*, unpublished M.A. thesis, Tübingen: Tübingen University, Institut of Political Science.

Standard & Poor's (2007a) *General Description of Corporate & Government Ratings Credit Rating Methodology*, http://www2.standardandpoors.com/spf/pdf/fixedincome/general_description_corpgovt_rating_methodology.06.26.07.pdf, date accessed September 3, 2008.

Standard & Poor's (2007b) *General Description of the Credit Rating Process*, http://www2.standardandpoors.com/spf/pdf/fixedincome/general_description_creditrating_process.06.26.07pdf.pdf, date accessed September 3, 2008.

Standard & Poor's (2007c) *Principles-Based Rating Methodology Criteria for Global Structured Finance Securities*, http://www2.standardandpoors.com/spf/pdf/fixedincome/principlesbased_methcriteria_global_sf_securities.06.26.07.pdf, date accessed September 3, 2008.

Standard & Poor's (2008) 'Standard & Poor's Rating Definitions', http://www2.standardandpoors.com/portal/site/sp/en/eu/page.article_print/2,1,1,4,1204838693805.html#ID5369, date accessed September 4, 2008.

Stiglitz, Joseph (2002) *Die Schatten der Globalisierung*, Berlin: Siedler.

Strange, Susan (1996) *The Retreat of the State: The Diffusion of Power in the World Economy*, Cambridge: Cambridge University Press.

Streeck, Wolfgang (1997) 'German Capitalism: Does It Exist? Can It Survive?' in Colin Crouch and Wolfgang Streeck (eds.) *The Political Economy of Modern Capitalism: Mapping Convergence and Diversity*, London: Sage, 33–54.

Strunz-Happe, Anne (2004) 'Externe Rating-Agenturen – Marktregulierung durch Basel II', *WM (Zeitschrift für Wirtschaft und Bankrecht)* 58: 3: 115–20.

Strunz-Happe, Anne (2005) 'Ein Ordnungsrahmen für Rating-Agenturen: Bericht über die internationalen und nationalen Bestrebungen', *Betriebswirtschaftliche Forschung und Praxis (BFuP)* 57: 3, 231–45.

Süddeutsche Zeitung (2008) 'Steinbrück attestiert den USA Versagen', *sueddeutsche.de*, September 25, http://www.sueddeutsche.de/politik/698/311619/text/print.html, date accessed September 25, 2008.

Summers, Lawrence (2007) 'Darf's noch etwas Staat sein?' *Financial Times Deutschland*, September 13, http://www.ftd.de/meinung/kommentare/247007.html?mode=print, date accessed June 13, 2008.

Sydow, Jörg (1992) *Strategische Netzwerke: Evolution und Organisation*, Wiesbaden: Gabler.

Sylla, Richard (2001) *A Historical Primer on the Business of Credit Ratings*, http://www1.worldbank.org/finance/assets/images/Historical_Primer.pdf, date accessed May 19, 2008.

Take, Ingo (2001) 'Allianzbildungen zwischen Staat, Zivilgesellschaft und internationalen Organisationen im Nord-Süd-Verhältnis', in Achim Brunnengräber, Ansgar Klein and Heike Walk (eds.) *NGOs als Legitimationsressource: Zivilgesellschaftliche Partizipationsformen im Globalisierungsprozess*, Opladen: Leske+Budrich, 239–57.

Tallberg, Jonas (2002) 'Delegation to Supranational Institutions: Why, How, and with What Consequences?' *West European Politics* 25: 1, 23–46.

Taylor, Simon (2008) 'Credit Rating Agencies Blamed for Market Losses', *European Voice*, September 4, 20.

Thatcher, Mark (2002) 'Delegation to Independent Regulatory Agencies: Pressures, Functions and Contextual Mediation', *West European Politics* 25: 1, 125–47.

Thatcher, Mark and Alec Stone Sweet (2002) 'Theory and Practice of Delegation to Non-Majoritarian Institutions', *West European Politics* 25: 1, 1–22.

Theiner, Patrick (2008) *Lessons from Internet Governance: Explaining Institutionalisation in a Heterarchical World*, Working Paper Prepared for a Joint Workshop of the Hebrew University of Jerusalem and the University of Tübingen, Tübingen, May.

Thompson, James D. (1967) *Organizations in Action*, New York: McGraw-Hill.

Tomlinson, Richard and David Evans (2007) 'CDOs Mask Huge Subprime Losses, Abetted by Credit Rating Agencies', *International Herald Tribune*, June 1, http://www.iht.com/articles/2007/05/31/bloomberg/bxinvest.php, date accessed June 30, 2008.

Trebesch, Christoph (2008) *Economic Governance,* SFB 700 Governance Working Paper Series No. 11, May, Berlin: FU Berlin.

Tsingou, Eleni (2008) 'Transnational Private Governance and the Basel Process: Banking Regulation, Private Interests and Basel II', in Andreas Nölke and Jean-Christophe Graz (eds) *Transnational Private Governance and its Limits,* London: Routledge, 58–69.

Ulrich, David and Jay B. Barney (1984) 'Perspectives in Organizations: Resource Dependence, Efficiency, and Population', *Academy of Management Review* 9: 3, 471–81.

Van de Ven, Andrew H. (1976) 'On the Nature, Formation, and Maintenance of Relations Among Organizations', *Academy of Management Review* 1: 4, 24–36.

Van de Ven, Andrew H., Dennis C. Emmitt and Richard Koenig (1975) 'Frameworks for Interorganizational Analysis', in Anant R. Neghandi (ed.) *Interorganization Theory,* Kent, OH: Kent State University Press, 19–38.

Van de Ven, Andrew H. and Gordon Walker (1984) 'The Dynamics of Interorganizational Coordination', *Administrative Science Quarterly* 29: 4, 598–621.

Van Evera, Stephen (1997) *Guide to Methods for Students of Political Science,* Ithaca, NY: Cornell University Press.

Vitols, Sigurt (2001) 'Varieties of Corporate Governance: Comparing Germany and the UK', in Peter Hall and David Soskice (eds.) *Varieties of Capitalism: Institutional Foundations of Comparative Advantage,* Cambridge: Cambridge University Press, 337–60.

Wahl, Peter (2008) 'Finanzmärkte als Entwicklungshemmnis', *Aus Parlament und* Zeitgeschichte 7, 33–38.

Wamsley, Gary and Mayer N. Zald (1973a) 'The Political Economy of Public Organizations', *Public Administration Review* 33, 62–73.

Wamsley, Gary and Mayer N. Zald (1973b) *The Political Economy of Public Organizations: A Critique and Approach to the Study of Public Administration,* Lexington, KY: Heath.

Wenturius, Nikolaus, Walter Van Hove and Volker Dreier (1992) *Methodologie der Sozialwissenschaft: Eine Einführung,* Tübingen: Francke.

White, Lawrence J. (2001) *The Credit Rating Industry: An Industrial Organization Analysis,* http://papers.ssrn.com/sol3/papers.cfm?abstract_id=267083#PaperDownload, date accessed August 16, 2008.

Williamson, John (2000) 'What Should the World Bank Think about the Washington Consensus?' *The World Bank Research Observer* 15: 2, 251–64.

Wood, Duncan R. (2005) *Governing Global Banking: The Basel Committee and the Politics of Financial Globalisation,* Aldershot: Ashgate.

World Federation of Exchanges (2008) 'Statistics, 1996–2007', http://www.world-exchanges.org/WFE/home.asp?action=document&menu=27, date accessed September 14, 2008.

Wyatt, Edward (2002) 'Credit Agencies Waited Months to Voice Doubt About Enron', *The New York Times,* February 8, http://query.nytimes.com/

gst/fullpage.html?res=9F01E5DA143CF93BA35751C0A9649C8B63, date accessed August 15, 2008.

Zürn, Michael (1992) *Interessen und Institutionen in der internationalen Politik: Grundlegung und Anwendung des situationsstrukturellen Ansatzes*, Opladen: Leske + Budrich.

Zürn, Michael and Mathias Koenig-Archibugi (2006) 'Conclusion II: The Modes and Dynamics of Global Governance', in Mathias Koenig-Archibugi and Michael Zürn (eds.) *New Modes of Governance in the Global System: Exploring Publicness, Delegation and Inclusiveness*, Basingstoke: Palgrave Macmillan, 236–54.

Zydra, Markus (2008) 'Standard & Poor's besänftigt die Kritiker', *sueddeutsche.de*, February 7, http://www.sueddeutsche.de/finanzen/artikel/206/156791/print.html, date accessed June 11, 2008.

Yuchtman, Ephraim and Stanley E. Seashore (1967) 'A System Resource Approach to Organizational Effectiveness', *American Sociological Review* 32: 6, 891–903.

Index